KT-573-475

Introduction to Local Area Networks

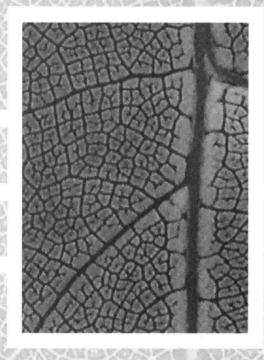

Robert M. Thomas

PARK CAMPUS
LEARNING CENTRE
C & G C.H.E. P.O. Box 220
The Park
Cheltenham GL50 2QF
Tel: (01242) 532721

San Francisco • Paris • Düsseldorf • Soest

NETWORK PRESS
SYBEX

Associate Publisher: Guy Hart-Davis
Acquisitions Manager: Kristine Plachy
Acquisitions & Developmental Editor: Guy Hart-Davis
Editor: Brenda Frink
Technical Editor: Mary Madden
Book Designer: Patrick Dintino
Graphic Illustrator: Inbar Berman
Desktop Publisher: Maureen Forys
Production Coordinator: Amy Eoff
Proofreaders: Katherine Cooley, Charles Mathews, Eryn Osterhaus, and Duncan Watson
Indexer: Nancy Guenther
Cover Designer: Archer Design
Cover Photographer: The Image Bank

Screen reproductions produced with Collage Complete.
Collage Complete is a trademark of Inner Media Inc.

SYBEX, Network Press, and the Network Press logo are registered trademarks of SYBEX Inc.

TRADEMARKS: SYBEX has attempted throughout this book to distinguish proprietary trademarks from descriptive terms by following the capitalization style used by the manufacturer.

TEL Keyboard 1090 copyright ©1989 Thomas Enterprises, Ltd. All rights reserved. Used with permission.

Netscape Communications, the Netscape Communications logo, Netscape, and Netscape Navigator are trademarks of Netscape Communications Corporation.

The author and publisher have made their best efforts to prepare this book, and the content is based upon final release software whenever possible. Portions of the manuscript may be based upon pre-release versions supplied by software manufacturer(s). The author and the publisher make no representation or warranties of any kind with regard to the completeness or accuracy of the contents herein and accept no liability of any kind including but not limited to performance, merchantability, fitness for any particular purpose, or any losses or damages of any kind caused or alleged to be caused directly or indirectly from this book.

Photographs and illustrations used in this book have been downloaded from publicly accessible file archives and are used in this book for news reportage purposes only to demonstrate the variety of graphics resources available via electronic access. Text and images available over the Internet may be subject to copyright and other rights owned by third parties. Online availability of text and images does not imply that they may be reused without the permission of rights holders, although the Copyright Act does permit certain unauthorized reuse as fair use under 17 U.S.C. Section 107.

First edition copyright ©1996 SYBEX Inc.

Copyright ©1997 SYBEX Inc., 1151 Marina Village Parkway, Alameda, CA 94501. World rights reserved. No part of this publication may be stored in a retrieval system, transmitted, or reproduced in any way, including but not limited to photocopy, photograph, magnetic or other record, without the prior agreement and written permission of the publisher.

Library of Congress Card Number: 97-67762
ISBN: 0-7821-2099-7

Manufactured in the United States of America

10 9 8 7 6 5 4 3 2 1

LEA
RE
npus
?20 T

Introduction to
Local Area Networks

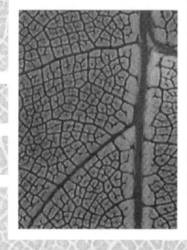

370011937 5

To Tully Bascomb, with admiration

Acknowledgments

This book has been produced not so much by an author as by a team of skilled editors and production people. I would like to thank three people in particular. Guy Hart-Davis, Associate Publisher at Sybex, was generous with his time and energy, first in finding a way to make this project possible and then in offering abundant suggestions and insights with the result that this edition is such a tremendous improvement over the first. I am deeply grateful to Brenda Frink at Sybex for so skillfully editing the raw manuscript and remaking it into a clear book text. I offer added thanks for her patience and support throughout. Also, I am thankful to have had the benefit of many helpful ideas and suggestions from Mary Madden, Technical Editor. Virtually all of the thoughts and insights from these three kind people have found their way in one form or another into this book. It is a much better book for them.

I am exceedingly grateful as well to the many people who worked behind the scenes to make a genuine book out of an ignoble manuscript: Thanks to Inbar Berman, who found a way to convert my oftentimes unclear sketches into lucid illustrations. Thanks to Amy Eoff, Production Coordinator, to Production Assistants Katherine Cooley, Charles Mathews, Eryn Osterhaus, and Duncan Watson, and also to Patrick Dintino for his book design. And, finally, thanks to Maureen Forys, who handled the desktop publishing.

I am very excited about how well this project has turned out; these people deserve the lion's share of the credit.

A bit closer to home, thank you Krista, my dear wife, for your patience and love while I obsessed over this project. And finally, as always, my thanks to Roscoe and Elaine, who connect and communicate just about as well as anyone.

—BT

Contents at a Glance

Table of Contents

Introduction

If you wanted to build your dream home yourself but did not know where to begin, you might start by learning about various tools and techniques that are available for getting the job done. With that first step in mind, you could go to your local bookstore and pick out a book that shows you home-construction tools and describes methods for building a house.

Introduction to Local Area Networks tells you about the hardware and software tools and methods you use to construct a computer network. This book won't turn you into a networking consultant overnight; but when you are finished you will be a lot more comfortable with the subject, and you'll have a solid basis for designing and constructing your own "dream network."

This book offers an overview of computer networking for people who are approaching the subject for the first time. It demystifies the networking process using non-technical terms. After reading this book, you will be comfortable with the networking process and able to talk knowledgeably with colleagues, consultants, and system vendors about installing or upgrading a computer network for your business.

Who Should Read This Book?

If you do everyday business tasks using a desktop computer, you have all the necessary background you need to read and understand this book.

This book was written for you if:

- You believe that your business could do better by connecting computers that currently reside on desktops, allowing your users to share information electronically.

- You have a network but don't understand enough about how it works to determine whether it's working at peak efficiency.

- You are not certain how to begin moving from stand-alone desktop computers to an integrated, networked system.

- You believe that computers are business tools whose purpose is to save or make money for your business, and you want to find out if a network will help your computers to do that.

How This Book Is Organized

The book has seventeen chapters grouped into five parts, plus two appendices:

- Part I, "Making Computers Communicate," gives a general overview of what networks do, how they go about doing it, and who benefits from them.

- Part II, "Network Hardware," introduces the hardware components of a networked computer system: cabling, network interface cards, workstations, servers, and the like.

- Part III, "Network Software," describes software, such as databases, e-mail, and groupware, that is especially designed for networks.

- Part IV, "Network Management," ties the hardware and software concepts together, showing you how to design and manage a local area network. This section also looks in greater detail at databases because they are integral to so many networks.

- Part V, "Intranetworking," shows you how Internet-based technology has revolutionized the way networks are used for communications and collaboration.

- Appendix A offers advice on selecting and hiring a networking consultant; Appendix B is a handy list of network-related terms and their meanings.

What's New to This Edition? Intranets!

Since the release of the first edition of *Introduction to Local Area Networks*, there has been a "virtual explosion" in the widespread use of Internet technologies to support the collaborative functions of computer networking. More than one hundred fifty pages of new material have been added to this book to account for this revolutionary phenomenon. Inside this book you will find everything you need to know to make intelligent choices about browsers, Web servers, and operating-system platforms for connecting a local area network to the Internet and for creating and maintaining intranets.

In addition, all of the network operating system material has been revised and expanded to account for changes and upgrades to the most popular networking systems available today. Special attention has been paid to Microsoft's Windows NT and Windows 95, Novell's Intranetware, Macintosh networks, and UNIX.

Finally, because information technology develops faster than the speed of book publication, you will find within these pages the resources you need to stay abreast of the latest developments in the world of local area networking. The information available on the Internet is of special importance in this regard, so I've included a list of helpful network-related Web sites.

Typographical Conventions Used

If you are an experienced reader of computer books, you will be familiar with the typographical conventions used in this book:

- File names appear capitalized (for example, COMMAND.COM).

- Internet domain names, newsgroup names, and software commands appear in their own typeface (for example, `www.sybex.com`, or `net use I:\`).

- Jargon and network-specific terms appear in italics the first time they appear, at which point they are also defined. (For example, you will often see statements like this: "*logging in* is a process by which you establish the connection between your workstation and the network at large.") If at some later point you encounter an unfamiliar networking term or piece of jargon that is not defined right there in the text, you can find a short definition in the glossary in Appendix B.

- Each chapter includes "For Further Reading" section, a short list of books to consult should you be interested in exploring a given subject on a deeper, more technical level.

- Most chapters include a "Case Study" section, a short descriptive illustration of the concepts discussed in that chapter.

Along the way, I have highlighted certain ideas as Notes, Tips, or Warnings:

A *Note* gives you extra information about the current topic.

A *Tip* is a bit of practical advice for applying the current subject matter to your own experience.

A *Warning* will help you to avoid a common pitfall.

One goal of this book is to convey a specific attitude toward networking and toward business computing in general: Computers and networks are tools, not ends in themselves. Computers and networks facilitate what makes doing business worthwhile: forming fulfilling relationships between people and making some money along the way. Learning is an adventure. Enjoy!

PART

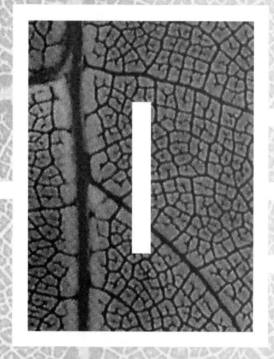

I

MAKING COMPUTERS
COMMUNICATE

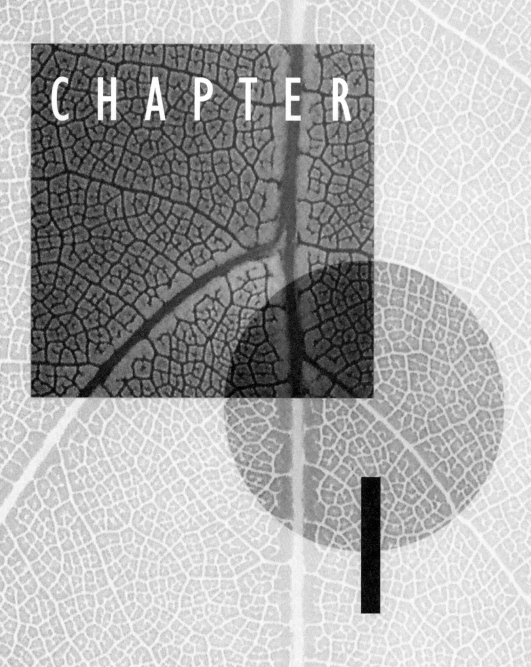

CHAPTER

1

Networks in the Workplace

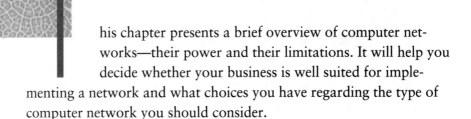

his chapter presents a brief overview of computer networks—their power and their limitations. It will help you decide whether your business is well suited for implementing a network and what choices you have regarding the type of computer network you should consider.

Why Networks Exist

In the early 1980s, when desktop computers began to proliferate in the business world, the intent of their designers was to create machines that would operate independently of each other. The computing ideal was summed up with the phrase, "One User, One Computer," which meant that individuals were free to manage information on their own desktops any way they liked.

This attitude was a reaction to the business-information environment of the time, based on large mainframe computers controlled by technical specialists and programmers. If you wanted information—a report on the aging of your accounts' receivable, for example—you made a request to the Information Services (IS) Department, who would program the computer to provide the report for you. The report could take any length of time to produce, depending on its complexity, and your only choice was to wait while IS massaged your report out of the mainframe. Once you got the report, if you didn't like its format or if the information in it wasn't clear for any reason, you would make another request to IS, wait some more, and hope the revised report was useful.

Desktop computers changed that. With a computer on your desktop, you could enter the information yourself, manipulate it to your heart's content, and produce the report you really wanted. (Of course, information stored on the mainframe would have to be re-entered at the desktop, but this inconvenience was often considered a worthwhile trade-off for the freedom to manipulate the data at will.)

IS departments were slow to realize the value of the desktop computers and through the early 1980s regarded them as toys rather than as worthwhile business information machines. By the time IS realized something serious was afoot, desktop computers had become more powerful and applications for desktop computers included simple spreadsheets, databases, and word processors.

The market for desktop computers exploded, and dozens of hardware and software vendors joined in fierce competition to exploit the open opportunity for vast profits. The competition spurred intense technological development, which led to increased power on the desktop and lower prices. Desktop computers were soon outperforming older, slower mainframe applications, accomplishing what appeared to be miracles in desktop publishing, graphics, computer-aided drafting, more powerful databases, and sophisticated user interfaces. Small businesses in particular were able to benefit from information management services that, a few years earlier, had been available only to wealthy corporations.

Something interesting happened as the desktop computer took over the way the world conducted its business: The ideal of "One User, One Computer" became an obsolete handicap rather than the liberating idea it was intended to be. Marketplace competition created large numbers of computers from different manufacturers and vendors, large numbers of applications, and the unimaginably vast amount of information stored in desktop systems.

Businesses soon rediscovered an old axiom: Business information is useful only when it is communicated between human beings. They also discovered a frustrating bottleneck: The process of distributing and communicating information among individuals, each with an independent desktop computer, is slow and prone to error.

Because of the large volume of information now being handled, it was impossible to pass along paper copies of information and ask each user to reenter it into their own computer. Copying files onto floppy disks and passing them around was a little better but still took too long and was impractical when individuals were separated by great distances. And you could never know for sure that the copy you received on a floppy disk was the most current version of the information—the other person might have updated it on their computer after the floppy was made.

For all its speed and power, the desktop computing environment was sadly lacking in the most important element: communication among members of a business team.

The obvious solution was to link the desktop computers together and link the group to a shared central repository of information. The problem was, desktop computers were not designed with this capacity in mind, and there were now thousands of these machines in the marketplace representing billions of dollars in business assets. Few users were willing to scrap their desktop machines altogether and replace them with new, redesigned machines (and new software) that would communicate with each other this way.

Besides, computer manufacturers were quite clever, and they were able to create additional components that users could attach to their desktop computers, which would allow them to share data among themselves and access centrally located sources of information. Unfortunately, the early designs for these networks were slow and tended to break down at critical moments.

The desktop computer continued to evolve. As it became faster and more powerful, capable of addressing much larger amounts of processing memory and thereby incorporating more sophisticated and complex features, communications between desktop computers gradually became more reliable. The idea of a Local Area Network (LAN) became a practical reality for businesses.

Computer networks, with all their promise and power, are more complicated to maintain than simple stand-alone machines. They require ongoing attention from managers whose job it is to oversee the networks and keep them running smoothly. Ironically, this concept looks a lot like the old mainframe paradigm, where a specialized cadre of technical insiders held near-absolute power to make information available. In some ways, it now appears as if business computing has come full circle, from IS to desktop and back to IS again.

But IS departments look a lot different today than they did ten years ago. Users are more sophisticated or at least more demanding. They want the same instant access, flexibility, and independence they became used to with their stand-alone desktop machines, plus access security and data accuracy throughout the business enterprise, plus access to other sources of digital information using the global capacities of the Internet.

Over the past few years, Internet technology has become more cost-effective and easier to use. Internet access sites have proliferated. As the Internet has grown and evolved in just a few years, it has become host to the *World Wide Web*, a community of thousands of business, educational, and personal information sites. Users can tap into these Web sites using special software, called *Web browsers*.

Web browser technology is evolving into the platform of choice for all levels of computer communications and resource sharing. Web browsers can be used as the foundation of *intranets*, which are a form of "private Internet" that eases the process of sharing information in a networked environment, and *extranets*, which expand the browser-based concept to include connectivity between networks at various and distant locations.

Networks now take a whole variety of forms: They can exist within a single room, an entire building, a city, a country, the world. There are networks of networks, and there are networks that access each other at will or at the whim of individual users who can contact them any time over telephone lines.

IS personnel have evolved from "high priests," with exclusive access to sensitive business information, to "manager/mechanics," whose chief function is to keep the data flowing smoothly among users. They also function as "security guards," who keep data safe from accidental (and sometimes deliberate) damage and loss. In some cases, the entire IS department has been replaced by a Network Administrator, a single person with responsibility for training, problem-solving, and technical support throughout the enterprise. The job is a demanding one. Network administrators are accountable for the integrity of critical data in an environment that works against their ability to maintain control over that data.

The proliferation of manufacturers and vendors, each vying for the loyalty of the hardware and software consumers, makes the new IS manager's job more difficult. The intense competition is in some ways beneficial, in that it keeps prices low and fosters technical innovation, but it also has its drawbacks. There are conflicting technical standards for exactly how all these billions of bits of electronic data are to be transferred quickly and accurately between dozens of different types of machines. Each type handles data in its own unique way, and the technical standards must define how to avoid typical network problems: electronic collisions along the data pathways, corruption of the data into meaningless electronic gibberish, lost data, or misdirection of data to unintended destinations.

For the time being, the world of networking looks like a Tower of Babel, at least until certain manufacturers and vendors who do the best job of filling the information and communication needs of the business marketplace emerge and narrow the spectrum of choices.

Is it worthwhile simply to wait? The answer depends on your own circumstances and how profitable your business can remain in the advancing information age. In the computer world, waiting while the technology evolves has always been rewarded: Prices tend to come down, technology to become more powerful. But waiting can be punished as well: Businesses with access to modern information technology enjoy a significant competitive advantage over their more technologically limited counterparts.

Networks allow more efficient management of resources. For example, multiple users can share a single top-quality printer, rather than putting duplicate, possibly lesser-quality printers on individual desktops. Also, network software licenses can be less costly than separate, stand-alone licenses for the same number of users.

Networks help keep information reliable and up-to-date. A well managed, centralized data storage system allows multiple users to access data from different locations and to limit access to data while it is being processed.

Networks help speed up data sharing. Transferring files across a network is almost always faster than other, non-network means of sharing files.

Networks allow workgroups to communicate more efficiently. Electronic mail and messaging is a staple of most network systems, in addition to scheduling systems, project monitoring, on-line conferencing, and groupware. All of these things help work teams to be more productive.

Networks help businesses service their clients more effectively. Remote access to centralized data allows employees to service clients in the field and clients to communicate directly with suppliers.

Networks greatly expand a business's marketing and customer service capability. Using Internet technology, a business can automate its ability to inform customers about its products and services, take orders directly from customers, and provide up-to-the-minute facts and figures to be accessed at the customer's whim, anytime day or night.

Who Needs to Network?

Along with all the overheated competition in the computer business comes a deluge of hype. Vendors, with a sharp eye out for your limited technology budget, are shouting over each other about how you cannot possibly survive without their system and how their system will transform your business from a plodding, unprofitable tin box into a fast, impregnable money machine.

Will it? If you are the leader or IS manager of a business considering the switch to a networked computing environment, you may be wondering if all the trouble and expense will be worth it. Here are some questions to ask yourself, which will help you decide if your business can benefit from a networked environment or if your current networked environment is living up to its promises:

Are you spending money on redundant hardware upgrades for each desktop machine? For example, modern software packages require immense storage space; the typical package uses 50–100 megabytes, plus the space required to store the associated data. It seems wasteful to buy larger and larger hard disks and redundant peripheral upgrades for each machine throughout your enterprise. Networks can reduce the cost of hardware by sharing resources and reducing redundancy. (Bear in mind, however, that you will make a trade-off eventually, between saving money by using shared software and saving money by optimizing your network's performance. Some of your applications will remain on workstation hard disks because the system runs faster that way.)

Are employees unable to share data because of software incompatibilities? While application data is frequently transferable from an earlier version to a later one, it often doesn't work the other way around. For example, an employee who develops a document on the latest version of a page-formatting program may not be able to pass that document along to another employee who has not chosen to make the upgrade. And if employees have become used to different applications from different vendors, the data may not be sharable at all. Networks provide the opportunity to create application standards and centralize the upgrade process.

Are support and training costs on the rise? The trend among software vendors is to charge for support. Training has always been costly and frequently not as effective as a manager would hope. Networks can reduce the cost of training and support by centralizing and reducing the number of applications used throughout the enterprise.

Are a great many vendors servicing your information management needs in a piecemeal fashion? A networked environment can reduce administrative overhead by streamlining the supply process. For example, you can use a network to pass ordering information to a central database of approved vendors and combine or time requests to take advantage of discounts.

Are business bottlenecks created because people must wait for information before they can act? For example, do your customer service representatives have immediate access to customer account histories, payment information, ordering trends, and the like, or must they place customers on hold or call them back after combing other departments for answers to questions or solutions to problems? A networked environment—especially one with Internet capabilities—can reduce the workload of service representatives by allowing customers to access basic product and service information directly.

Finally, there are some everyday signs that networking would help your business function more efficiently:

- Lost data because some individuals don't make backups as well as others

- An increasing number of files being transferred via floppy disks (often called "sneaker net," referring to individuals wearing sneakers, carting disks around a building)

- Routine business communication being conducted in an ad-hoc, haphazard fashion, or by arranging formal meetings to discuss everyday issues

- Important messages being passed via adhesive note pad, report margins, or scraps of paper, being lost or simply not noticed until it is too late

If you recognize your own business in the above questions and scenarios, you could benefit from establishing a networked system (or seriously redesigning your current system). Later chapters in this book will give you the information you need to choose the best system for your business from among the most common systems available or to develop a strategy for making your existing system work as intended.

Networks in the Workplace

While computer networks can make a business more productive and efficient, they are hardly a panacea. Despite vendors' claims that computers are miracle machines capable of transforming businesses, computers can only optimize existing systems, they cannot turn bad systems into good ones.

In stand-alone computer environments, each individual user is responsible for the performance of his or her machine. Each user devises a personal method for getting results from the machine. Some users are simply more talented or enthusiastic than others, and these users tend to be called on for support when things break down. As valuable as talent and enthusiasm are, they are no substitute for hard information. In a stand-alone computer environment, inefficiency and underutilization of resources become a part of everyday routine simply because people are able to get by and expertise is difficult to share.

A networked environment, on the other hand, is only as good as its administrator. A network administrator must have good training and be able to draw on a deep store of factual, detailed information about every aspect of the system. Talent and enthusiasm alone will not suffice. A computer network requires daily maintenance and supervision if it is to function as advertised and keep its vast data stores secure. The network administrator is by far the most critical component in any system, getting the most out of a system that may be less than state-of-the-art or bringing the most advanced system in the world to its knees.

If you are now making the switch from a stand-alone to a networked environment, the best place to begin is with the hiring of your network administrator. The administrator should be brought on board first and should become involved in every aspect of the system's design, selection, and implementation. The search for a suitable administrator should be done slowly and carefully. Interview fully, check references carefully, and hire only that candidate with a proven track record and credentials.

Alternatively, you can make an investment in training an existing employee who has demonstrated serious aptitude. Such an employee should demonstrate a focus on achieving real-world results; look for ways to maximize results from existing technology; avoid money-wasting, impulsive acquisition of leading-edge technologies; and understand the difference between the tool and the task.

The Tool and the Task

The "tool" is the machine and also the style by which the machine achieves its ends. The "task" is the process of achieving an intended purpose as efficiently as possible. An employee who spends hours making a report look pretty is wasting company time if the task is merely to transmit some necessary information to its destination. On the other hand, if the purpose of the report is to both impart information and impress the receiver (for example, an advertising flyer), then the extra time spent may be worth it.

Some computer enthusiasts spend more time teaching their computer new tricks than getting real jobs done. They may appear to be experts or "computer wizards" to those who find the world of computers daunting. In reality, "the Wiz" can often be someone who has merely confused the tool with the task. The Wiz can be useful on occasion but can break down in situations where substance is favored over style, when the mundane necessity of getting real work done interferes with computer experimentation and exploration.

A good network administrator can command an annual salary of fifty thousand dollars or more, depending on the complexity of the system and its location. The system administrator's salary could easily be the most expensive single aspect of your system. You do not want to waste this large an investment on dilettantes, part-timers, or hobbyists-turned-consultants. Seek recommendations from other network professionals who have credibility and track records of their own. Insist that candidates speak plainly and avoid a litany of jargon. The time and trouble you take at this stage of the process is trivial compared to the time and trouble you will save once your system is up and running.

Depending on the complexity of your network, you may require additional personnel, who also must be chosen with great care:

Database administrator   Responsible for programming and maintaining a large multi-relational database in a networked environment and facilitating direct access to the database by individuals on the network.

How to Become a Network Guru

So you have decided that your next career move is into the exciting world of computer network support. You believe you have the necessary aptitude. You understand the fundamentals of desktop computing, operating systems, and hardware. Your intention is to use technology to increase your business's productivity. You have extraordinary patience, can cope with high levels of stress, and work well with other people. You still need two more things: an understanding of the technical aspects of networking and experience using them.

You must undergo training to acquire the necessary understanding. Network training is becoming more and more formal. Novell, for example, has set up authorized training centers that teach the technical details to beginners. A Novell training center can certify you for two levels of networking expertise: A Certified Novell Administrator (CNA) can provide day-to-day support to users on a Novell network; a Certified Novell Engineer (CNE) has more detailed knowledge of the hardware and software and is qualified to design and install complex network systems. Microsoft, using local training centers and educational institutions, offers credentials as a Microsoft Certified Systems Engineer (MCSE) as part of its Microsoft Certified Professional (MCP) program. To become an MCSE, individuals are required to pass a number of certification exams proving their ability to implement and maintain computing environments using Microsoft networking products, such as Windows NT Server, Windows NT Workstation, and Microsoft BackOffice.

Local colleges and universities may offer classes and degree programs in data communications. Local dealers and vendors may offer training in the products they sell. If you have the required aptitude, it can take about a year to acquire enough training to qualify you for hands-on experience.

You acquire the necessary experience the old-fashioned way: hunting for a low-end job, working for less pay than you would like, and slowly working your way up. The field is already a crowded one, full of people who believe that the future of technology is built around networking, so expect competition. Your job is to impress all potential employers and keep your eyes open for opportunities to advance—just like any other job. Good luck!

Workgroup manager   Responsible for problem-solving, implementing standards and solutions, reviewing performance, facilitating the efficiency of a specific group of individuals who are connected, as a group, to a larger network environment.

Support staff   Responsible for technical assistance to the system administrator in large, complex network environments. Provides routine problem-solving and spot training to end users.

Maintenance contractor   Responsible for hardware repairs and upgrades; often this position is filled by contracting with a third-party service provider or with the vendor.

Webmaster or Web site administrator   Responsible for implementing and maintaining the content and style of the company's Internet site, keeping the information accurate, up-to-date, and interesting.

Where to Go from Here

By answering the questions and applying the information in this chapter to your business, you can develop some notes regarding the strengths and weaknesses of your current business information and communication technology. Your goal is to determine whether building a network would improve your business efficiency and profitability enough to justify the investment.

After answering the questions in the section "Who Needs to Network?," meet with your fellow workers about how you will distribute the responsibility for managing a new, more complex business tool. You will want to identify current workers who are interested in spending extra time to learn new skills and, if necessary, begin a search for new employees or outside consultants.

Later chapters in this book will help you learn the basics of the network world and speak its language. This information will enable you to work with your network system administrator to implement a cost-effective network system; one that justifies your investment of time, trouble, and money with measurable increases in productivity, efficiency, communication, competitive advantage, and profitability.

For Further Reading

- Derfler, Frank J. *How Networks Work*. Ziff-Davis, 1996.

- Heath, Steve. *Effective PC Networking*. Butterworth-Heinemann, 1993.

- Moncur, Michael, and James Chellis, with James Chavez. *The CNA Study Guide for NetWare 4*. Sybex, 1996.

- Moncur, Michael, and James Chellis. *The CNA Study Guide for IntranetWare*. Sybex, 1997.

- Mossberg, Walter. *The Wall Street Journal Book of Personal Technology*. Times Books, 1995.

- Rhodes, Peter D. *Building a Network*. McGraw-Hill, 1995.

In the next chapter, we will move on to more technical information: how networks connect desktops, what those connections look like in the real world, and what options are available to you for making the best connections for your business.

CASE STUDY

Generic Accounting & Bookkeeping (GAB) is a small, independent accounting firm. Over the last eight years, they have established a reputation for quality work and have grown slowly and steadily from a two-person firm to a sophisticated small business employing an owner, an office manager, and twelve full- and part-time bookkeepers. They provide timely and accurate financial reports, tax returns, budgeting, and analysis to about 35 small and medium-sized business clients.

The business now occupies a wing on one floor of a high-rise office building. Bookkeepers share administrative information, and more than one bookkeeper may be assigned to a client, but individual client accounts are confidential. Each bookkeeper has a computer and a dot-matrix printer. The bookkeepers would like to upgrade to a laser printer to print high-quality reports and graphs for clients and internal use.

Recently, the Owner and Office Manager met to discuss the company's future plans. In the course of that meeting, they made the following observations:

- Employees are sharing administrative information via memos, conversations, and meetings.

- It is often difficult to arrange meetings and coordinate staff schedules, despite an ugly Who's Here/Who's Away bulletin board near the main entrance.

- When staff persons exchange digital information, they do it by means of floppy diskettes. This is inefficient and sometimes confusing. On one occasion, current data was overwritten by past data because an individual used the wrong disk to update their data.

- Data backups have been left to the individuals. In many cases, staff persons have learned the value of backing up the hard way: by losing valuable data. Some staff are better at maintaining reliable backups than others.

- Individual clients require their financial information in a variety of digital formats. Software incompatibilities make it difficult for staff to exchange information when required.

- Often projects are delayed because a stand-alone computer that stores critical information is in use on another client project. Transferring client software and data files to a new machine can sometimes take an hour or more and ties up both machines in the process.

- Over time, the company's stand-alone computers have been purchased from a variety of vendors: a local retail store, a mail-order firm, and a large discount office supply warehouse across town. When technical support or upgrades for older machines are required, staff does not always know who was the vendor of a particular machine.

- Everyone knows that two or three staff persons are real "computer nerds"—they are frequently interrupted in their work when other, less sophisticated staff have technical problems.

The Owner and Office Manager have determined that they will consider investing in a computer network, provided that it meets the following goals:

- Provides a consistent and reliable system for backing up critical data.

- Provides a consistent and simple track for obtaining upgrades, technical support, and day-to-day administration.

- Saves on outsourced printing costs and speeds up the process of producing high-quality reports, by allowing staff to share two or three high-quality, high-speed laser printers in house.

- Allows staff to share access to client information from a centralized location but allows that access only to those who are authorized to work with the data.

- Allows different software packages to be used across the network when required but locally whenever possible.

- Creates efficient and consistent communications between staff.

- Centralizes a system for scheduling staff meetings and conferences.

CHAPTER

2

Network Topologies

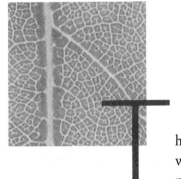

This chapter takes a bird's-eye view of the landscape of the networked environment. It discusses how networks go about connecting computers and transferring data between them. It also defines some basic terms used to describe networks and how they work.

If you are new to networking, it is important to understand the different ways computers can be connected to one another. They are connected physically, via cables, phone lines, or wireless microwave transmission; and they are connected logically, using software to manage the flow of data across the physical connections. In both the physical and logical realms, different types of connections are suitable for different types of businesses and budgets. This chapter explores the fundamental options that are available.

Making the Connection

The process of setting up network hardware is relatively straightforward, at least when compared to the process of setting up the software. Although there are different types of networks, they do have certain hardware characteristics in common. (Technical details of individual network hardware components are discussed in Chapter 4.) An overview of the workings of network hardware follows.

Network Interface Cards

A *network interface card* (NIC) must be installed in each computer on the network. This card is inserted into a slot inside the computer. There are several types of cards manufactured by different vendors, but they all perform the same fundamental operation: They manage the flow of network information to and from the computer in which they reside. Figure 2.1 shows a typical NIC. As you can see, it looks pretty much like any other plug-in computer card, except for one item—the jack for a cable connection. (We'll get to that in a moment.)

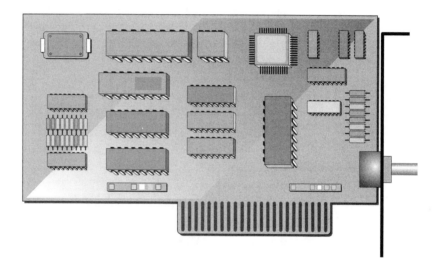

FIGURE 2.1

A network interface card

The differences among various NICs are based first on the type of computer with which they are designed to work. For example, IBM-compatibles require one type of card, and Macintosh computers require another. NICs also differ in the speed and efficiency with which they manage the information flow. For more details on network interface cards, see Chapter 4.

Cables and Connections

A user-accessible computer on a network is called a *workstation*. A connection to the network made by any type of device (including workstations, shared printers, modems, and the like) is called a *node*. Each node on the network must be able to communicate in some fashion with the others. Most networks whose nodes reside within a reasonable distance of each other (say, for example, on the same floor of an office building, or perhaps between a few adjacent floors) make this connection using *cables*.

A cable is an insulated wire that is attached to each NIC in the network and thus becomes the pathway along which the network data traffic travels. Figure 2.2 shows how an NIC is installed in a workstation and how a cable is attached to it.

There are, as you might already suspect, different types of cables that can handle the flow of information at varying speeds and with greater or lesser efficiency depending on the physical environment in which they are used. See Chapter 5 for more technical information on different types of cable.

F I G U R E   2.2

An NIC installed in a workstation, with cabling attached

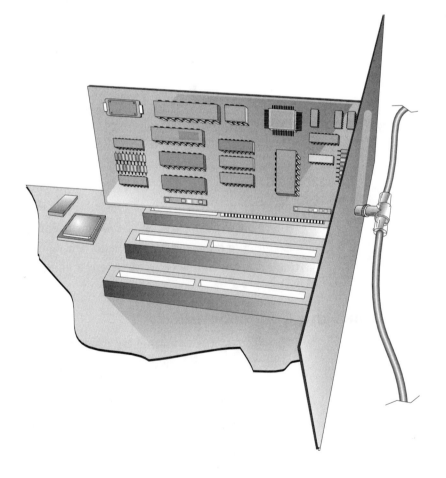

If the network is spread out over an extremely wide area (for example, between different government office buildings in a town or state), cabling becomes impractical. These wide-area networks may use existing telephone lines to establish the connection. If the wide-area network is handling especially large volumes of information or requires exceptional speed, it may require its own dedicated telephone system cables (called T1 or T3 lines) to handle the traffic.

A third alternative for establishing the connection is called *wireless transport services*. This technology consists of hardware that manages the connection using radio or infrared signaling devices, eliminating the need for cables altogether. Wireless networks are expensive and require additional support services to insure reliable communications; they are usually operated by large corporations with compelling needs for them and the budgetary resources to afford them. A wireless network may be required in areas where cabling is extremely difficult or impossible. Some cable-based networks may use a wireless connection for temporary connections from remote locations (see Chapter 7 for more information on remote access). A wireless network can make use of existing cellular telephone technology, satellite communication systems, or commercial paging systems.

Hubs and Repeaters

A *hub* is a useful device that facilitates the physical connections between network nodes. There are many different types of hubs. Some are simple hardware devices that accept multiple cable connections and accept the network data signal—these are called *passive* hubs. Other hubs are more complicated; they analyze and control the flow of information to various network locations—these are called *active* hubs.

A *repeater* is a special device, similar to a hub, whose function is to amplify and reduce electrical interference with the flow of network data

Networking without NICs

If you need to connect only two computers (or intend to connect a computer to a workstation on another network), you may be able to accomplish this cheaply and easily using a *Direct Cable Connection* (DCC).

DCC uses either a parallel or serial cable to connect two computers, using their built-in communication ports. Both machines must use the same operating system, which must support this type of connection (for example, Windows 95). Although DCC is not a network in the usual sense, the operating system does use a network protocol to manage the flow of data between the machines. For example, Windows 95 supports either NetBEUI, IPX/SPX, or TCP/IP protocols for DCC.

Once DCC is installed and configured, you will be able to use one machine as a *remote* and the other as a *host*. The remote machine accesses files and runs programs on the host machine.

If the host machine is on a network that supports IPX/SPX or TCP/IP, a DCC can use one of these protocols and access the wider network from the remote machine.

DCC is useful for making temporary connections between laptops and network workstations. DCC is much slower than dedicated networking hardware, especially if you use a serial cable for the connection. Parallel ports on modern machines will deliver better performance.

DCC is not automatically installed when you install Windows 95; if you have previously installed Windows 95 and decide to try this option, access Add/Remove Programs in the Control Panel to install the DCC capability. Click the Communications icon, then the Details button, and finally click the Direct Cable Connection check box. The first time you use DCC, Windows 95 will start a "DCC Wizard" that guides you through the initial configuration process.

and to relay the data from one segment of cable to another. Repeaters are used on large networks, where the nodes are located so far apart that a single long cable could degrade the signal.

Topologies

*T*opology is a term used to describe the way in which computers are connected in a network. The *physical topology* describes the actual layout of the network hardware; the *logical topology* describes the behavior of the computers on the network, from the perspective of its human operators.

Physical Topologies

On the simplest level, most networks use one of three types of physical topologies, *linear bus*, *ring*, or *star*:

Linear bus   (See Figure 2.3.) In this common layout, a single main cable connects each node, in what amounts to a single line of computers accessing it from end to end. Each node is connected to two others, except the machines at either end of the cable, which are each connected only to one other node. The network operating system keeps track of a unique electronic address for each node and manages the flow of information based on this addressing scheme. (See Chapter 8 for more information on network operating systems.) Linear bus topology has the advantage of simplicity and of not requiring that every user workstation be up and running in order for the network to function. In client/server systems, (where one or more machines are designated as *servers*, meaning that they are dedicated to the distribution of data and are not usually used for information processing) a linear bus topology can be useful because of its ease of implementation and because workstations can log on and off the network and access servers at will. However, because a single cable is dedicated to all the information traffic, performance can be slow at times.

Ring   (See Figure 2.4.) This layout is similar to the linear bus, except that the nodes are connected in a circle using cable segments. In this layout, each node is physically connected to only two others. Each node

FIGURE 2.3

A linear bus topology. Computers are connected by a single cable, end-to-end.

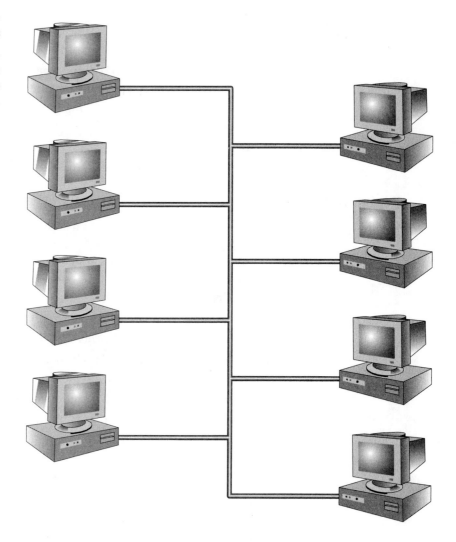

passes information along to the next, until it arrives at its intended destination. Performance can be faster on this system because each portion of the cabling system is handling only the data flow between two machines. The disadvantage to the ring topology is that the failure of one machine can affect the entire network. For this reason, ring topology is usually found in smaller *peer-to-peer* networks, in which

FIGURE 2.4

A ring topology.
Computers are
connected to a single
cable, in a complete circle.

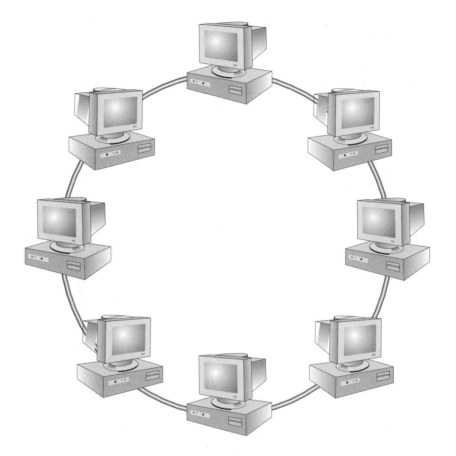

each machine manages both information processing and the distribution of data files. In this case, the faster topology helps compensate for the increased amount of processing required.

Star   (See Figure 2.5.) In a star topology, each node is connected to a single, centrally located data control device, usually a hub, using individual segments of cable. This topology has the advantage of minimum data traffic along the cables (node-to-hub only), for optimum performance. Also, because each machine has an independent connection to the central hub, the network can continue to function if any of the individual nodes fails.

FIGURE 2.5

A star topology. Computers are connected to a single hub, using many cables.

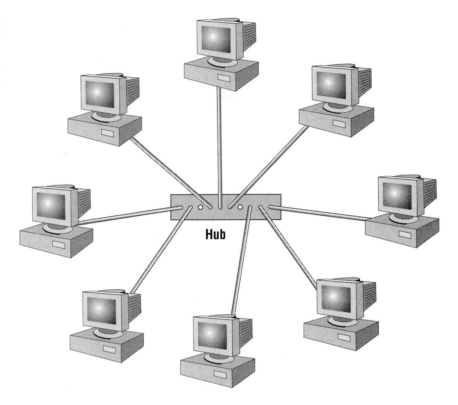

Hybrid Topologies

Larger, more complex networks can combine different physical topologies. Here are two common examples:

Star bus   Two or more star topologies are linked together using a linear bus trunk (called a *backbone*).

Star ring   Two or more star topologies are linked together using a central hub. At first glance, this configuration looks like a star topology joined into a larger star topology. However, in a star ring the central hub accesses the individual star hubs in a sequential loop, acting like a ring.

FIGURE 2.6

A star bus topology, linked by a backbone; and a star ring topology, linked by a central hub.

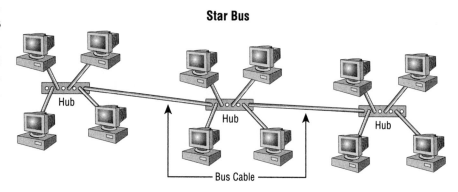

Star Bus

Bus Cable

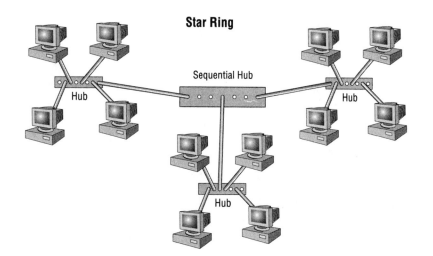

Star Ring

Sequential Hub

Logical Topologies

Logical topology describes how the network's operating system manages the flow of information between nodes. The operating system's communication scheme influences how people using the workstations visualize the way their computers are communicating with each other.

Most network operating systems use one of two basic kinds of logical topology:

Linear   (See Figure 2.7.) This communications scheme functions like the linear bus topology and is common in Ethernet-based systems. Each node has a unique address, and the addresses are accessed sequentially. Information is passed up and down the list until the right destination address is found.

Token ring   (See Figure 2.7.) This scheme can be found on both linear bus and ring topologies. Each node has a unique address, and the addresses are accessed in a circular fashion. Notice that there isn't necessarily a correspondence between the logical addresses and the physical location of the computers relative to each other.

FIGURE 2.7

The difference between physical and logical topologies. In the Ethernet system, the logical addresses correspond to the physical location of the computers. In the token ring system, the logical addresses do not have the same correspondence to the linear bus layout.

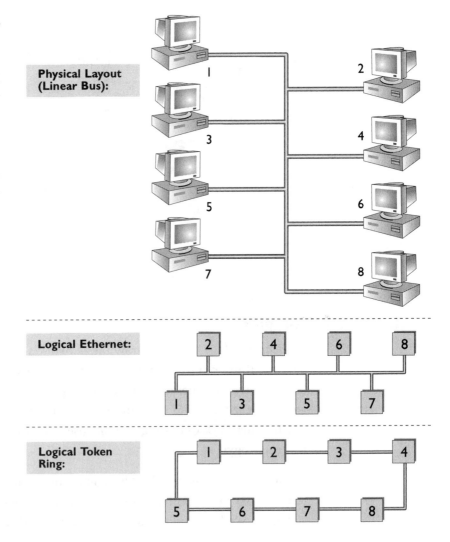

Clients and Servers

The terms *server* and *client* are used somewhat loosely in discussing networks. In general, any machine that stores and sends out data along the network can be called a server, whereas a machine that receives and makes changes to that data can be a client.

More specifically, the term *file server* refers to a computer whose chief purpose on the network is to store and send out data files. It does not process or make changes to the files it stores and sends out. It may not even have any intelligence regarding what kinds of files it sends. In other words, the server doesn't have to know whether a file is a text document, a graphic picture, or a financial spreadsheet. Instead, the server busies itself answering requests from client machines for files that it keeps stored and leaves it to the software on the client machine to know what the file is, what kind of data it contains, and what to do with it. Figure 2.8 compares a file server to a workstation.

FIGURE 2.8

A file server. Notice the absence of keyboard and monitor. Some file servers can be accessed directly using a keyboard and monitor, but this particular server is accessed only from client nodes across the network.

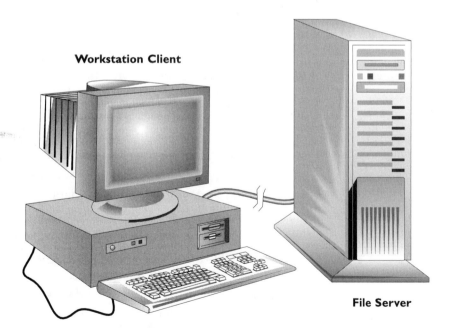

Workstation Client

File Server

In this system, clients are usually computers on the network that are operated by human beings, making changes to the data files they receive and, when those changes are complete, sending the files back to the file server for storage.

This arrangement has the virtue of processing efficiency, especially on large networks with dozens or even hundreds of machines. With the full processing power of a very powerful computer allocated solely to sending and storing files, individual clients are not kept waiting for data, and the clients can process different files with different software independently of each other.

A single file server may be made even faster and more efficient if it contains more than one central processing chip so that complex requests for data from dozens of different clients can be allocated to different processors running concurrently. These servers are called *symmetric multiprocessor units* (or SMU for short).

If the network is extremely large, it may employ more than one file server, each server handling specialized requests for specific types of files. For example, one file server may handle requests for customer database records and another for company budget information. Figure 2.9 shows the layout of a basic file server system.

Clients on a network don't have to be other computers. The server also can direct data to and from other automated devices, such as printers (in which case the server is called a *print server*). On large networks, dedicated *mail servers* may be used to handle e-mail traffic, and *Web servers* may be used to manage Internet Web browser–based connections. We will discuss Web browsers in more detail in Chapter 14.

Most servers handle security issues such as limiting access to certain kinds of data or devices, or access to data by select users, or at specific times of the day.

Systems like these are called *client/server* systems, and they are distinguished by a high degree of data centralization. This creates the need for a system administrator or specialized group of support staff who understand the system as a whole and take responsibility for the safety, accuracy, and availability of the data stored on the server.

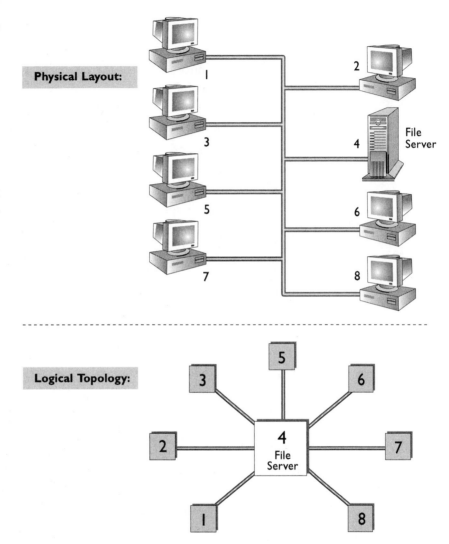

FIGURE 2.9

A fundamental client/server system. One computer is dedicated to sending, receiving, and storing data files, also managing the system. Notice that, although the system is physically connected as a linear bus, most of the network data traffic passes to and from the server.

Physical Layout:

Logical Topology:

Networks like these are suitable for large organizations with large budgets who require that many users have access to the same general data, and that current, updated information be available to all users at any given time. For details regarding client/server operating systems, see Chapter 8.

Peer-to-Peer Networks

Not every business needs the power of a complex client/server system. Many smaller companies can do well using a network of computers in which each machine sends and receives data files and processes data using those files. Because each computer has the same potential to access and process data, these types of networks are called *peer-to-peer* networks.

A peer-to-peer network (as shown in Figure 2.10) has the virtue of simplicity in both design and maintenance. It is usually less expensive to set up. However, it is also slower and less secure than the client/server network. It is suitable for smaller organizations with limited budgets where security is less of an issue, and where the number of computers on the network is limited (usually twenty or less). With fewer computers on the network, performance and speed are not noticeably degraded. This type of network is also well-suited for groups of users who must freely access data and processing abilities that reside on other computers across the network.

Maintenance of a peer-to-peer system can be tricky. Although this type of system can be configured to offer some measure of security and limited access to data, it cannot offer the robust security features of a client/server system. Because all individual peer-to-peer network users are capable of storing and accessing data files, they share greater responsibility for maintaining both the smooth operation of the system and the integrity of the data.

Peer-to-peer technology is improving because the market for it is growing among smaller companies with smaller budgets. Peer-to-peer systems are connecting more and more powerful computers with larger RAM and vastly increased data storage capacity. With these advances come better and more reliable performance, more features like intra-network communications (also called electronic mail, or e-mail), and temporary connections from remote sites via telephone lines. Although client/server is

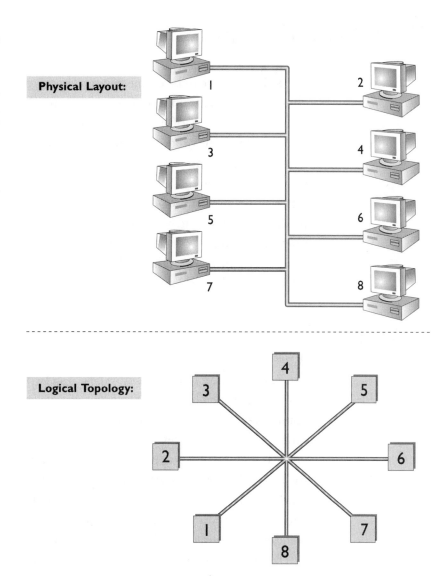

FIGURE 2.10

A peer-to-peer system. All computers send, receive, store, and process data files. The absence of a dedicated file server lowers hardware and maintenance costs. Performance is slower, especially if the network has many nodes.

Physical Layout:

Logical Topology:

still the system of choice among network power users, the peer-to-peer model can deliver quite satisfactory results for these smaller companies or for client workgroups that attach to larger networks.

For details regarding peer-to-peer operating systems, see Chapter 8.

Complex Networks

Networks can be connected to other networks; and networks can consist of different types of machines from different vendors, each with its own unique way of handling electronic information, not directly understood by the other machines on the network. Special software and hardware can be attached to the network to handle this complicated setup. These devices, called *bridges, routers,* and *gateways,* perform in different ways the task of "translating" the electronic information supplied by one machine into a format that can be understood by another. Once installed and configured, these devices can operate in a way that does not require any additional work by each machine's operator. Let's look at each device in turn.

Bridges

A *bridge* consists of a computer with two or more network interface cards, connecting two different types of networks. For example, one interface card might connect to an Ethernet system, while a second card connects to a Token Ring system. These two systems speak two entirely different data languages and require the bridge to translate the node address supplied by one network into an address that is recognized by the other. The bridge uses special software that accepts data from the sending network, recognizes the address as one belonging to the other network, translates the address so the receiving network can understand it, and sends it to the receiving network.

The bridge examines all the traffic on both networks, but it can distinguish between "foreign" data, which is sent between the two networks, and "domestic" data, which is sent between nodes on the same network. Data that does not require translation is allowed to pass through the bridge unchanged and is not routed to the other network at all. This process, called *filtering*, increases efficiency by reducing unnecessary data traffic between the two foreign networks. The filtering mechanism sees to it that the two networks handle each other's data only when they have to.

Networking the World

The first complex networks were computer bulletin board services, which proliferated at the beginning of the desktop computer revolution because they were a convenient means for users to share information, oftentimes centered around some area of common interest, using modems and telephone lines. A single user, often an extremely dedicated enthusiast, would offer their machine as a central sending and receiving point for anyone with the necessary hardware, software, and knowledge required to call up and access the information stored there. Computer bulletin boards are still a good source of advice and support for specific hardware and software products, and you might look for one that has information and advice regarding local-area networks. Check retail computer stores in your area and local computer newspapers for more information.

Large commercial enterprises took the bulletin board idea to the next evolutionary step, the *on-line service provider*. These large, mainframe-based enterprises offered access to huge databases of information, plus on-line messaging between users, and charged a monthly subscription fee. For example, CompuServe and America Online are two commercial on-line services.

More and more desktop computer users are connecting to the *Internet*, a loosely organized, world-wide network of computers connected by telephone lines. To access the Internet from a stand-alone desktop computer, you must use that computer's modem to make a telephone call to another computer that is already connected to the Internet system. Once connected, you can establish contact with any other computer on the Internet. In the networking world, LANs can make direct or modem connections to the Internet, and once connected, each node on the network can be assigned access rights to Internet connections. Internet connections are discussed in detail in Chapter 14.

Routers

A *router* is similar to a bridge but can handle more complex types of communications between dissimilar networks. Routers are usually employed by Wide-Area Networks, which often connect networks using different communication protocols and dissimilar addressing schemes. A router maintains a table of pathways between nodes and can select an optimal route of node addresses over which to send data. If the router detects an error condition after attempting to send data over one selected pathway, it can try again using an alternate.

A router is programmed to understand the communications protocols of its attached networks. However, some complex networks can be accessed by remote networks using any possible protocol. In these situations, routers can function as bridges. The router simply translates the address and passes the data along the network data path to the receiving node.

Gateways

A *gateway* is used when simply transferring raw data between networks is not enough. Some network systems (in particular mainframe- or minicomputer-based systems) require specific instructions on how data is to be managed once it is received onto the network. A gateway is also required when connecting two or more networks that are running on top of different operating systems. A gateway incorporates the functions of routers and bridges but in addition can translate the instruction set of the sending network into the corresponding instruction set of the receiving network. For example, a nationwide on-line database service, running on a large mainframe system, would employ a gateway system because it is open to telephone connections from dozens of different types of computers and networks. The gateway translates requests from the connected computers (for example, a request to download a file) into instructions the mainframe can understand. The gateway also translates messages from the mainframe (starting and ending the download, monitoring progress and possible error conditions, and the like) into instructions the receiving computer can understand. All of this is transparent to the human being sitting at the receiving computer. From this person's point of view, it appears as if the entire process is taking place in their native format.

Enterprise Computing

It is common for networks to grow in complexity as the needs of an organization evolve over time. What starts out as a small peer-to-peer LAN can, in a few years, grow into a far-flung network composed of other networks, dozens of different machines speaking their own electronic "language," and individuals with portable machines accessing central repositories of data from anyplace in the world with cellular or pay phones. This type of "network of networks," usually organized around some large business model, is called an *enterprise*, a loosely-applied term referring to any complex network. In enterprise computing, shared data is usually stored in several different locations; in technical jargon, it is *distributed* throughout the enterprise, producing the frequently-heard terms *distributed data*, *distributed processing*, and *enterprise computing*.

Enterprise computing represents a middle ground between the absolutely centralized world of mainframe computing and the completely decentralized world of stand-alone desktop PCs. Ideally, enterprise computing attempts to maximize individual productivity while keeping its foundation of raw data as tightly controlled, safe, and reliable as possible.

Where to Go from Here

When you first set up a network, you need to choose the type of hardware, software, and network operating system to be used, and the physical and logical topologies. These choices are interdependent and together make up the *network configuration*. You can make these choices by balancing such factors as:

Cost	What is the most efficient system your business can afford?
Speed	How fast does the system need to be?

Environment   Are there environmental factors (for example, the presence of electrical fields) that will influence the kind of hardware required?

Size   How big will the network be? Will it require a dedicated file server or servers?

Connectivity   Will other users (for example, field representatives using laptop machines) need to access the network from various remote locations?

You will find that your decisions tend to revolve around money: the cost of the number of nodes on your network, distances involved, and whatever future plans you envision for your business.

Here are some general guidelines for selecting an appropriate network topology:

Topology	Pro	Con
Bus	✔ Easy to set up.	✘ Difficult to troubleshoot.
	✔ Economical.	✘ Slow when network traffic is heavy.
	✔ Reliable; widely-used.	✘ Broken cable downs entire network.
Ring	✔ All computers have equal access.	✘ Reconfiguration suspends entire network.
	✔ Robust even with many users.	✘ One node failure can impact entire network.
Star	✔ Centralized Management.	✘ Manager must support multiple users.
	✔ Easy to add new users.	✘ Large networks more time-consuming to support.
	✔ Failure of one node doesn't affect the whole network.	✘ Failure of the central hub downs entire network.

From an information-management standpoint, nearly every business has certain unique characteristics. Each business must take the time to design a suitable information-management system. An experienced network design consultant or responsible vendor can help you analyze your business needs and explain your options in detail, showing you which options are most suitable for your particular business. Above all, proceed slowly in these early stages. Don't hesitate to get a variety of viewpoints from different vendors. Take your time so as to fully understand the systems you are offered; in this way you will save time and money in the long run and be assured of getting the solution your business really needs.

For Further Reading

- Charles, Gerald T. Jr. *LAN Blueprints: Engineering It Right*. McGraw-Hill, 1995.

- Derfler, Frank J. Jr. *PC Magazine Guide to Connectivity*. 3d ed. Ziff-Davis, 1995.

- Martin, James. *Local Area Networks*. 2d ed. Prentice Hall, 1994.

- Senn, James A. *Information Technology in Business*. Prentice Hall, 1995.

Subsequent chapters in this book will take up a more detailed exploration of network hardware, software, and design. This knowledge will serve as a platform on which you can base good buying and configuration decisions and create—or remake—a reliable, cost-effective network for your business.

CASE STUDY

GAB's office manager identifies the most computer-savvy of the company's employees and enlists them in helping to research and plan the network. After studying the available options, they come to the following conclusions:

A fast peer-to-peer system could be useful for quick and easy transfer of data files and facilitate the sometimes free-flowing communications between staff. It also has the advantage of being relatively inexpensive to implement and support. But GAB's particular challenge is that it must share information while maintaining a reasonable level of client confidentiality. GAB needs security as well as flexibility, and it wants to grow. Not only might a peer-to-peer system present security problems. it might become cumbersome, if not obsolete, before the company grows too much larger.

For this reason, they decide that a server-based system would better achieve the company's goals of backup, support centralization, shared resources, data security, communications, and future growth. They soon decide against a ring topology for this system, as it would be more appropriate for the already-rejected peer-to-peer system and unnecessarily complex for a server-based system. They consider a linear bus topology because it would be relatively easy to install the main cable from one end of the office wing to the other and drop extension cables to the computers in each office. But they are leery of potential difficulties troubleshooting a large, bus-based system. They also have concerns about downtime for the entire company should problems occur with the main cable. In the end, they settle on a hub-based star topology. Although more complicated to install, it will be easier to centralize the network administration and over time could be converted into a star/ring if the company grows very large and if individual workgroups would benefit from that kind of evolution.

CHAPTER

3

Communication Protocols and Standards

ommunication among human beings depends upon agreement about the meanings of words and the rules for using them. The closer and more consistent these agreements, the greater the chance for understanding. Nevertheless, one charm of human communication is its inexactitude. Most of the time, we don't need to spell out exactly what we mean because we know the listener or reader can infer a great deal from context. We understand (and sometimes misunderstand) one another because of the assumptions we make about what our words and style of communication mean. For example, if I tell you I think a certain person is "cool," you would have to know me fairly well, know the context in which I am speaking, or at least interpret my tone of voice, before you could determine if I'm offering high praise, taking a temperature reading, or simply describing a personality type.

Computers, alas, are not so good at drawing inferences, and computer network communications cannot afford any degree of inexactitude. Consequently, network vendors establish a *protocol*, or set of rules that govern the electronic communication process. These rules must govern every aspect of network communications, down to the smallest details. For example, separate protocols must apply to how data communication begins, continues, and ends. Protocols have been established for different types of hardware, software, and data. When all these different protocols work together to make data communication possible, the set of protocols is called a *protocol suite*.

It is the responsibility of the developers of hardware, network operating systems, and application software to develop their products so that they conform to the rules of communication. When a product conforms to a particular protocol suite (or set of different suites), the product is said to *support* those protocols.

In a simplistic world, there would be only one protocol suite, which would by necessity use a limited set of hardware and software, and networks would have to conform to it. Life would be easier; every network would be able to communicate predictably with every other network; and, once the necessary hardware and software were installed, all the computers in the world would be easily able to talk to each other.

In the real world, there are multiple vendors competing with each other for your money. They are continuously developing and refining network systems that work better, faster, and sometimes even cheaper, and that customers can apply to all sorts of unique circumstances. Manufacturers, industry leaders, researchers, developers, and vendors all pay close attention to the way systems work, what customers respond to, and what aspect of computing and networking offer a competitive edge in the marketplace. Experts gather together to work out a balance between adopting standard rules of communication and maintaining the kind of competitiveness that leads to improved products. All this activity results in support for different protocols that apply to different types of networks.

Some of these evolving protocols have become *de facto standards*, meaning that they are in such widespread use that network vendors try to develop new products that are consistent with them. It is a difficult task, since protocols put constraints on how network products work. As the need grows for more powerful networks, the hardware, software, and standards evolve and become more complex. Old networks become obsolete, businesses feel the pressure to upgrade to newer systems, protocols evolve along with everything else, and the vendors make more money.

This chapter discusses some standard communication protocols in use today. These protocols are likely to be the reference rules for new communication standards that will evolve in the future. It is important to have an understanding of standard protocols because computers cannot communicate without them, and vendors will use these terms and concepts as a way of promoting the advantages of their products over their competitors'. If you understand the protocols your system uses, you can make better decisions regarding selection of hardware and software, avoid incompatibility problems, and manage your system's evolution with less anxiety and more productivity.

OSI/RM and the Seven Layer Model

In an effort to develop a structured model for computer network communications, the International Standards Organization (an international body of experts who define a variety of different technical standards for governments) set up the *Open Systems Interconnection Reference Model*, or *OSI/RM*.

The purpose of OSI/RM is to demonstrate how the parts of a network communication system should work together. The model specifies only what needs to be done—it does not specify how those needs are to be implemented. Actual implementation is left up to individual developers and programmers who work out the protocols that conform to the OSI/RM model.

The OSI/RM model organizes communication services into seven groups called *layers*. Each layer specifies a greater degree of functionality in network services, building on the services of the previous layer. Together the OSI/RM forms a complete *Seven-Layer Model* (SLM) for network communicating. The layers are:

Layer 1: The physical layer   Describes the electrical, mechanical, and functional specifications for handling network data. It describes processes that handle data as streams of binary bits flowing through hardware but does not include standards for the hardware itself.

Layer 2: The data link layer   Describes processes for detecting and correcting low-level data errors during transfer of data between the physical layer and the layers above the physical layer.

Layer 3: The network layer   Describes processes for routing data between network addresses and for verifying that messages are sent completely and accurately.

Layer 4: The transport layer   Includes functions for establishing appropriate connections, initiating data transmission, and releasing the connection after a transmission is complete.

Layer 5: The session layer   Includes processes for controlling the transfer of data, handling transmission and transport errors, and managing records of transmissions sent.

Layer 6: The presentation layer   Controls rules for formatting data transmissions. For example, this layer includes specifications for encoding and decoding character sets.

Layer 7: The application layer   Describes specifications for the environment in which network applications communicate with network services.

The OSI/RM provides a way of thinking about network communications. It is a general-purpose model. Its significance derives from its use by governments. Governments can select standards from the OSI/RM model that meet their needs and issue a profile of OSI/RM standards, called a *Government Open Systems Interconnection Profile*, or *GOSIP*. The GOSIP is made available to manufacturers who intend to sell products to these governments. Governments have heavy financial clout in the marketplace, so manufacturers who service government markets pay serious attention to OSI/RM specifications. These OSI-compliant products, often with some degree of modification, can be distributed in private-sector markets as well.

TCP/IP

TCP/IP stands for *Transmission Control Protocol/Internet Protocol*. TCP/IP is more than twenty years old; it was first used to link government computers and is now the basis for the Internet, the largest network of computer networks in the world. Its evolution as a standard was boosted when it was incorporated into the UNIX operating system in the early 1980s. Nowadays, TCP/IP has the advantage of being compatible with a large number of different hardware and software systems.

The primary responsibility of the Transmission Control Protocol is to receive an electronic message of any length and break it into 64K sections. (The last section can be smaller.) By breaking up the message into sections, the software controlling the network communication can transmit each section and subject it to verification procedures one section at a time. If a section is corrupted during transmission, the transmitting program need only repeat the transmission of that section—it does not have to repeat the transmission from the beginning. Since data corruption can occur from time to time, especially over long distances, transmitting a section at a time is more efficient in the long run.

The Internet Protocol (IP) takes the sections, verifies each section's accuracy, addresses them to their intended destination, and makes sure they are sent in the proper order. The IP includes information on many different addressing schemes and uses the correct addressing scheme based on the intended destination. This feature allows TCP/IP to be compatible with different types of networks. TCP/IP is discussed in greater detail in Chapter 14. All network operating systems in widespread use today support TCP/IP.

NetBIOS

NetBIOS stands for *Network Basic Input/Output System*. The IBM Corporation developed it to provide a standard way of using the computer's underlying operating system to access network services.

NetBIOS can be used by any IBM-compatible network system. Because different systems have unique ways of tapping the features of the underlying operating system, individual implementations of Net-BIOS tend to differ just enough to make them incompatible with each other. In other words, if you are using NetBIOS and change your network operating system, there is some chance you'll have to use a new version of NetBIOS as well.

Still, NetBIOS has the advantage of hiding all those arcane and idiosyncratic aspects of network/operating system communication from the user. Instead, the user sees a more understandable set of network functions.

Network software can access NetBIOS functions by instructing the operating system to perform some network function. The software accomplishes this by sending a small chunk of data called a *network control block* (NCB). The NCB is passed to the operating system, which is programmed to understand it and respond with the correct network service; for example, to send a message to another computer.

NetBIOS has several useful functions. Here are some examples of those most commonly accessed:

Configuring the NIC   This function allows you to make changes to the settings of your network interface card or obtain information on its current configuration.

Message broadcasting   This function allows you to send a single message simultaneously to every other computer that happens to be connected at the time.

Node names   This function allows you to attach meaningful names to various nodes on the network. For example, you could name a shared printer "LaserPrint1" and forward printing documents to this name instead of some arcane node address.

Virtual circuits   This function allows you to establish a direct connection between two computers, bypassing the other nodes on the network. This can speed up two-way communication between a pair of nodes in a complex network. When the two-way communication is complete, NetBIOS deletes the virtual circuit.

NetBIOS Redirector

The Redirector is software that acts as a network "traffic cop." Its purpose is to control the flow of data between the various nodes on the network. It is responsible for seeing to it that the printers, servers, and clients all get data intended for them and for handling the flow in such a way as to eliminate bottlenecks along the network's data path.

The Redirector accomplishes this task by using a *Server Message Block* (SMB) protocol. This protocol intercepts requests by computers on the network and creates instructions that NetBIOS can understand. We might paraphrase such instructions like so: "Send this chunk of data to the screen on Roscoe's computer, send that chunk of data to the printer connected to Elaine's computer," and so on.

NetBIOS is a common standard for peer-to-peer networks such as LANtastic and Invisible NET/30. Microsoft's LAN manager also uses a form of the SMB protocol. NetBIOS is not generally used for very large or complex network systems. Figure 3.1 charts the NetBIOS protocol suite.

FIGURE 3.1

The NetBIOS protocol suite, showing relationships between protocols and their functions. Notice that data is passed to NetBIOS' operating system from software.

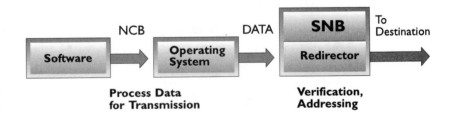

XNS

XNS stands for *Xerox Network System*. The Xerox Corporation developed it for use by smaller local area networks as a simplified protocol suite. It does not support the more complex functions of other protocols that are generally not required in small, local systems.

The basic protocol in XNS is the *Internet Datagram Protocol* (IDP), which handles data verification and addressing responsibilities similar to those found in TCP/IP. This protocol is a suite of smaller, dedicated protocols:

Clearinghouse translates device and user names to internal network addresses.

Packet Exchange Protocol (PEP) processes messages for reliable transport along the network.

Remote Courier Protocol (RCP) allows instructions by software to access and run services available on other network nodes. To the local software program, these services appear as if they are running on the local terminal. This allows programs without network-specific functions to access network services.

Routing Information Protocol (RIP) establishes the best data path for messages from one node to another.

Sequenced Packet Protocol (SPP) verifies that data is transmitted accurately.

The XNS protocol suite is used by Banyan VINES. A subset of these protocols is implemented in Novell NetWare versions 2.*x* and 3.*x*.

AppleTalk

AppleTalk is a suite of protocols for Macintosh systems. The suite is complicated and involves many integrated protocols that manage the various detailed aspects of the Mac's data communication system. Macintosh, in keeping with its ease-of-use philosophy, keeps these protocols well out-of-sight of the everyday user. Still, it is important to understand some Mac-specific jargon used to describe the Mac's networking services.

The heart of the AppleTalk suite is the *Datagram Delivery Protocol* (DDP). Each message sent to the DDP is accompanied by data indicating a specific computer on the network and an address in the computer's operating system that stores a procedure for handling that message. The computer is called a *station*, and the procedure address is called a *socket*. DDP receives messages and routes them to stations and sockets, where the processing takes place. Several protocols are used to facilitate and monitor the process:

AppleTalk Data Stream Protocol (ADSP) monitors the flow of data between two computers, to verify that it is not interrupted or corrupted by internal errors.

AppleTalk File Protocol (AFP) handles requests for data files, and it manages file security—for example, not allowing overwrites of read-only files.

AppleTalk Session Protocol (ASP) checks messages that are sent in sections. It tests to see that the sections are the correct size and are received in the correct order.

AppleTalk Transaction Protocol (ATP) verifies the accuracy of network messages.

Echo Protocol (EP) repeats each message back to the sending node to confirm that it has been sent completely, to gather information on delays, and to test the data path for maximum efficiency.

Name Binding Protocol (NBP) translates user-defined network node names into network node addresses.

Page Description Language (PDL) is a set of functions used by printers to control the formatting of text on paper. For example, Macintosh-compatible printers understand a PDL called PostScript.

Printer Access Protocol (PAP) monitors the flow of data that is sent in a continuous stream instead of sections.

Routing Table Maintenance Protocol (RTMP) monitors the location of nodes on the network and maintains a database of reliable connections between them. If one node fails, RTMP can establish an alternate route.

Zone Information Protocol (ZAP) analyzes the network configuration and collects device addresses into groups, or *zones*, to establish efficient access.

AppleTalk is specific to Macintosh networks. It is noteworthy in that it is integrated into the Macintosh operating system and is largely transparent to the user. Figure 3.2 charts the functions of the protocols in the AppleTalk suite.

AppleTalk supports two variations of its proprietary implementation, which allow it to coexist with other LANs: EtherTalk, also known as the EtherTalk Link Access Protocol (ELAP), and TokenTalk, also known as the TokenTalk Link Access Protocol (TLAP). Simply put,

FIGURE 3.2

AppleTalk protocol suite, showing relationships between protocols and their functions

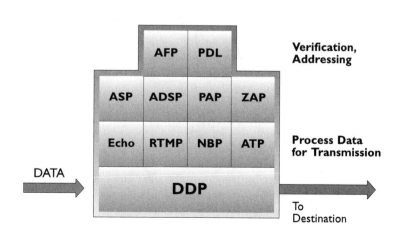

EtherTalk is AppleTalk linked over Ethernet at the physical and datalink layers. TokenTalk is AppleTalk linked over Token Ring at the physical and datalink layers. These variants require a special adapter card, which can be found in the more powerful Macintosh machines (such as the Mac Quadra).

NetWare Protocols

Besides its support for the standard protocols listed above (except AppleTalk), NetWare has introduced some additional protocols that are specific to itself. These protocols often duplicate functions found in standard protocols, but they are integrated more fully into NetWare's own system. NetWare protocols are for use on NetWare networks only, are additional to standard protocols, and are designed to give NetWare a competing edge over other systems that confine their implementations to standard protocols only.

Internetwork Packet Exchange (IPX) handles data verification and addressing responsibilities similar to those found in TCP/IP. This protocol can handle *internetwork messages* (messages sent between NetWare and other networks).

NetWare Core Protocol (NCP) manages the flow of data between NetWare clients and file servers for maximum efficiency.

Sequenced Packet Exchange (SPX) uses NetWare NOS functions to verify the accuracy of data.

Server Advertising Protocol (SAP) monitors the process of logging on and off the network, and it manages the transfer of messages between nodes throughout the entire internetwork.

Novell's strategy of providing proprietary protocols in exchange for more robust performance was dealt a blow in the mid-1990's, when Internet technology began making its presence felt in the world of business networking. Novell was already hard at work integrating their own proprietary TCP/IP gateway, called NetWare Internet Access Server (NIAS), into NetWare. But other companies had developed standardized TCP/IP gateways, bundled with Web servers and e-mail protocols that took advantage of TCP/IP's ability to function well on a wide variety of platforms. Novell realized belatedly that a proprietary TCP/IP gateway would not be competitive and hurriedly bundled together NetWare 4.11, NIAS, plus additional software such as NetWare Web Server, Multi-Protocol Router (MPR), and NetWare/IP into a product named IntranetWare. Their intent was to market IntranetWare as a complete networking and intranet solution, but the speed of change and deluge of intranet hype had taken their toll on the market—IntranetWare was already a me-too product in late 1996, and Novell was forced to play catch-up. Computer systems marketing is a cruel game.

Windows NT Protocols

Windows NT Server supports four protocols:

TCP/IP   Windows NT Server included TCP/IP protocol support well before Novell. This helped NT Server obtain a competitive advantage in intranet development features. TCP/IP is discussed in detail in Chapter 14.

Microsoft NWlink   A version of Novell's IPX/SPX protocols, discussed in the previous section of this chapter, included for compatibility between Windows NT and NetWare.

NetBEUI   An extension of the NetBIOS protocol. NetBEUI uses NetBIOS as an interface to the network but adds functions (support for Data Frame Format) that enable it to work with a wider range of hardware and software.

Data Link Control   A limited protocol, designed for connections to IBM Mainframe computers or for hardware devices that connect directly to the network cable, instead of a workstation or server.

Where to Go from Here

The important thing to remember about protocols is that they are the rules by which networked computers understand each other. The protocols discussed in this chapter are standard and in widespread use.

Computer networks have a tendency to evolve over time into larger and more complex systems, containing more nodes and devices and increasingly sophisticated software. It is helpful to know about protocols and to know what vendors mean when they advertise support for various protocols in their networking products. Also, if you know the rules your current system uses, you can decide whether future upgrades and changes to your system will be compatible.

For Further Reading

- Apple Computer, Inc. *Planning & Managing Appletalk Networks.* Addison-Wesley, 1991.

- Chappell, Laura A., and Dan E. Hakes. *The Complete Guide to NetWare LAN Analysis.* Sybex, 1996.

- Henshall, John. *Opening Up OSI.* Ellis Horwood, Ltd., 1993.

- Krochmal, Jim. *Banyan VINES Professional Reference.* New Riders, 1994.

CASE STUDY

GAB's owner and office manager meet again to discuss how to proceed now that they have settled upon the type of network they are interested in. The owner indicates that she has been reading articles in trade magazines and newspapers about the growth of the Internet and wonders if they should be developing an Internet presence. In addition, she has concerns about how to ensure that the network will deliver full performance for the money.

They agree that when they reach the stage where they are ready to receive quotes from vendors, they will ask each vendor to explain what communication protocols their proposed network will support. They agree that the vendor must make it clear how the proposed system will support local data-sharing protocols and Internet protocols as well. Finally, they agree that a vendor who can clarify and explain a system to them in terms they can understand would likely deliver the most reliable technical support as well.

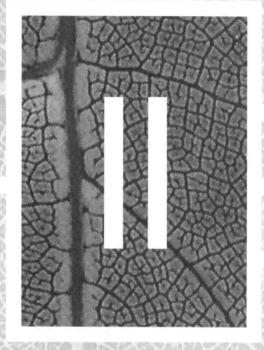

PART

II

NETWORK HARDWARE

CHAPTER

4

Workstations

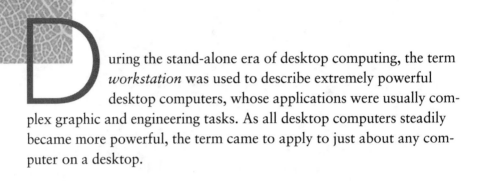

uring the stand-alone era of desktop computing, the term *workstation* was used to describe extremely powerful desktop computers, whose applications were usually complex graphic and engineering tasks. As all desktop computers steadily became more powerful, the term came to apply to just about any computer on a desktop.

Network Workstations

In a networking context, a workstation is any node on a network that is accessed and used by a human being (at a keyboard, for example). At a minimum, the workstation includes the standard items we normally associate with a desktop computer: a keyboard for entering commands, a monitor for displaying output, and a central unit for processing data. The central processing unit (CPU) includes random-access memory (RAM) for making changes to data and managing data communication instructions. Most network workstations also include a hard disk for data storage, although in certain circumstances they may not need one—for example, if a high-security application requires that all data reside on a remote file server. The workstation includes an internal transport system, called the *bus*, which moves data between keyboard, RAM, monitor, and hard disk.

Other optional equipment may be connected to the workstation—for example, a *mouse*, a pointing device used with graphic user interfaces like Windows, OS/2, and the Macintosh, or a *digitizer*, a drawing device often used with computer-aided drafting applications.

The key issues that affect a workstation's performance on a network are processing speed, memory, and bus performance. These issues are interrelated, and their relationship is discussed in detail in the following sections.

Choosing Your Workstation

Keep in mind that every user's needs are special in one respect or another. If your network is going to run only word processing and spreadsheet software, your workstation needs are going to be cheaper and easier to fulfill than if your network is going to run space-engineering design software. When in doubt about which workstation design is best, extend your implementation deadline and go over available options in detail with your vendor. Give yourself time to test a variety of workstation configurations to determine the best workstation for your own situation. The extra time you invest now will save much more time and money in the future.

Processing Speed

Each new microprocessor design released by a manufacturer does its work faster than the previous one. The only theoretical limit on the speed of a processor is the speed of electricity, so processors will continue to get faster and faster until we have reached the ideal of nearly instantaneous processing.

Speed is a burning issue for all computer users, more so now than ever before because recent software has become inordinately complex and graphics-driven. This software includes billions of separate computer instructions that must be processed inhumanly fast. Computer vendors have exploited this need for speed by heavily promoting microprocessor speed ratings in their advertising.

Microprocessor speeds are measured in *megahertz* (MHz). One MHz equals one million cycles of a vibrating crystal in the microprocessor, which controls its internal flow of instructions and is thus known as the *clock*. At the time this book is being written, microprocessor speeds of 200 MHz, or 200 million cycles per second, are common, and higher speeds are well under development.

Is Processor Speed the Whole Story?

In the most simplistic terms, the higher the MHz, the faster the processor, and the better the software performs. However, the actual speed of a workstation depends not just on the speed of its central microprocessor but also on its slowest individual component. In other words, if the microprocessor is fast but the hard disk is slow, or if the microprocessor and hard disk are fast but the video display system is slow, then the speed of the fast components is wasted while they wait for the slower components to catch up. (Later in this chapter we'll look at other components that can affect performance.)

The lesson to be learned here is to pay attention to the ratings of *all* the system components before you buy any computer. If you spot a "bargain" computer with the latest and greatest microprocessor and a temptingly low price, be certain the low price does not mean that some inferior component is lurking inside.

Microprocessor vendors are continually working to increase their products' performance by optimizing their chips' internal architecture. Powerful chips now available include Reduced Instruction Set Computing (RISC) chips such as the IBM PowerPC, Sun SPARC, and DEC Alpha; or Complete Instruction Set Computing (CISC) chips such as the Intel Pentium Pro and AMD K6. Intel has further optimized more recent Pentium chips by incorporating MMX technology (a set of 57 new instructions that increase multimedia performance). Chips now under development include Intel's Klamath (266Mhz) and Deschutes (333Mhz), Cyrix's M2 (225Mhz), and Digital's Alpha 21264 (500Mhz).

RISC chips are favored by users who depend on calculation-intensive tasks, such as engineering and high-end graphics applications. The major drawback of RISC chips is that they do not offer the widespread software compatibility of CISC. Intel and Hewlett-Packard have begun a joint project to develop a new instruction set, called IA-64. This 64-bit instruction set will attempt to combine RISC performance with CISC compatibility. Intel intends to produce an IA-64 chip (originally named the P7, now code-named Merced) before the end of the century. Its debut processing speed is currently unknown.

Memory

Memory speed and size are also crucial to workstation performance. It is a common misconception to believe that you can save money and install a relatively small amount of memory on a workstation and then run applications remotely across the network. This is possible but will usually cost you more—in terms of lost productivity because of slow performance—than you will save skimping on workstation RAM.

RAM size is measured in *megabytes*, a megabyte being space sufficient to hold one million bytes of data. At the time this book is being written, sixteen megabytes (16MB) are usually considered the practical minimum for networking, with 32MB a likely standard for machines running sophisticated graphic user interfaces such as Windows 95.

The amount of RAM each workstation requires depends on the size and complexity of the operating system and applications that you intend to run on it. Each workstation will devote a certain portion of its local RAM to those parts of the network operating system that it must access locally. The remaining RAM will be used to store software applications while they are running, plus the data being processed by those applications.

Applications specify their RAM requirements on their packaging, usually in very small print so you won't be deterred from purchase by reading them carefully. Squint and read them carefully anyway. While you're at it, check to see if the application is programmed to be network-aware, if it requires a specific network operating system to run, and if it has any esoteric hardware requirements.

Most recently-developed software will make use of *virtual memory*; in other words, if the software detects that there is not enough RAM available (above a certain required minimum need to run at all), it will store excess operating instructions in temporary files on your hard disk. Then, if it needs instructions stored on the hard disk, it will swap the needed instructions into RAM and swap out some unneeded instructions to make room for the needed ones. This process allows the software to function in less-than-sufficient RAM, but it is grindingly slow. Such a situation is at best a stopgap measure, and you would be well advised to consider adding more RAM to your workstation.

Something Is Easy?

Fortunately, adding RAM to modern workstations is a fairly easy thing to do. Modern RAM is supplied on small cards called SIMMs (Single Inline Memory Modules), as illustrated in Figure 4.1. These small cards snap into slots on workstation motherboards.

Just be sure that the SIMM you are installing is compatible with your motherboard. Some older SIMMs are designed for 30-pin slots, while more recent models are designed for 72-pin slots. Also, some older motherboards require that SIMMs be installed in pairs. Check your workstation's reference manual if you have it, or contact your workstation vendor to get answers to questions about the SIMM your machine requires. If you don't have a manual or if the vendor is no longer available, a qualified vendor or consultant will be able to advise you.

F I G U R E 4.1

Modern RAM for workstation memory is contained in a single inline memory module (SIMM) that can be easily installed in a workstation slot. A SIMM holds a series of DRAM chips that together add up to between 8 and 64 megabytes of RAM

72 pin

Ideally, each workstation on your network would have sufficient RAM to access and run every application *locally* (that is, in its own random-access memory). However, it is not absolutely necessary. In situations where it may be deemed practical, a single copy of an application can be stored remotely, accessed once by the workstation and run out of its own local RAM. This is not usually the best alternative as it tends to increase network traffic.

RAM, Storage, and Licensing

Be aware that most network software is sold based on *user licensing*. This means that the software vendor requires that a separate software license be purchased for each user of an application on the network. The license is not sold for the actual physical copy of the application. If you have ten people using a software program and they all access a single copy on a central server, you will in all likelihood be expected to purchase ten licenses. Some vendors offer *site licensing*, which permits an unspecified number of users to run an application at a single physical location. Site licensing can be limited. Read your licensing agreement carefully before agreeing to purchase any network application.

RAM chips come in a few different varieties:

Dynamic random-access memory (DRAM)   This is the most common type of memory chip. DRAM chips are low-cost and easy to manufacture. They use tiny capacitors to store electrical charges that represent data in binary format. Capacitors by nature lose their electrical charge very quickly, and the chip must continually refresh the charge to retain the memory image. Some chips, depending on their design, can refresh the charge more quickly than others. The faster a chip's *refresh rate*, the more efficiently the computer's processor can access the chip's stored data image.

Extended data-out random-access memory (EDO RAM)   These chips are specially designed to take advantage of fast motherboards, like those found on high-speed Pentium systems. They incorporate a more efficient data access scheme than standard DRAM chips, which results in a significant (20-30 percent) improvement in performance.

Static random-access memory (SRAM)   These chips are much faster and larger than DRAM chips because they do not require capacitors and do not need to refresh their electrical charge. However, they are much more expensive than DRAM chips and are generally reserved for special applications, such as hardware-based cache memory. (See Chapter 6 for more information about cache memory.)

Video random-access memory (VRAM)   These specialized SRAM chips are used on video controller cards to process the digital graphics data that is in turn converted into an analog signal for display on the system monitor.

Window random-access memory (WRAM)   These chips are found on expensive high-performance workstations. They intercept and process Graphic User Interface (GUI) data, freeing more of the system's on-board resources for general information processing.

The speed at which RAM chips function can have a noticeable effect on your workstation's performance. Memory speed is measured in *nanoseconds*, a nanosecond being one-billionth of a second. The smaller the number, the faster the chip. For example, 70-nanosecond chips are faster than 120-nanosecond chips. The faster the chip (as you might have expected), the more expensive it is. Still, if you are buying a workstation with an ultra-fast processor, buy the fastest RAM you can afford. Check with your dealer to determine the best RAM for your chosen microprocessor.

WARNING Memory speed is an often-overlooked feature and, knowing this, some vendors may attempt to lower their prices by shipping workstations with slower-than-required memory. The speed of a fast microprocessor is wasted by slow memory chips; be wary of the memory chips you might find lurking in these very low-priced machines.

File Server Memory

If you are running a client/server system, you will be running the network operating system from the file server while simultaneously sending and receiving both applications and data between the server and its various clients. These operations require vast amounts of RAM, and the requirement will only increase as your network operating system software becomes more robust and complex, more users are added, more applications are added, and existing applications are upgraded.

Server systems vary a great deal in their RAM requirements—anywhere from 32MB for a small system to virtually unlimited amounts for complex, high-end systems. Be sure that any file server you consider for purchase can accommodate additional RAM in the future. Ask your vendor to explain expandability issues before you approve the purchase of any machine.

Bus Performance

The *bus* is an electrical pathway inside a workstation's CPU. Data travels along this pathway between the CPU's components—keyboard or mouse to video card to hard disk to network interface card to other optional add-on controller cards and back again if required. Data flows along this path continuously while the computer is in operation.

There are two features of the data bus that determine its performance effectiveness: data transfer speed and the width of the data path. The rate at which data can move along the bus is set by the manufacturer. It is important that fast microprocessors use a correspondingly fast bus, otherwise the processor speed is wasted. In addition, bus speed is important when selecting add-on cards for the machine; a card designed for a slower bus will not work with a fast bus.

In the earliest desktop computers, the width of the data path was 8 bits. This meant that the data moved between components along eight parallel tracks of copper that were printed onto the computer's main circuit board (or *motherboard*). The 8-bit bus width allowed data to move one byte at a time. This system was soon replaced by a 16-bit data bus, using 16 parallel copper tracks so that data bytes could move between components in pairs, called *blocks*, making the data flow that much faster. The latest systems, such as those built around 80486 and Pentium microprocessors, use a 32-bit data path, which increases the speed of data transfer by an order of magnitude, using 4-byte blocks.

The data bus is constructed according to a standard physical architecture. The most obvious aspect of the bus architecture is the shape of the slots into which the peripheral cards must be inserted. Figure 4.2 compares different bus slots.

The network interface card in your workstation must be manufactured to fit with the type of bus architecture your workstation is using. There are five major types of bus architecture in use in networked systems:

Industry Standard Architecture (ISA)   This is the oldest standard bus still in widespread use. It is a 16-bit design but can handle peripheral cards designed for earlier 8-bit systems. It has the advantage of being less expensive than other bus architectures, but it is slow. ISA architecture can be found in IBM-compatible machines using 80286 processors or better.

FIGURE 4.2

Comparing bus connectors for different PC bus configurations. From left to right: 8-bit ISA, 16-bit ISA, 32-bit EISA, and 32-bit PCI.

16-bit ISA

8-bit ISA

32-bit EISA

32-bit PCI

Extended Industry Standard Architecture (EISA)   This is a 32-bit design that is an enhanced version of the ISA architecture, developed by Compaq Corporation in cooperation with other industry leaders, for use in IBM-compatible machines. Besides cards specifically designed for EISA, this bus can handle most cards designed for ISA machines. Its chief drawback is expense—EISA-specific network cards cost too much to make them popular for anything but file servers.

Macintosh NuBus   This is a proprietary bus used by the Macintosh and is not available on any other type of computer. It is a fast 32-bit system. Recently, Macintosh abandoned this bus in their new PowerMac machines, in favor of the PCI bus specification described below.

Micro Channel Architecture   This was a proprietary 32-bit design developed by IBM for its PS/2 line of desktop computers. It did not support any cards developed for any other bus. IBM developed micro channel architecture in hopes that it would become a new standard bus architecture and drive competing machines off the market. The system was very fast but did not catch on as well as it might have because of compatibility issues. The PS/2 computer has faded in the marketplace.

Peripheral Component Interconnect (PCI)   This is the most recent bus design. The Intel Corporation developed it to take advantage of the advanced processing power in systems that use 80486 or later microprocessors. It also borrows some concepts that were introduced in the micro channel architecture bus; for example, PCI cards have a direct connection to both the system's main memory and the CPU. This allows the card to function as a *bus master*, transferring information directly to the memory, bypassing the CPU. This bypass technique can speed up network performance dramatically. PCI cards also have the advantage of a lower price than comparable EISA cards. They use fewer hardware jumpers and configuration switches, making them easier to install and maintain. They are well suited for the plug-and-play architecture of operating systems like Windows 95 and Windows NT. Workstations differ in their support for PCI; some combine slots for PCI cards with ISA slots on the same machine. This type of bus allows you to use peripheral cards that take advantage of PCI's features (such as high-resolution video cards), together with older cards or cards that do not take advantage of PCI (such as modems).

Data Storage

Data storage on a network usually involves a compromise of one sort or another. Network designers have to weigh several concerns against one another when configuring network data storage systems. These concerns include access speed, convenience, application performance, and security.

Data on the network is stored on workstation hard disks, on the file server hard disk, or split between workstations and one or more servers. It is the responsibility of the network administrator to guide users on where to store data, as well as to keep track of what data is stored where, how to keep it secure, and how to be sure that its integrity and accuracy are upheld as the data moves throughout the system. See Chapter 12 for more details on network administration.

In a client/server system, the ideal data storage solution is to centralize all stored data on the file server and keep nothing of consequence on workstation hard disks. Some client/server workstations may have no hard or floppy disks of their own, requiring that all requests for data be handled by the central server, and preventing the workstation operator from copying any data off the network. For example, in a high-security environment (such as military defense or commercial research), such a diskless terminal would be a simple and practical means of preventing individuals from removing sensitive information on disks.

In most everyday circumstances, it is necessary to store some data on workstation hard disks, when security and data sharing are not issues and such local storage will reduce network traffic and speedup system performance. Client hard disks tend to be small (1–2GB), and file server hard disk are by necessity many times larger.

Peer-to-peer systems distribute data across a series of workstation hard disks, and it is up to the network users, in cooperation with a network administrator and sometimes with the help of internally-programmed access rights, to agree on systems to protect the data's integrity and accuracy.

The size of the hard disk on the server and workstations will be determined by the amount of data your system must handle weighed against the amount of money you can spend. However, there is a general law of computing that says that all stored data will eventually grow to fill any hard disk storing it. Unless you know there is a fixed upper limit on the amount of data you will handle, buy the largest hard disk you can afford.

A workstation's hard disk size is measured in *gigabytes* (GB). A gigabyte is the space it takes to store one billion bytes of data. These days, a 1GB hard disk on a workstation is considered small. On a network file server, such a size would be hopelessly inadequate. Nowadays, between 10 and 100 GB is common for file servers, using multiple hard disks.

Hard disks access data at varying speeds, measured in *milliseconds*, indicating the amount of time it takes the hard disk to find data. A millisecond is one-millionth of a second; the lower the hard disk's millisecond rating, the faster it is. Thus, a 10ms hard disk is faster than a 16ms hard disk. Because networks must access and store far greater amounts of data than stand-alone systems, buy the fastest hard disk you can afford. Fortunately, hard disk prices are falling and those made by the major manufacturers tend to be reliable. As long as you stick to the popular brand names (I've had good experience with MiniScribe and Western Digital), price can be your overriding concern when selecting hard disks for your system. For file server storage devices, choose one with a good warranty.

Network Interface Cards

The Network Interface Card was described generally in Chapter 2. This peripheral card is the key component of the network workstation. Its chief purposes are to send data out onto the network and to receive data sent to the workstation in which it resides.

Although several manufacturers produce network interface cards, they can all be used to talk to each other in any of the popular network systems (LAN Manager, NetWare, Windows NT, and others). A more important compatibility issue is the type of workstation bus in which they are being installed. For example, you cannot use a 32-bit card in a 16-bit bus. However, most 16-bit cards can work accurately, although more slowly, in a 32-bit bus. Cards are designed for specific bus architectures as well; many ISA cards will fit in EISA slots, but all other types of card will fit only into the specific bus slot for which they were built—PCI in PCI slots only, EISA in EISA slots only, and so on.

Each network card is manufactured with a unique, permanent electronic address. In accordance with standards set by the Institute of Electrical and Electronics Engineers (IEEE), manufacturers license blocks of addresses to encode onto their cards and, barring some egregious mistake on the manufacturer's part, this licensing system ensures that no address is ever duplicated. This address is a 16-bit binary code, which limits the total number of available addresses to about seventy trillion.

Network cards allow for a set of configuration options that ensure the card's ability to coexist with other peripheral devices in the workstation and to respond correctly to your network operating system. If you are using a Macintosh network, the hardware and software are already fully integrated and you need not concern yourself with configuration options. If you are using a PC-based network, you should consult your network operating system manual for information about the required settings for the NIC you are using and check the settings in use by other add-on equipment for each workstation to prevent conflicts.

Why Not Just Use the Defaults?

Almost all NIC vendors ship their cards with widely used standard configurations already set. Network software vendors, wishing to avoid customer support problems as much as possible, try to respect these default settings in their software. Still, take the time to check each board's configuration settings before you install it, even if you have decided to go with an "all default" configuration. Mistakes setting default configurations do creep in when a card is being manufactured; and once a incorrectly-configured card is in place and cabled up, the smallest incorrect setting can cause all kinds of mysterious and maddening behavior to occur. What's worse, these errors often seem to be software-related. Since you have assumed that all the NICs have default settings only, the NIC is the last place you expect to find the problem.

The two most important variables governing the behavior of an NIC are its *port address* and *interrupt*. The port address is different from the card's permanent address. Whereas the permanent address identifies the card throughout the network, the port address is a hexadecimal number used by the workstation to select a local electronic circuit through which it directs the NIC's incoming and outgoing data. A common default port address is 300h. The workstation must be configured to send network data to the correct port address; the NIC must be configured to recognize when data is sent to that address. If the hardware configurations do not agree, the data will get sent elsewhere (to the printer, to the mouse, or nowhere at all), the network will fail to respond, and the workstation may simply shut down.

The interrupt is also a local electronic switch used by the operating system to control the flow of data. The interrupt, as its name implies, is used by the workstation to stop the flow of data temporarily, allowing other data to pass through the system. Interrupts prevent different data flows from using the same physical circuitry simultaneously. PCs have a limited number of interrupts, and a workstation loaded down with many peripheral devices (such as modems, mice, page scanners, bar code readers, extra printers, dual monitors, joysticks, and more) must be carefully configured to allow all those devices to share interrupts without bringing the whole affair to a crashing halt.

Interrupt conflicts are a common cause of network problems. If you suspect that your workstation is locking up because of conflicts between network cards and other peripheral devices, the solution may be to take out one or more of the extra devices (bye-bye, beloved joystick), or to spend hours experimenting with various optional configurations until the whole mess finally works harmoniously together. In these circumstances, you may need the services of a network engineer, a person with the detailed technical knowledge necessary to straighten things out. Have the coffee ready.

Configuring an NIC usually involves setting *switches* or *jumper block connectors* (see Figure 4.3). It is always a good idea to set these devices before pushing the NIC down into its slot on the workstation's motherboard. If they need to be changed later, turn off all power, lift the card gently out of its slot, reset the switches, and gently replace the card.

Switches are usually found clustered together in a switchblock, a tiny plastic box. Switches are extremely small levers that must be set in combination to achieve particular configurations.

Switches are often too small for fingers to handle. Electronic supply stores carry miniature toolkits that contain tiny screwdrivers you can use to move switches.

Jumper-block connectors are set by pushing a separate small connector down on a pair of exposed pins. A good set of tweezers can help make this job easier. Move the connectors carefully—They have a tendency to fall away and hide in the recesses of your workstation's internal hardware. And if you handle them too roughly, they may bend or even break the pins.

FIGURE 4.3

A switchblock and pin jumper block. A switchblock sets configuration options by adjusting the positions of small switches. A jumper block sets configurations by shorting, or establishing a connection between, exposed connector pins.

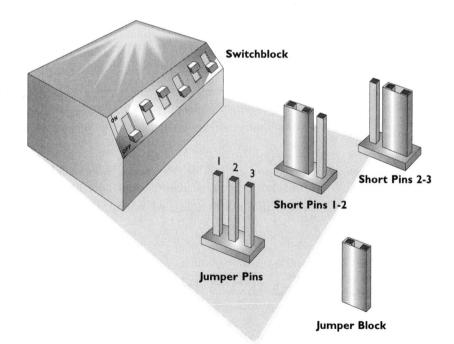

The switches and jumpers do more than set interrupts and port addresses. They can also configure the NIC to handle other optional features:

Cable   Some NICs can be configured for different types of cabling—thin Ethernet, thick Ethernet, 10BASET, and others. Refer to Chapter 5 for more information on cables.

Remote booting   Some NICs are designed to be used in diskless workstations and have special chips that allow the workstations to boot from file servers or other network nodes. A jumper or switch must be set to enable this kind of chip.

Direct memory access (DMA)   Some NICs have special circuits that allow them to bypass the microprocessor for certain data-transfer operations. These circuits can be enabled or disabled with switches or jumpers.

If you are using more modern NICs (for example, 3Com's EtherLink III, Addtron's AE-200, or Kingston's EtheRx), you can configure them entirely with software. This feature is a tremendous advantage over hardware-based configuration and can save hours of tedious problem-solving. It also allows a network administrator to change workstation configurations from a single node on the network.

Good workstation design can reduce the number of headaches you may encounter running your network. Keep copies of the NIC instructions handy, along with manufacturer's manuals for the workstation and the network operating system. Read the manuals carefully, take your time during installation, and test the results as you work. You will find that a little hands-on experience goes a long way and that the process will quickly become less daunting than it first appears.

Where to Go from Here

It is entirely possible that some, if not all, of your current desktop computers will be adequate as network workstations. Some may require only minimal upgrades in the form of increased RAM or storage space. Do a survey of the desktop computers your currently own. Open them up if necessary, or ask a qualified technician to do it for you. You will want to know their current RAM and hard disk size, their CPU type, video capabilities, operating system software, and what extra peripherals (for example, modems and printers) are attached.

This is a tedious job but well worth it. Your goal is to find ways to standardize the workstations on your network. The more alike they are, the easier they will be to manage and support. If your current machines are already suitable for your purposes, don't re-invent the wheel.

In previous chapters, you learned how to collect certain critical facts on which to base network design decisions: how your business handles information, what kind of network is most suitable, and who will manage the network. Armed with that information, a good listing of what you already own, and the guidelines in this chapter, you are ready to hack your way through that most treacherous jungle of the digital age: ads and catalogs from computer dealers promoting the latest and greatest in desktop technology. Compare them on the basis of price, features, and, most importantly, *reputation*. A dealer with a reputation for reliability and customer service is of great value.

The next chapter explores in detail the fundamental means by which all your workstations are able to communicate with each other: the network cabling that connects them.

For Further Reading

- Newman, Sally, and Allen Wyatt. *PC Magazine 1997 Computer Buying Guide*. Ziff-Davis, 1996.

- Pearson, Olen R. *Consumer Reports Guide to Personal Computers*. Consumer Reports Books, 1997.

- Thomas, Greg M. Jr. *The Ultimate Computer Buyer's Guide*. Wordware Publishing, 1995.

CASE STUDY

GAB's office manager has spent a long, difficult week going from office to office collecting information about the computers on hand. The company is the proud owner of three 80386-based machines, each with 8MB of RAM and a 500MB hard disk; four 80486-based machines with 8MB of RAM, which were recently upgraded with 1.2GB hard disks; one 80486-based machine with 16MB of RAM and the same size hard disk; and five 166-Mhz Pentiums, each with 16MB of RAM and 1.2GB hard disks.

The owner and office manager examine the results. None of the current computers is a good candidate for a server, as they all lack sufficient RAM and hard disk space, although one of the Pentiums may be upgradable to server capability.

They must also determine which network interface cards to use. They examine some catalogs from computer hardware supply houses and find a wide variety of cards available. The cheaper ones go for about twenty dollars, but others can cost more than a hundred dollars.

They agree to double the RAM in all the workstations and upgrade the smaller hard disks. This will allow them to run applications locally. After much discussion, they decide to purchase one new machine, with a 200MHz Pentium CPU, 64MB RAM, and one 2GB hard disk, plus room to grow and upgrade over time. This new machine will function as a dedicated server. The Pentium is a reliable CPU, a generally-accepted standard, and relatively inexpensive for its speed. 64MB of RAM appears to be an affordable minimum in light of GAB's anticipated usage (central file access and messaging, moderately heavy, with a small number of workstations). Expandability is extremely important; GAB may decide to upgrade once the network is up and running and they have a chance to see how they use it day-to-day.

The 80386 machines, however, require a closer analysis to determine if they can be used as workstations. If they have old-style RAM boards inside, it may be difficult to upgrade them. If additional RAM boards are not available, these machines could be useful dedicated to low-end applications. Before purchasing interface cards, the owner and office manager show vendors their summary of their workstation hardware. The vendor they use is able to tell them which cards are compatible with the bus of each machine they will be installed in and the cable they intend to use. Also, the vendor is able to ensure that the cards' software drivers are compatible with the network's proposed operating system. After talking with the vendor, the owner and office manager compare the features of acceptable cards and decide which cards provide the best value for the price. Because they are assuming growth and high traffic, they elect to install 100 Mbps Ethernet cards in their system.

CHAPTER

5

Cabling

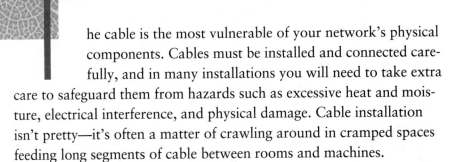

he cable is the most vulnerable of your network's physical components. Cables must be installed and connected carefully, and in many installations you will need to take extra care to safeguard them from hazards such as excessive heat and moisture, electrical interference, and physical damage. Cable installation isn't pretty—it's often a matter of crawling around in cramped spaces feeding long segments of cable between rooms and machines.

Cables are not exciting—they are often perceived as simple wires, and once installed they are easily forgotten. However, when an established, reliable network develops sudden problems, you should check your cabling first as a possible source of the problems. If you know what kinds of cables your system is using and understand their characteristics, you are better prepared to identify and solve problems that might arise.

This chapter will acquaint you with the language of cables and the basics of how they are installed and used. If you are installing a small system—for example, a system with less than ten nodes in a single room or small building—this chapter will give you enough information to select the proper cables and connect the network reliably. Bear in mind, though, that cabling issues become more complicated and elaborate as the size of your installation increases. If you are installing a very large system, covering several floors in a building or running between different buildings, you should leave the installation to a reputable professional cabling service. They have more experience designing intricate wiring schemes and avoiding potential hazards. And you will save money in the long run.

Cable Transmission Rates

The capabilities of different types of cable are described using a standard terminology that anyone involved in planning a network needs to understand.

A cable that transmits only one signal is called a *baseband* cable (often abbreviated to Base). Some cables can handle simultaneous transmissions of different signals by sending them at different frequencies. These cables are called *broadband* cables. Broadband cables are more expensive and require additional frequency-modulating equipment; baseband is the cable used for networking.

The terms broadband and baseband are related to a frequently-used piece of network jargon: *bandwidth*. Bandwidth is a general term describing the amount of data that can be carried on a network—the more data, the greater the bandwidth. Broadband cable can carry a network with a large bandwidth because a single cable carries simultaneous data transmissions along multiple frequencies. It is used, for example, by the telephone system to connect all those thousands of Mother's Day phone calls. But baseband, or Base cable, is what you will use for local area networking.

Cables are also described by the maximum speed of data transmission they are built to handle. Data transmission speed is expressed in numbers of megabits (one million data bits) transmitted per second. Thus, *10Base*, a common type, indicates that the cable is of the baseband type and is capable of transmitting data at a rate of 10 megabits per second (abbreviated as 10 Mbits/s).

Cables are also described by a numeral indicating the maximum length, in hundreds of meters, of any single segment you can use without degrading the electronic signal. For example, the term *10Base2* indicates that the cable is baseband, handles 10 megabits per second, and can be used to a maximum length of 200 meters.

Finally, if the cable is a twisted-pair type (discussed later in this chapter), the letter *T* is added to the end of this descriptive shorthand. Thus, 10BaseT (pronounced *Ten-Base-T*) describes baseband, twisted-pair cable that handles 10 Mbits/s.

Network technology developers are creating standards for faster transmission rates, with speeds up to one hundred megabits per second, to handle the heavy demands of larger and more complex networks. Currently, there are two standards for faster network performance: *100 Voice Grade(VG) AnyLAN* and *100BaseX Ethernet,* also called *Fast Ethernet.* Both standards are capable of speeds up to ten times faster than 10BaseT specifications. 100VG AnyLAN can support both Ethernet and Token Ring protocols. However, it requires its own hubs and cards; also, maximum cable lengths are limited compared to Ethernet specifications, even 10BaseT. For example, in a 100VG AnyLAN system, the total length of the two longest cables from a hub to a computer cannot exceed 250 meters.

Fast Ethernet, on the other hand, is simply an extension of the current Ethernet standards, making it easier to install or upgrade from existing Ethernet systems. However, Fast Ethernet does require specially-designed cable, described in the next section.

Cable Types

Besides the differences in their transmission capabilities, cables are classified according to their type of physical construction. There are several different types of cable, each suitable for specific network configurations and rates of data transport. The most common types of cable currently in use are coaxial, twisted-pair, and fiber-optic.

Coaxial

Coaxial (or *coax*, pronounced *co-ax*) cable is the most common type of network cable. This cable consists of an inner wire surrounded by a layer of insulating material, a conducting layer of woven wire, another layer of insulation, and a plastic covering. Figure 5.1 shows the structure of coaxial cable.

FIGURE 5.1

Different types of cable used to connect network systems

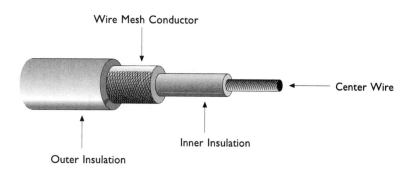

Wire Mesh Conductor

Center Wire

Inner Insulation

Outer Insulation

Coaxial

Type RG-58 cable (10Base2) is a thin coaxial cable in widespread use. It can connect many local area networks that are limited to a single office or small building and it is relatively inexpensive and easy to handle.

Older, larger, and more complex networks might use RG-11 (10Base5) cable. This is a coaxial cable that is much thicker and sturdier, can withstand more rugged surroundings, and as its descriptive type indicates, can be used with much longer segment lengths.

Twisted-Pair

Twisted-pair cable looks something like telephone cable. It consists of two pairs of wires twisted together. Figure 5.2 shows the structure of twisted-pair cable. There are two types of twisted-pair cable: unshielded twisted-pair (UTP) and shielded twisted-pair (STP). Higher grades of UTP can be suitable for data transmission on a computer network. STP is of higher quality and includes extra insulation to prevent electrical interference from degrading the signal.

Twisted-pair cable is less expensive than coaxial. However, coaxial has a reputation for greater durability because in older designs coaxial's

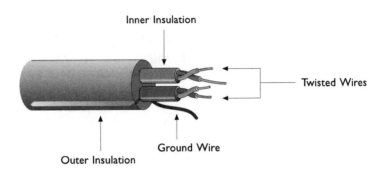

Inner Insulation

Twisted Wires

Outer Insulation

Ground Wire

Twisted-Pair

central wire was more durable and better-protected by the surrounding insulation and outer casing than twisted-pair. To see the difference in design for yourself, compare a cable TV wire (coax) to the wire between a desk telephone and the wall (twisted-pair).

In these older designs, twisted-pair wires were thinner than coaxial, more subject to breaks and line problems when the cable got twisted or creased. The outer casing was thinner, too. But more modern construction has produced very durable T-P cable. These improvements in cable manufacturing have made twisted-pair cable as reliable and durable as coaxial at speeds up to 100 Mbits/s. Another important advantage of twisted-pair cabling is its effect on the network as a whole: If a portion of a twisted-pair cable is damaged, the entire network is not shut down, as well may be the case with coaxial.

There are five categories of unshielded twisted-pair cabling:

Category 1   Ordinary telephone cable, used to carry voice, not data

Category 2   Certified to carry data up to 4 Mbits/s, using four twisted pairs

Category 3   Certified to carry data up to 10 Mbits/s, using four twisted pairs with three twists per foot

Category 4   Certified to carry data up to 16 Mbits/s, using four twisted pairs

Category 5   Certified to carry data up to 100 Mbits/s, using four twisted pairs of copper wire

The newer, faster LAN standards use unshielded twisted-pair cable. 100VG AnyLAN uses Category 3, 4, or 5 cable. Fast Ethernet uses one of two types of Category 5 cable: *100BaseT4*, which incorporates telephone-grade pairs of wires; or *100BaseTX*, which incorporates data-grade pairs of wires.

Fiber-Optic

Fiber-optic cable (shown in Figure 5.3) is becoming more common as demands for transmission speed increase. This type of cable consists of a thin glass or plastic filament, about as wide as a human hair, protected by a thick plastic padding and an external plastic sheath. Fiber-optic cable uses a pulsing laser light instead of an electronic frequency to transmit a signal.

Using light offers important advantages over using electricity; the light signal can travel farther, faster, and more reliably. This is because the light signal is not subject to electrical impedance from copper wires and can pulsate at faster rates than electric frequencies. In addition, the light signal is immune to external electrical interference. Fiber-optic cable can send reliable signals as far as 10 kilometers, at speeds approaching 100,000 Mbit/s. Both the 100VG AnyLAN and Fast Ethernet standards support special two-strand fiber-optic cable, called *100BaseFX* cable.

You may wonder why, if there is no electrical impedance to get in the way, fiber-optic cable has any distance limit at all. The answer is that after about 10 kilometers, the fiber has absorbed enough of the light to weaken the signal.

Fiber-optic cable is expensive to buy, install, and maintain. It requires special equipment (called *fiber line drivers*) to translate the electronic signals that are sent to and from workstations into pulsing light signals sent along the cable. Its use is limited to very large and extensive networks where distance, speed, and security issues are important enough to justify the extra expense.

FIGURE 5.3

Fiber-optic cable

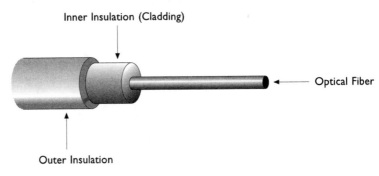

Inner Insulation (Cladding)

Optical Fiber

Outer Insulation

Fiber-Optic

Backbones

A backbone is a type of linear-bus cabling configuration, often found on widely-dispersed multiserver networks. The backbone's purpose may be to group each node closest to the server that holds the data it accesses most often; or to connect multiple servers close to each other; or to group nodes close to hubs, bridges, or routers.

Backbone cabling is effective on networks with nodes that are physically far apart from each other but still connected via cable—occupying several floors in an office building, for example. In such broadly-dispersed networks, the distances between nodes and servers can have a notable effect on performance. Fiber-optic cable is often used for backbone cables to improve transfer speeds. Figure 5.4 shows a typical backbone-style layout.

Backbones using fiber-optic phone lines are used to speed up connections between networks that must frequently communicate with each other. Although the connected LANs may be some distance apart, the use of a fiber-optic line over the wide area can mean a significant improvement in network performance.

FIGURE 5.4

A backbone-style cable layout. Notice that each node is no more than two nodes away from the server it will presumably access most often. Also, the servers are connected for fast data transfers between them.

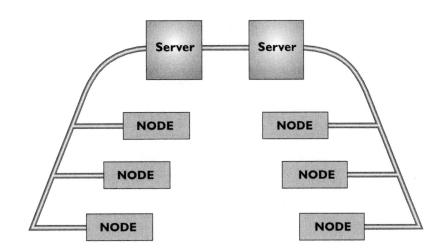

Selecting Cable

At one time, cable choices were determined by the chosen topology; for example, Ethernet used coaxial, and Token Ring used shielded twisted-pair. Nowadays, networks are more accepting of a variety of cable types, and thus your cable choices are a balancing act between budgets and performance needs. The selection is normally worked out on an installation-by-installation basis when you are initially designing and budgeting your proposed network. Here is an overview of how cable choices tend to be worked out:

Ethernet   This topology supports all cable types.

- Coaxial cables have the reputation of supporting higher data rates, longer distances, greater durability, and better protection from electromagnetic interference and electronic eaves-dropping (compared to unshielded twisted-pair cabling).

■ Modern shielded twisted-pair cables, however, have performance specifications virtually equal to coaxial, with the additions of greater flexibility and less impact on the network as a whole if they should suffer damage. For this reason, twisted-pair cabling is becoming more and more popular as the chosen cable for Ethernet networks.

■ Fiber-optic cable provides the highest data transfer rates, less susceptibility to transfer errors, and protection from electro-magnetic interference but is expensive and more difficult to install than the alternatives.

ARCnet   This topology uses coaxial, twisted-pair, or fiber-optic cables.

■ If you are working with one of the older ARCnet systems, chances are you will be using coaxial.

■ Some later variations of ARCnet support twisted-pair or fiber optic, with the same considerations as listed above.

Token Ring   If you are working with a Token Ring system, you will most likely use shielded twisted-pair cabling.

Fiber Distributed Data Interface (FDDI)   In this topology, if price is no object and high performance is the goal, you will use fiber optic cable.

Tables 5.1 and 5.2 summarize these considerations.

T A B L E 5.1	**Cable Type**	**Compatible With...**			
Choosing a cable type: network compatibility		**Ethernet**	**Token Ring**	**ARCnet**	**FDDI**
	coaxial	yes	no	yes; on later systems	no
	twisted-pair (shielded)	yes	yes	yes	no
	twisted-pair (unshielded)	no	yes	yes	no
	fiber-optic	no	yes	yes; on some later systems	yes

T A B L E 5.2	**Cable Type**	**Speed**	**Reliability**	**Price**	**Comments**
Choosing a cable type: network compatibility	coaxial	fast	good	midrange	used less often than twisted-pair in modern systems
	twisted-pair (shielded)	faster	good	lower	recent improvements in speed and durability
	twisted-pair (unshielded)	acceptable	subject to EMI	lowest	not often used in modern systems
	fiber-optic	fastest	immune to EMI	highest	technology still evolving and improving

Installing Cable

Cable is connected to workstations and other nodes along the network by means of special connectors. Connectors are specific to the type of cable being used. Figure 5.5 shows the most common types of connectors.

FIGURE 5.5

Cable connectors

BNC (Bayonet Connector) Plug

BNC T-Connector

Coaxial Connections

Coaxial cable requires a connection called a *BNC plug*, a metal cylinder with a slot cut in the side. The plug fits over a smaller cylindrical receptacle with a small knob. The slot in the plug slides around the knob as the plug is fitted into place. You secure the plug by turning it, tightening it against the knob.

A special BNC connector, called a *T-connector*, is used to join workstations in a ring or daisy-chain topology. A T-connector (shown in Figure 5.2) is attached to each network interface card and protrudes from the back of each workstation. The network is linked by cables that are attached to the open ends of the T-connectors. In a daisy-chain topology, two workstations (one on each end of the chain) will have only one cable attached. On these end workstations, the open end of the T-connector must be capped using a *resistor plug*, a small cap that absorbs the signal and prevents distortion along the line. This type of connection is fairly easy to set up and maintain.

Ethernet bus topology networks, which share a single cable, are connected in a different way. In this topology, a cable is connected directly to each network interface card and extended to the shared cable. The shared cable is marked every 1.5 meters to indicate where a *tap connector* (sometimes called a *vampire tap*) can be installed. A tap is a small device that stabs a hole into the shared cable and makes a connection to the core (hence the "vampire" nickname). The tap is used to attach a device called a *transceiver* (or *media attachment unit*, or *MAU*) to the shared cable. This device includes an attachment for a special nine-wire cable that connects the shared cable with the network workstation. This type of connection requires more precise and careful handling to ensure that solid connections are made at exact locations along the shared central cable. Imprecise connections lead to signal distortions and bad network communications, and therefore this job is best left to a professional.

Twisted-Pair Connections

Twisted-pair cables use connectors that look like the plugs commonly found on telephone wires inside homes. These connectors are called *RJ connectors*. They are built to different specifications for different types of twisted-pair cable. The most familiar type, called RJ-11 (shown in Figure 5.6), is the type used for telephones. A larger version of this connector is the RJ-45, which can handle cables with as many as eight wires. The RJ connector is simply inserted into a corresponding socket on the network interface card until it locks in place. This type of cabling technology is improving and can equal coaxial-cable performance at reduced cost.

Fiber-Optic Connections

Fiber-optic cable is made to order and comes equipped with its own connectors (shown in Figure 5.7). These connectors fit into special receptacles and lock in place. If you are connecting a workstation with

FIGURE 5.6

An RJ-11 connector, used with twisted-pair cabling

RJ-11 Connector

FIGURE 5.7

A fiber-optic connector

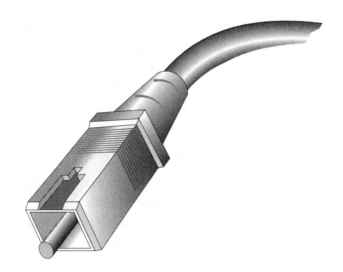

Fiber-Optic Connector

equipment that is not compatible with fiber-optic cable, you must attach the workstation to a conversion device called a *fiber-line driver* (Figure 5.8). This device takes the light signal and converts it to an electronic signal and vice-versa. It can become expensive to install a lot of extra equipment in order to provide compatibility between the nodes on your network and the cable, and the extra equipment requires additional maintenance as well. But if you have a very large system and need the enhanced performance, this option may be worth it.

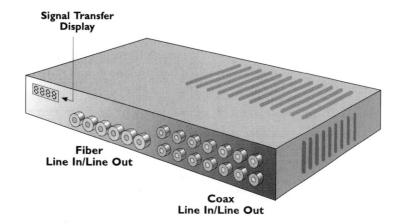

F I G U R E 5.8

A fiber-line driver

Signal Transfer
Display

Fiber
Line In/Line Out

Coax
Line In/Line Out

Handling Cable

Unlike other kinds of electrical wiring, network cable is subject to performance problems because of bending and pinching. For aesthetic reasons, people like to install cable out of sight—behind walls, above ceilings, and in crawl spaces. This is fine, provided that you protect the cable from hidden damage. Water leaks (from old plumbing, worn roofs, or whatever) and heat (from nearby heater vents, sunlight through windows and skylights, and so on) can ruin cable and shut down a network. In addition, cable signals are subject to distortions from nearby electrical appliances. Fluorescent lights have been known to cause problems; other potential problem spots are elevator shafts and nearby industrial machinery. When necessary, you may have to protect your cable from environmental interference by installing special insulating pipes and running the cable through them.

Common Cable Problems

Many network problems can be traced to cable problems. If you are experiencing bizarre network behavior, check the cable first. Some problems are easy to solve: The cable connection simply has shaken loose or has become disconnected. If all the connections are still solid, check the cable for signs of damage. If you find such evidence (for example, torn or sliced insulation), replace the entire cable.

Some network systems have built-in diagnostic procedures that can send signals down a cable and report on the status of the transmission.

Sniffing Down a Cable

Because cabling problems are frequently the source of network problems, it makes sense to inspect the cables when troubleshooting almost anything— from intermittent slow-downs to the terrifying, out-of-nowhere system crash.

- Check the cable connectors first. Loose or disconnected cables cause big problems and are often easily reconnected.

- Check for signs of physical damage. Cables can get cut or broken (when heavy objects move across them, for example), and the damage is usually easy to spot.

- If the cables are not easy to inspect (they are threaded through air ducts or behind building walls, perhaps), you can use a device called a *time-domain reflectometer* (informally, a *cable sniffer*) that transports a signal down a cable and measures the time it takes the signal to reflect back from blocked points. The elapsed time is translated into cable distance, and you then have a pretty good idea where the trouble is.

Cabling Ethernet

Ethernet is a flexible topology supporting a wide variety of hardware and configurations. It can use both coaxial and twisted-pair cabling. Coaxial cable can be RG-11 (also called *thick Ethernet*), using transceivers to connect to workstations, or RG-58 (also called *thin Ethernet*), using T-connectors to link workstations directly. Thin Ethernet is good for relatively small local networks, especially using peer-to-peer topologies. Thick Ethernet is good for larger, more demanding systems, such as client/server systems with a lot of nodes and data traffic. Twisted-pair cables are used to make direct links between workstations and a central hub. Regardless of the physical topology that you choose, Ethernet functions as a logical bus topology.

If you are using thin coaxial cable with T-connectors, the following rules apply:

- The longest allowable cable segment between nodes is 300 feet.

- The shortest distance between T-connectors is 1.5 feet.

- The maximum number of nodes on a network (without repeaters) is 30.

- The total cable length along a network (without repeaters) cannot exceed 607 feet.

- Up to four repeaters can be used, joining a maximum of five cables and 138 nodes.

- The total cable length along the entire network (with repeaters) cannot exceed 3,035 feet.

If you are using thick coaxial cable, the following rules apply:

- The longest allowable cable segment between nodes is 300 feet.

- Special nine-wire cable is used to connect the workstations to the shared cable.

- The shortest distance between transceivers is 1.5 meters (8 feet).

- The maximum number of nodes on a network (without repeaters) is 100.

- The total cable length along a network (without repeaters) cannot exceed 1,640 feet.

- Up to four repeaters can be used, joining a maximum of 488 nodes.

- When using repeaters to join cables, up to five cables can be joined, but only three can have computers attached to them. The other cables must be empty and serve only to extend the overall length of the network.

- The total cable length along the entire network (with repeaters) cannot exceed 8,200 feet.

If you are using twisted-pair cable, the cabling rules are determined by the type of hub used to make the connections to the workstations. In general, you should be allowed up to 300 feet of cable between the hub and each workstation.

Some Ethernet hubs can be connected to other hubs using coaxial cables. In such cases, the rules for coaxial cabling apply.

Cabling Token Ring Systems

Token ring networks use a ring topology to support large, complex systems. These systems use shielded, twisted-pair cables in most cases. Workstations are connected using a special Token Ring hub called a *multi-station access unit* (MSAU). Each MSAU contains up to 24 ports for network nodes. In addition, each MSAU has two special ports, called Ring-In (RI) and Ring-Out (RO). If you choose, you can use these ports to connect several MSAUs together. Figure 5.9 shows a simple token ring cabling topology.

If you are using shielded twisted-pair cables, the following rules apply:

- If you choose to connect more than one MSAU to your network, you must connect each MSAU's RO port to another MSAU's RI port, thus chaining them all together in a physical ring. If you are using only a single MSAU, the RI and RO ports are ignored.

- The longest allowable cable segment between an MSAU and a workstation is 150 feet.

FIGURE 5.9

Cables and connections in
a Token Ring topology

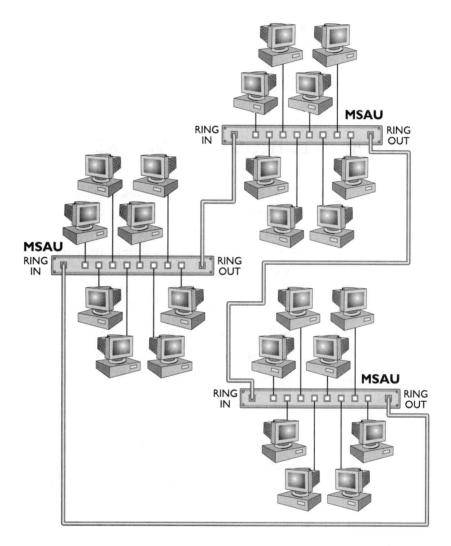

- The maximum distance between two MSAUs is 150 feet.

- The maximum number of nodes on the network is 260.

- The maximum number of MSAUs is 33.

Token Ring networks can become quite complicated, more so if you use bridges, routers, and gateways. Connecting these types of devices to a Token Ring network can force changes and exceptions to the above rules, and such an installation should be undertaken by an experienced professional.

Cabling Macintosh Networks

Macintosh networks use shielded, twisted-pair cables. Each workstation uses a *drop cable* to connect to a small connector called a *LocalTalk connector*. Other cables connect the LocalTalk connectors to each other. The system is simple and easy to set up. Cabling rules are simple as well:

- The maximum total length of cable along the network is 1000 feet.

- The recommended maximum number of nodes is 32. (LocalTalk hardware supports up to 254 nodes, but with this many nodes performance would be seriously degraded; therefore, it's not recommended.)

Other types of cable can increase the recommended specifications. For example, you can use Farallon's PhoneNet cabling system to increase the size of your Macintosh network. This system uses unshielded twisted-pair cabling and standard phone connectors. It allows a maximum of 48 nodes and 1800 feet of cable total along the network.

Where to Go from Here

Speed, speed, and more speed is the Holy Grail of networking. Network hardware design is centered around making things faster than ever, and cabling specifications may change to accommodate newer and faster networking systems. Expect to see lower prices as different standards and specifications emerge. This chapter has given you guidelines for selecting and installing cable, plus a foundation for understanding what changes may be made in the future.

For Further Reading

- Derfler, Frank J. and Les Freed. *Get a Grip on Network Cabling*. Ziff-Davis, 1993.

- Trulove, James. *LAN Wiring, An Illustrated Guide*. McGraw-Hill, 1997.

CASE STUDY

Now that they have made important decisions about the topology of their proposed network, GAB's owner and office manager find the selection of cable relatively easy. They know they plan to implement a hub-based star topology. Most hubs use twisted-pair cable. They are planning to implement a 100-Mbps system, so they agree to use 100BaseTX cable. No one at GAB has any experience installing cable, so they plan to hire an experienced cable installer for the job.

As the proposed system takes shape, it is clear that more and more of the decisions regarding network components are based on how they work together, not just on the strengths and weaknesses of each individual component. The network must be viewed as an integrated system whose components are coordinated to work together.

CHAPTER

6

Servers

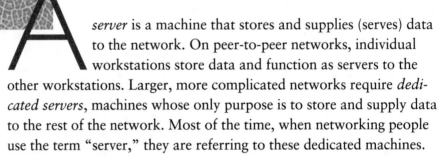

server is a machine that stores and supplies (serves) data to the network. On peer-to-peer networks, individual workstations store data and function as servers to the other workstations. Larger, more complicated networks require *dedicated servers*, machines whose only purpose is to store and supply data to the rest of the network. Most of the time, when networking people use the term "server," they are referring to these dedicated machines.

(By the way, a machine that receives the data from a server is called a *client*. Networks that depend on dedicated servers are thus called *client/server* systems. You will learn more about clients in Chapter 9.)

There are different types of servers, distinguished by the type of data they store and supply. *File servers* are the most common. They are discussed in previous chapters, especially Chapters 2 and 4, in relation to other network technologies. This chapter explains in detail what file servers do, how they do it, and how they came to be. Understanding something about file server technology will help you decide whether a client/server network is the right kind of network for your business.

How Servers Came to Be

The computer revolution has yet to fulfill its ideal of a paperless office. As computers have become more powerful, they produce increasingly sophisticated information. However, most of this information, sooner or later, is put back on paper. With today's word processing programs (or even spreadsheet and database software), any computer user with a sufficient understanding of page design can produce professional-looking documents incorporating various fonts and page layouts, tables, charts, graphic images, equations, and the like—all intended to be printed on paper.

A Server for Every Client

A file server can store any type of data, and on simpler systems, may be the only server necessary. On larger and more complicated systems, server responsibilities may be distributed among several different types of servers. For example:

Print server   This machine manages user access to shared output devices, such as printers. These are the earliest type of server and are discussed in the next section of this chapter.

Application server   This machine manages access to centralized application software; for example, a shared database. When the user requests information from a database, the application server processes the request and returns the result of the process to the user. For more information on shared databases, refer to Chapter 13.

Web server   This machine stores and retrieves Internet (and intranet) data for the enterprise. For more information, refer to Chapter 15.

Mail server (also called communication server)   This machine manages the flow of electronic mail, messaging, and communications with mainframe systems on large-scale networks. Electronic communications are discussed in Chapter 10.

Fax server   Similar to the mail server. This machine manages flow of fax information to and from the network.

Directory services server   On large-scale systems with data that is distributed throughout multiple servers, this machine functions as an organization manager, keeping track of what is stored where, enabling fast and reliable access to data in various locations.

Sophisticated printed information requires sophisticated printing hardware. Printers have evolved in response to this need, but the most powerful (for example, high-resolution, full color) printers are also the most expensive.

This problem has existed since the first days of desktop computing. Because a printer connected to a single computer often sat idle for hours at a time, it was a natural response on the part of information experts to look for a way to make expensive printers more cost-effective by allowing a number of users to share the same printer.

Sharing a printer presented scheduling and resource problems: It wouldn't be cost-effective to tie up computer time waiting in line to print. Printer sharing required an intelligent management scheme to store and line up ("spool") print jobs separately, allowing computers to continue other processing while the printer churned out information on paper. The solution was a *print server*, a separate computer that received printing instructions from several computers, stored the instructions, and fed them to the shared printer in turn.

Management eventually caught on to the idea that the print server could save resources (read: money) and increase productivity (read: profits). They increased demand for more sophisticated print services. In large organizations, print servers could manage several printers. Print servers could run in unattended batch mode, at night, leaving more time for human workers to focus on company business. Print servers could analyze the printing process and offer information that could be used to streamline printing. In this way, the print server was the beginning of client/server networking.

Enter the File Server

If it worked for printing, why not for data? Storage media were also expensive. Why not share a single storage location? This would save money, simplify access to the documents needed by many different users, and eliminate the inconsistencies that arise when copies of the same document are scattered on hard disks throughout the organization. The goal of achieving consistency and reliability of information throughout an organization was the business ideal of desktop computing's infancy.

File sharing, unfortunately, was a much more complicated and expensive process than printer sharing. Whereas print services involved mostly one-way transfer of data (computer-to-printer), file sharing would involve transfer back and forth throughout the organization. Bottlenecks and collision would have to be avoided, and centrally-located, shared information would have to coexist with local, individually-owned information. These were immense technological problems to solve.

The solution was the *file server*, a computer dedicated to storing shared information and managing (by means of software and transmission hardware) the distribution of that information throughout the enterprise.

How Many Servers Is Enough?

File servers must be doing something right. The demand for these powerful computers increases each year. According to the Bureau of the Census, there are over 11 million business establishments (defined as a location with at least one worker) in the United States. By the turn of the century, nearly every business establishment in this country and in the world will have at least one computer, and many will have more than one.

These computers are linking together. As a conservative estimate, there are easily 30 million business locations worldwide now in the process of linking up and transmitting data. Some experts estimate that the business world will make use of more than 50 million file servers before the turn of the century.

File Server Functions on the Network

If the local area network is the nervous system of a business, the file server is the system's brain, as illustrated in Figure 6.1. Software on servers process orders, manage inventory, schedule shipments, balance accounts, issue paychecks, manage schedules, update personnel records, and analyze the organization's use of its resources, including the network itself. Overall, file servers provide the following general services:

1. They function as a central repository for shared business data solutions.

2. They enforce enterprise-wide rules that (ideally) transform this data into consistent, meaningful information.

3. They facilitate communication between work team members.

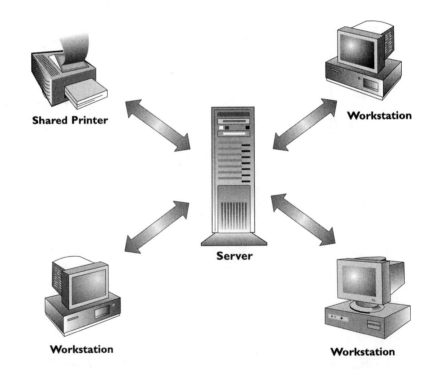

FIGURE 6.1

In a network with a single file server, the server stores data and distributes it throughout the enterprise. This model balances convenient access, consistency, and security. Notice that this model is a logical model and is independent of the physical topology of the network.

Shared Printer

Workstation

Server

Workstation

Workstation

Storing Shared Data

Servers, to a large extent, follow a hierarchical model of information storage and retrieval as it evolved in the pre-computer world. In the pre-computer world, the fundamental building block of business information (the first level) was a sheet of paper on which information was printed. At the next level, sheets of paper could be gathered together and secured with a staple or clip of some kind. Related documents could be gathered into file folders, file folders gathered together into larger hanging folders, hanging folders in file drawers, drawers in cabinets, cabinets in rooms, rooms in buildings. If a document was relevant in more than one context, physical copies of it needed to appear in each appropriate file folder.

Servers translate the ink/paper storage model into an electron/magnetic media storage model, but the fundamental arrangement is the same. The basic building block (the computer equivalent of information-on-paper) is called *data*. Data is information in its simplest form, meaningless until related together in some fashion so as to become meaningful. Related data is stored on a server's disk under a unique name, called a *file*. Related files are gathered together into directories, and related directories are gathered together into larger and larger directories until all the required information is stored in a hierarchy of directories on the server's hard disk.

The server's "filing cabinet" is a database; it offers a number of advantages over the paper model. You can search electronically for a particular file, even if you can only remember a tiny portion of what the file contains.

Using a database, you can *tag* data, relating it to other data in several different ways, without having to replicate the data in different physical locations. This ability to access and organize data in a flexible manner without making physical copies of it (and thus preserving the integrity of the information at its most basic level) is what has led to the increasing use of client/server technology as a widespread business information model.

The Server and the Database

Servers exist primarily to manage databases of information in various formats. Without the database, servers would be impractical as business tools. True, you could still use them to share resources and facilitate communication; but, in the absence of business databases, a peer-to-peer network would be a more cost-effective tool to handle these jobs. So the question of client/server becomes a question of whether or not your business needs centralized databases. Sharing and communications are built on top of that.

The Database

A database, generally defined, is a flexible, hierarchical structure for storing raw data, which facilitates its organization into useful information. Under this definition, just about all data on computers is stored in one kind of database or another. A spreadsheet is a database, arranging data in a grid of rows and columns. A word processing document is a database, storing data in an arrangement of characters and formatting instructions.

What a database does, then, is break down information into its most fundamental components and then create meaningful relationships between those components. We depend on databases of varying configurations and complexity for all our computerized information needs.

A specialized form of the database is the *relational database*, which follows the hierarchical component model to its logical conclusion. The relational database breaks down a series of related forms of data into fundamental units, which are arranged according to common attributes, called *fields*. Then it arranges the fields into sets called *records*, and the records into sets called *tables*. It also forms relationships between tables based on links between different fields. All of this data crunching is handled by a piece of software called a Database Management System (DBMS), which you will learn about in Chapters 10 and 13.

Many people, when they hear the term database, think of a DBMS. But in the client/server context, the term database is extended to include any hierarchically-arranged data. And, as you'll see in Chapter 10's discussion of network applications, the concept of information sharing embraces tools such as e-mail and discussion media as well as databases.

Data Distribution

Distributed data and *distributed processing* are terms used widely in the world of client/server networking. Figure 6.2 shows a graph of the difference between these two terms.

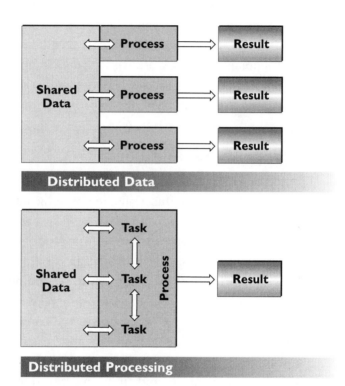

FIGURE 6.2

Distributed data
(shared access) and
distributed processing
(shared tasking)

Distributed data and distributed processing are two sides of the same coin:

Distributed data refers to the basic data stored in the server, which is distributed to different members of the work team.

Distributed processing refers to the way different tasks are organized among members of the work team. If a set of information-handling tasks is thought of as a single step-by-step process and is split among members of the work team so that they can handle the steps more efficiently, that process is distributed.

Here's an example: Imagine that a customer's ordering and payment information is stored in a central customer record on the server. This record is accessed by many departments in various locations throughout the company (accounting and shipping/receiving, to name two). Thus, this data is an example of distributed data. In addition, because accounting and shipping/receiving work with the data in unique but related ways in order to accomplish a specific goal (updating the customer record), their activities are an example of distributed processing.

Enforcing Enterprise-Wide Rules

In addition to centralized storage, the file server performs a less-understood, but equally important, function: preserving the integrity of the data by enforcing rules about how it may be processed and communicated.

For example, practically every business derives its income from invoicing customers. A well-run business follows generally accepted rules for handling invoices in order to determine how best to record charges and payments. Charges must be related to both customers and products ordered, records must be stored consistently and accumulated accurately, and payments must be applied against the correct customer and correct invoice. Back orders, late charges, and other anomalies must be accounted for, and all this must be done in a consistent manner to avoid the kind of confusion and mistakes that will alienate the customer and undermine the business. If everyone in the business could access the data and make whatever changes to it they deemed appropriate, it would be impossible to maintain consistent, reliable information for the enterprise.

Throughout any business, rules are set up for handling all sorts of different information. These rules can be formally designed, like those for bookkeeping and accounting, or they can evolve out of the day-to-day handling of the business, but they are there and their consistency is vital.

What's a Business Rule?

The concept of *business rules* is so important in the world of networked computing that it's worth defining in some detail.

In general terms, a business rule is a process that specifies some action (or set of actions) that occurs as the result of another; to put it in computer-specific terms, a business rule is an *if/then* process. An example: *If the minimum shipping order is 25 items, then orders of less than 25 items must be combined to meet the minimum.* If the minimum is met, then we ship the order.

Business is full of these rules. Together, they form a series of steps that define the nature of business and keep it running. And, of course, business rules are organic—they tend to evolve and become more complex over time.

If you are running a one-person business (or at least a very small one), the rules may be informal, kept in your head (*If it's Tuesday, then I stay open an extra hour*) and subject to momentary exceptions. A medium-size or large business cannot afford to keep informal or constantly-shifting rules because employees would waste time determining a course of action instead of taking it. ("*What were we supposed to do with government purchase orders again?*" "*How do we account for customer defaults?*")

The short-term if/then decisions of a business work together to become the real policy and business plan of an enterprise, more so than idealized mission statements or advertising copy. To whatever extent you have formalized the business rules you work by and communicated those rules clearly throughout your enterprises, you can expect to have pretty much that same extent of success using computers to model your business procedures.

Centralized data storage provides a narrow access point through which data is made available to the enterprise and through which the enterprise transmits data for storage. It is at this point that the server can be programmed to accept or reject the transmission if the information does not conform to vital rules. For example, the server can assure that charges are not billed to customers without an accompanying order for products. Also, the server can perform necessary security operations, such as preventing data from being lost or making sure that sensitive business information is not available to competitors.

A business's competitive advantage is often based on specialized knowledge (access to information). Centralized data storage and retrieval often involve a delicate balancing act between ready access to information by those who need it and securing proprietary information against those who might use it against the enterprise. For example, a company is well justified in keeping its new-product research and development information confidential. It has, after all, invested significant resources in its creation. The company needs to be sure that those who are developing new products have access to the research results, while keeping competitors' eyes away.

The balance between access and security is seldom perfect. Most companies will tend to make data more secure than accessible, and thus day-to-day accessibility issues can take up a significant amount of a network administrator's time. We will discuss data security in greater detail in Chapter 11.

Facilitating Communication

The file server, because of its centralized nature, is a natural repository of ad-hoc information between work team members. Software on the server can send a single copy of a business memo from one team member to selected other members, or to the entire enterprise, nearly instantly. Server software can inform team members that a message exists for them, provide access, and keep track of who has received the message and who hasn't.

Network communications systems (also called e-mail) have evolved into complex messaging systems that provide sending, storing, and receiving services for a virtually unlimited number of potential users, as well as managing complicated security and access issues. If the system is large enough, a separate server may be dedicated to managing communications. Electronic communications are discussed more fully in Chapter 10.

Resource Sharing

Finally, the original purpose of the server, allowing shared access to expensive peripherals, remains as important a function as ever. These days, however, more than just printers are involved. A server can manage access to such devices as high-speed, multi-line modems that permit simultaneous access to the network from remote sites; data scanners for more efficient data input; sophisticated graphic output devices, such as pen plotters; and high-speed data backup devices. In effect, just about any information-processing device can be attached to the server and shared, provided that it is cost-effective to provide the necessary supporting technology to make the connection. We have come a long way from the lowly print server, but the principle remains the same.

Print Servers: Then and Now

From its beginning as a dedicated workstation, the print server has evolved into as much a logical process as a hardware device. For example, in NetWare, a dedicated workstation can run software named PSERVER.EXE to manage the flow of data to printers on the network. However, as a process running on top of a file server or router, the print server is software—named PSERVER.NLM (a NetWare Loadable Module)—that does the same job without dedicated hardware (at the cost, however, of using up some of the file server's RAM and disk space).

The Server's Technical Requirements

If the business benefits just discussed sound interesting to you and you believe that you are in the market for client/server networking, be ready to open your wallet. File servers must be capable of handling thousands upon thousands of requests from users. This means that servers need:

Massive storage   (Not only to hold data that is to be shared by many individuals, but also to hold network application/management/communication/interface data.) Furthermore, the need for storage space is increasing because all software becomes more feature-laden and complex as vendors compete to provide upgrade incentives. We are already at the point where immense storage capacity is required for software applications alone. It isn't unusual for some server disks to use more space for application software files than for the data files they manipulate.

Massive Random-Access Memory   From the user's point of view, graphic interfaces and advanced application features make data processing easier and more intuitive. From the computer's point of view, they are diabolically complex, involving billions of individual data-processing instructions. An ocean of RAM is now required to keep vast amounts of data processing instructions, plus the data being processed, in a place where they can all be handled efficiently.

Blazing speed   What good are billions of instructions if the machine executes them slowly? At the positively glacial pace of one second per instruction, a computer would take more than 31 years to process a billion instructions, and a billion instructions aren't nearly enough to do any serious processing on your network. Computers must therefore execute billions of instructions in scant seconds. They must also be able to transfer data between storage and RAM fast enough to keep up with their processing speeds. This means hard disks that are not only big, but also can access stored data as close to instantaneously as possible.

Bigger and faster servers are more expensive. The larger your network, the more speed and storage you need, and you (or your trusted network engineer) must determine your exact requirements. For purposes of comparison and as a thumbnail estimate, consider that a 20-node client/server network running an average database for a company of that size, with room for individual applications and standard communication features, might want to start with a single-processor, 200-MHz Pentium server, with 2 or more GB hard disk storage and 64MB RAM. But these figures are not hard and fast. Every business is different. Your server will be custom-designed.

Of course, you can wait, and today's power machine will be cheaper next year. That's the good news. The bad news is that it may be obsolete as well. To keep today's servers from falling by the wayside, more and more hardware designers are building upgradable servers, meaning servers that will accept more powerful or additional processors, additional RAM, and larger or additional hard disks, as they are needed and become available. This type of server promises to have a longer life span, and may well be worth the additional money.

Servers, like workstations, tend to feel obsolete after about three years. It is wise to know before purchase that the server you are considering includes a clear upgrade path, in order to maintain the usefulness of your investment.

Servers and Mainframes

There is some controversy as to whether servers will someday replace mainframes. They may, but not any day soon. Mainframes still serve a purpose in managing the complex business rules of very large organizations and enterprises that are spread out over a very large area. But the increasing processing power of servers combined with their lower cost make them the logical replacement to mainframe-based systems in the future.

In the interim, client/server networks will often find it necessary to connect to mainframe-based systems. This is because some data can only be found in the mainframe environment, usually because the business rules for handling it are sufficiently complex or because the data itself is massive or sensitive enough that as a practical matter it remains stored there.

Connecting to a mainframe requires some form of network-like access. Even if you are using a telephone and modem as your access hardware, you still require special software to make your workstation appear to the mainframe to be just another network terminal. Many vendors can provide the necessary software to handle this type of network extension.

Reading Server Ads

Because servers are computers, much of their sales promotional literature deals with the same specifications touted for workstation computers: processing speed measured in megahertz (MHz); hard disk capacity measured in gigabytes (GB); data transfer rates measured in milliseconds (MS). There is some server-specific jargon that is useful to know, however. Following are some common terms you're likely to run across.

RAID

RAID stands for Redundant Arrays of Inexpensive Disks. Borrowed from mainframe technology to provide security for data, RAID systems utilize a set of hard disks to write data onto more than one disk simultaneously. If one disk fails, the operating system can retrieve the data from a backup disk. The more disks (and thus the more redundancy), the safer the system.

RAID can also speed up disk access. If a file server uses only a single disk, any request from a user for data must wait until all previous requests from other users have been accommodated. Using RAID, because redundant copies of data are stored on multiple disks, requests for data can be accommodated simultaneously, speeding up access. Figure 6.3 illustrates this process.

FIGURE 6.3

RAID technology, in addition to providing data security by simultaneously creating multiple copies of data, allows data to move more efficiently by providing the means for different subsets of data to be distributed simultaneously along the network.

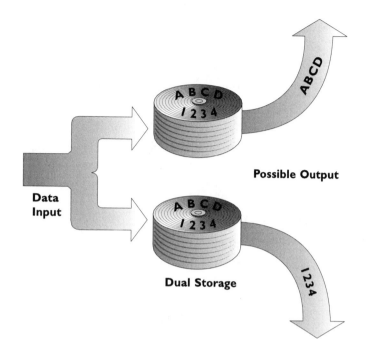

Data Input

Dual Storage

Possible Output

Symmetrical Multiprocessing

Symmetrical multiprocessing (SMP) was discussed in Chapter 4. Briefly summarized, SMP is a feature that adds power by integrating more than one central processor into a single file server, along with the necessary additional hardware and software to divide processing chores between them. Other terms for this same feature imply the number of processors involved: *bi-processor* (two processors); *tri-processor* (three processors); *quad-processor* (four processors); and so on.

Using multiple processors can have a dramatic effect on server speed, although it is not as simple as doubling speed with two processors, or tripling speed with three. SMP involves additional processing overhead to manage the distribution of processing among those multiple processors, and this does cut back on performance somewhat. SMP, as expected, is expensive. It is a feature suited to large-scale networks.

EDC Memory

EDC stands for Error Detection and Correction. EDC memory is configured at the hardware level with special circuitry that verifies RAM
output and resends output when memory errors occur. This type of
memory is becoming standard equipment on modern servers and boosts
overall reliability. Vendors include this type of memory to remain competitive in the marketplace, so its impact on the price of the server
depends on what price the vendor believes the customer will pay.

Memory Cache

Memory cache sets aside a portion of the server RAM to store the most
frequently-used network instructions so that they can be accessed as
quickly as possible. Cache storage is constantly updated while the
server is in operation. During network processing, instructions that are
accessed less frequently are pushed out of cache, replaced by instructions
that are accessed more frequently. The larger the size of the memory
cache, the more instructions the server can keep on hand for fast access.

Memory cache uses specialized, high-speed memory chips called *static
RAM* (SRAM) chips. These chips are more expensive than *dynamic RAM*
(DRAM) chips used for standard computer memory.

On many existing networks, you can find cache sizes of up to 2MB per
processor. In general, if you have a great many nodes on your network or
rely on your server for application processing, you will probably benefit from
a large memory cache. If your network is relatively small (20 nodes or less),
you can achieve satisfactory results with about 512KB memory cache.

Rack Mounting

A rack-mount server usually refers to multiple servers stacked on top of
one another in a single cabinet to save space. Rack mounts can be found
in very large and powerful client/server systems that require more than a

single file server. This type of configuration is for highly centralized and complex systems and further blurs the distinctions between network and mainframe technology. As such, it is beyond the scope of this book. If you have the budget for this kind of networking muscle, you should allocate a significant portion of that budget to experienced, professional consultants and support personnel. You will need them.

Power Protection

A *redundant power supply* (RDS) is good idea for businesses that can afford insurance against downtime. The power supply is the unit that distributes electricity within the server. As the name implies, a redundant power supply is a backup power supply that takes over in the event that the main power supply fails. This feature is different from an *uninterruptible power supply* (UPS), an external device that provides continuous electrical power to the server, usually for a short time, in the event of an electrical power failure. The RDS keeps the network running indefinitely, as long as electricity is being fed to it; the UPS keeps the network running just long enough after a power failure to store and protect your data before shutting down.

The *line conditioner* is another important form of power protection. This device monitors the electrical current and compensates for extreme fluctuations, called *spikes* (bursts of too much voltage) or *brownouts* (sudden drops in voltage). Spikes and brownouts can damage your hardware. If your building is old and the wiring is suspect (and you cannot afford to rewire your building), a line-conditioner can offer you some peace of mind.

Where to Go from Here

Computing technology only facilitates and hastens the flow of information. You can effectively computerize your information services to the extent that you have standardized the means by which information is used and communicated throughout your enterprise, and that you have implemented consistent business rules for organizing and communicating that information. Only then will computing technology make your information services more productive.

Measure the volume of information you must carry day-to-day. You already know if you carry a significantly larger amount of one type of information over another. For example, if every day you send and receive hundreds of critical faxes, a fax server would be a good investment. If you plan to manage a large, complicated database, an application server might be in order. If you are fortunate enough to have access to information about companies similar to your own, check out their degree of satisfaction with their solutions as one way of determining your own needs. If this is impossible, a good consultant can show various standard network solutions that have been applied to situations like your own and then make alterations as necessary to suit your unique needs.

A server-based system will require some degree of daily administration, so give special attention to securing the services of a reliable individual to carry out these tasks. Remember that, in the client/server environment, your network administrator is responsible for designing automated systems that enforce the business rules that secure your data's integrity and assure that it has meaning.

Servers are about finding a balance between empowering users to access needed information immediately, and at the same time protecting the integrity and consistency of that information. Servers do this by allowing work teams to access information directly, instead of applying for access to information through centralized, mainframe-based information management services.

The next chapter will discuss remote access to your network, technology that increases its power and allows you to connect your network to larger networks around the world.

For Further Reading

- Vaskevitch, David. *Client/Server Strategies*. IDG, 1993.

- Lowe, Doug. *Client/Server Computing for Dummies*. IDG, 1995.

CASE STUDY

GAB's owner and office manager have a lot to think about. Over the life of the company, information flow has evolved into a loosely-applied set of rules in which individuals are free to discuss accounting issues informally but must keep hard data secure in locked cabinets. Some of the company accountants have gone so far as to password-protect their desktop machines to keep unwanted users out. The switch to a server-based system will involve some adjustment. Still, there is some good news. The fact that GAB is an accounting business means that it already must conform to some specific, hard-and-fast business rules and legal requirements. As the network causes changes to GAB's administrative culture, the employees will find it easier to adjust if the new rules are developed so as to conform with standard accounting practice.

The owner and office manager review their stated goals for a network system and agree that, from the standpoint of determining their server needs, their most important considerations are (1) the ability to access data from a highly secure centralized source and (2) facilitating employee communications. The volume of accounting data is large, but it doesn't appear at this time that the actual volume of critical communications data (mostly memos and scheduling) is so large that a dedicated communications server would be cost-effective.

There is one other consideration. In the near future GAB would like to develop an Internet presence and have their network take full advantage of Internet-based technology.

Under these circumstances, it seems for now that a single powerful server could handle their data-sharing and communications traffic, but that they should configure the system so that their communications functions can be transferred to a Web server at a later date when GAB is ready for Internet access.

The owner and the office manager agree that it would be helpful, now that they have clarified their needs, to solicit suggestions from local vendors for the types of servers that would match their needs. But they don't rush into any actual purchasing at this point. Deciding what server hardware to buy can wait until they have settled on their most suitable network operating system and application software. At that point, a short meeting with a good consultant could be quite helpful in selecting the best possible overall solution.

For now, it appears that they could do with a single-processor, 166Mhz Pentium server with about 10GB of storage space on multiple hard disks. Because GAB deals with critical accounting data, they agree to include a redundant storage system, mostly for backup purposes but with the added nicety of more efficient access to data; also an uninterruptible power supply to give them some insurance against power failures; and some form of unattended tape backup as well, just to be sure.

CHAPTER

7

Remote Connections to Your Network

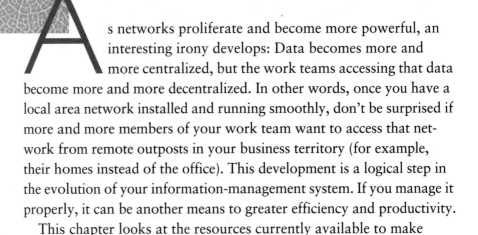

As networks proliferate and become more powerful, an interesting irony develops: Data becomes more and more centralized, but the work teams accessing that data become more and more decentralized. In other words, once you have a local area network installed and running smoothly, don't be surprised if more and more members of your work team want to access that network from remote outposts in your business territory (for example, their homes instead of the office). This development is a logical step in the evolution of your information-management system. If you manage it properly, it can be another means to greater efficiency and productivity.

This chapter looks at the resources currently available to make remote connections to your network and at some of the problems and pitfalls you will want to avoid.

Decentralizing the Team

When data is centralized, all access to it across network lines can be viewed as remote—some access is simply more remote than others: Across town is conceptually more remote than across the hall. However, the time required to access the centralized data does not necessarily reflect the actual physical distance between user and storage.

The Rise of the Portable PC

The evolution of the portable PC has done a lot to widen the market for remote access products. Portable PCs have expanded the concept of remote access beyond the process of connecting from fixed remote sites (for example, telecommuting from a home office) to highly flexible systems of access from mobile remote sites.

At first, the portable PC was not practical because of the bulk and weight of early hard disks. Early portable PCs, weighing eight pounds or more, with 40 MB hard disks, could not store the large amounts of data capable of being stored on desktop systems. Nowadays, the best of these portable machines are every bit as powerful as desktop systems—as well as small, reliable, and lightweight enough to carry nearly anywhere. In addition, networking technology has evolved to the point where it can be adapted to make direct connections over existing communication lines. In fact, you have several methods of remote access from which to choose. Once you've decided, modern software and graphical user interfaces make the connection easier to establish.

Who Needs to Connect?

There are four types of users who make use of remote access to centralized data:

Home users, also called *telecommuters* More and more individuals no longer travel from home to office every day of the week. Instead they access the office via a workstation at home.

Mobile users These individuals have jobs that demand their presence at work sites away from the office. They bring the office with them via remote access using portable PCs.

Remote office staff These users are working at a remote site that is too far away from the base office to make direct network connections practical.

Remote clients These individuals (for example, purchasers of products direct from the manufacturer through on-line catalogues) access centralized data directly because business considerations like speedy customer service, high volume, or customer convenience make offering such access profitable.

Establishing a Remote Connection

When it works right, remote access can produce enormous gains in business productivity, reliability, and efficiency. But this is true only when reliable remote connections can be made. Reliable, cost-effective connections require you to understand which of several variations of remote access are best for your type of business and (as usual) your budget.

Currently, people looking to access their LAN from a remote location have a choice of two basic types of connection services: *direct access* and the *dial-up connection*. There is also the *wireless* connection, but this is—for the time being, at least—simply another form of dial-up connection, using radio and cellular technology to replace wire lines. Right now, the advantages and limitations of wireless technology are, from the end-user's standpoint, the same as wire-based dial-up technology.

For dial-up connections, there are for the present time two communication methods: analog (the most widely available) and ISDN (increasing in popularity and gradually becoming as available as analog). These connection technologies and communication methods are described in detail in this chapter.

Direct Access

Direct-access connections are the most reliable. They also tend to be the fastest, and they connect the remote PC directly as another node on the network. Direct access connections are expensive, and they are best suited for connections being made to remote sites that are long-term or permanently established and need near-constant availability of LAN services. Direct access uses a dedicated, leased telephone line to complete the connection. The line is sturdier and made of higher quality materials than what is normally used for voice communications. Also, unless the distances are too great, the line does not usually traverse a series of analog switches as voice-only lines do but instead forms a direct link between the nodes.

Once the dedicated line is installed, you make the final connection between the cable, your host network, and the remote PC using dedicated hardware devices or high-speed modems. With a dedicated line, the choice of appropriate connecting devices will depend on the type of network you are using and the communication protocols it supports. Your network vendor will inform you of what options are available and you will work out appropriate choices together.

The obvious disadvantage of direct access is its high cost, which is dependent on the distances involved and the degree of difficulty installing the dedicated line but can normally run into thousands of dollars. However, it can be cost-effective if you have sufficiently large needs for fast and reliable transfer of high volumes of data. Most small business owners and departmental managers will prefer to make the connection using the less-expensive dial-up options.

Dial-Up Access

Dial-up access is based on the idea of tapping into existing communications technology to establish remote connections. Using this method, establishing a remote network connection is like making a telephone call to your network. In general terms, there are two dial-up options and both use standard modems to make remote connections using telephone lines: You can make the link using *remote-control software* or using a specialized hardware device called a *remote access server* to accept the incoming telephone connection and establish the remote user as a node on the network.

Remote-Control Connections

Remote-control access is the easiest and least expensive means of remote access to your LAN. This solution uses specialized software to establish a connection, via modems and standard analog telephone lines, to a host workstation connected to the LAN. Once the telephone connection is established and the remote-control software takes over the host workstation, the remote user can access LAN services as if the user were sitting locally at the host. There are several relatively inexpensive software products that will do the trick. Windows NT includes this software, called remote access services. If you require an add-on product, you might look at Carbon Copy (Microcom) or Norton pcANYWHERE (Symantic), among others. The remote-control process has some limitations, however:

- The connection is strictly one-to-one. Each remote connection will tie up a workstation on the network as a separate, dedicated host PC. As more users want to connect remotely, remote-control access becomes decreasingly practical.

- Only those services available to the host PC are available to the network. While this can provide some measure of security, it also can be inconvenient for some remote users who might need fuller access to the network.

- The host workstation must be powered up and running the same software as the remote PC.

- Performance is likely to be slower than other types of connection, especially when using graphical interfaces.

Performance is critical. A remote-control connection normally does not send network data over the telephone line. Instead, traffic over the remote link consists of remote commands to the LAN and host screen changes sent back to the remote PC. In most cases, the remote user only monitors processing on the network. If the remote user has an application on the remote machine and wants to use the local application to process data on the host network, then the remote user must resort to entire-file transfers to and from the network or put up with slow data communications across the remote link. The former puts data at risk and limits local access; the latter is likely to be frustratingly slow, especially if there is a lot of other traffic on the host network.

Setting up a remote-control connection requires that the software be installed, properly configured for the modems being used, and running on both ends of the connection. When the remote PC dials the host workstation, the software sets up the necessary digital handshaking and transfers control to the remote PC. When the connection is ended, the software senses this and returns the host PC to normal operation. This process is illustrated in Figure 7.1.

FIGURE 7.1

A remote-control connection. The remote PC takes over for a host PC and directs its behavior at a distance. Any process available to the host PC is available to the remote.

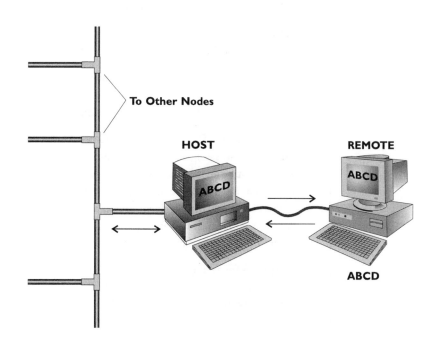

Remote Access Servers

A remote access server is a hardware device that allows a remote PC to function as a full-fledged member of the LAN, operating network applications and accessing network data directly across the remote link.

Computers, Talking on the Phone

Computer modems are well-established devices with a language all their own. Here's a quick run-down on common modem jargon:

Baud rate   The speed of the data transfer, expressed in kilobits-per-second (Kbps). These days, 28.8 Kbps (28,800 bits per second) is a practical minimum; for Internet access, 33.6 Kbps is recommended, and the newer, faster 56K modem is preferred if your Internet service provider supports it. Expect modems to get faster as the telephone system updates its technology to fill the increasing demand for faster data transmission.

Data bits   The number of bits used to send one character (for example, a single letter or number) over the line. Characters are sent using either seven or eight bits.

Duplex   A display control setting for the display of transmitted characters. In Full Duplex mode, characters you type at the keyboard are not displayed on your screen. In Half Duplex, they are displayed.

Handshaking   The process by which two connected modems analyze each other's transmissions and exchange data without conflict. A sending modem interrupts its transmission when the receiving modem indicates that it has received a maximum allowable number of characters. Then the receiving modem becomes the sending modem and the transmission goes the other direction. This back-and-forth process occurs at very high speed so that the communication appears smooth and steady to the user.

Parity   A form of error checking that interacts with the number of data bits. When you use 7 data bits, you can set Even or Odd parity, to coincide with the parity setting at the other end of the communication. If you use 8 data bits, parity is set to "None."

Port   The connection point between the computer a peripheral device. Most modems communicate through *serial ports*. A PC can have up to four serial ports, named COM1, COM2, COM3, and COM4. A modem is configured to use one of these ports to transmit data.

Stop bit   A delay after a character is sent, to indicate to the receiving modem that the single-character transmission is complete. The modem's stop bit setting is always set to 1, unless you have been instructed to set it to some other value.

Figure 7.2 shows how a remote access server is set up. Remote access servers have distinct advantages over simple remote-control access:

- The host LAN can support a single access point to multiple remote sites, without tying up the services of a dedicated LAN workstation.

- The same access point can be used to provide an array of network services to the remote PC.

- Easier-to-manage network security. For example, the remote node server can identify callers and allow different levels of access.

- Better performance through the use of local network interfaces on the remote PC.

- Access across different networking environments and protocols (in effect, the remote node server acts as a bridge to other networks).

FIGURE 7.2

A remote access server. The remote access server can establish a direct connection to the LAN and allow different users different levels of access to the network.

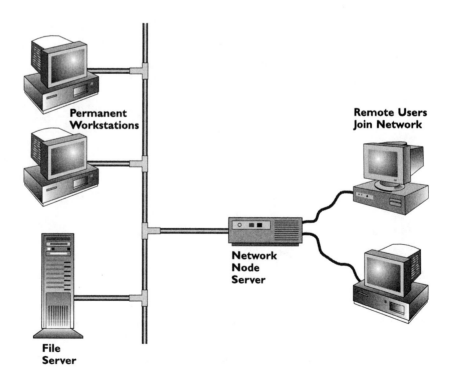

Permanent Workstations

Remote Users Join Network

Network Node Server

File Server

Remote-Connection Security

Providing secure access to valid remote sites involves special configurations to your host LAN. For remote-control connections, you should secure the host PC as if it were available to any walk-up user. Remember that any access available to the host machine is automatically available to the remote machine as well. The remote-control software will provide a certain amount of basic password protection at connect time, but you should not rely on this level of security alone.

It is easier to provide security for remote access servers or remote connections to other networks. Products for these types of connections normally include protocols that limit the initial connection to authorized users. You should verify that any remote connection products include compatible security protocols. Some readily-available standard security protocols include:

Password Authentication Protocol (PAP)   A no-frills, Internet-standard protocol for verifying passwords from remote callers.

Challenge Handshake Authentication Protocol (CHAP)   This is an Internet-standard protocol for verifying encrypted passwords.

Call Line Identification (CLI)   This protocol identifies the calling number and checks against a stored list of authorized callers before making the link.

You'll learn more about security in Chapters 11 and 16.

In theory, remote access server connections are fairly easy to set up:

1. Acquire the server box from your hardware vendor.

2. Connect it to your LAN using the included connection hardware.

3. Install however many modems you are using (the number will depend on how many remote users must have access at the same time).

4. Configure the server using the LAN remote access administration software supplied by the vendor.

5. Distribute the access software to your remote users.

In practice, however, you can expect that some fine-tuning will be required before things run smoothly. This is another case where an experienced network administrator, one who understands your network design and its communication protocols, will ease the installation and configuration process.

Data Signals: Something Old, Something New

There are two types of electrical signals that carry data: analog and digital. Analog signals are represented as regular waves of varying voltage. These variations are the signal's *amplitude*. The voltage cycles between a maximum and minimum level a given number of times per second. The length of the cycle is the signal's *frequency*. Analog signals are sent over a transmission medium—for example, over a telephone line—or as a wireless signal, like cellular microwaves. Multiple analog signals can coexist on the same sending medium if each one starts and completes its wave cycle at a different voltage level.

Computers send and receive binary data (data coded into ones and zeros; in other words, computer data) using analog signals. To do this, specific levels of frequency or amplitude are assigned meaning. For example, amplitude above a certain level may mean one; below that level, zero. Alternatively, a given frequency can mean one; otherwise, the signal means zero.

The technology for sending and receiving analog signals has been around for a long time and is well established. Analog signals can travel great distances (an international telephone call, for example). However, analog signals are susceptible to static and other electrical "noise," called electromagnetic interference (EMI). This interference is the cause of some distortion you may hear on a long-distance telephone call and can create errors when sending computer data.

Digital signals work differently, by alternating between the presence of a given electrical state (one) or a contrasting state (zero). For example, a digital signal can consist of a positive electrical polarity changing to no polarity (meaning one), or a negative electrical polarity changing to no polarity (meaning zero). Digital signals are better suited for sending binary data because the binary encoding is locked directly into the signal. They are less susceptible to EMI, so they tend to be clearer. They are sent over digitally-aware transmission mediums, which can be either wires, or as digital wireless transmission signals.

> However (and here's the meat of the matter) analog circuitry does not handle digital signals very well. If you have an analog signal and digital equipment (like an analog telephone signal coming in to a PC) or digital signal and analog equipment (like a CD-ROM sending musical signals to a set of non-digital speakers), some conversion of the signal is needed. Analog-to-digital conversion equipment analyzes the amplitude and frequency of the analog signal, in a process called *sampling*. The equipment tests the signal many thousands of times per second and creates a digital representation of the analog signal, then sends the digital signal along to the digital equipment. In the reverse conversion, the digital signal can be used to generate waveforms directly.
>
> The most efficient and least expensive means to work with binary data is to use digital equipment to send and receive digital signals. In this scenario, the equipment does not have to perform complex signal processing. For this reason, digital wireless communications have become desirable for remote access. But because a tremendous amount of analog equipment is installed throughout the world, analog-based communications (and analog-to-digital conversion) will remain part of our remote-access world for the time being.

Telephone Line Communications

The two most commonly-used methods for dial-up data connections over the telephone line are standard analog and ISDN. Following are brief descriptions of each.

Analog Connections

Analog communication is the most widespread communication method available. When you use the telephone to make a local call, you are using analog technology to carry the voice signal. Analog telephone technology (which can be carried over wire and cellular telephone lines) may seem old-fashioned in this high-tech age, but it offers some advantages for remote LAN users:

- Remote access links can be established from any spot in the world that has telephone service.

- Long-distances charges are inexpensive compared to ISDN charges.

- Analog-compatible modems are low-priced and easy to configure, use, and maintain.

- The technology is traditional and is therefore supported by vendors and application developers.

Analog has some disadvantages as well:

- The transmission rates are slow compared to direct network or ISDN access. Currently, the fastest analog modems handle 56.6 kilobits per second (Kbps).

- Connections can be noisy, with line static and echoes that cause communication failures.

ISDN Connections

ISDN is a set of technologies (circuits and upgraded telephone lines) that allow specialized data pathways to coexist with voice pathways. It is, in effect, an upgrade to the existing analog system. To use ISDN lines, you must use ISDN-compatible modems and connecting devices to establish the remote link to your LAN. ISDN offers some significant advantages over analog communications:

- Processing speed is nearly as fast as direct connection to the host LAN.

- Usually lower cost for the performance, compared to direct-access. However, if you have a choice of ISDN providers, by all means compare rates; they can vary a great deal.

Telephone systems are gradually upgrading to ISDN. All vendors of remote-connection systems support ISDN. However, no firm standards yet exist for optimizing ISDN's communication features at local connection sites. This means that, if you intend to make use of ISDN (especially to connect networks to one another), you are likely to find that vendors' current product offerings are proprietary. Proprietary technology will limit, at least for the time being, your ISDN links to those remote LANs that support your vendor's products or have licensed your vendor's proprietary standards.

Connecting via the Internet

If your remote link is primarily for e-mail, messaging, and transferring data files, it would be practical to use the Internet. In this case, the LAN and its remote access sites connect, via modems, to one or more local Internet Service Providers and establish permanent Internet addresses for storing transmitted data.

Instead of making direct links to the LAN, all parties to the communication send data to the desired receiver's Internet address, which is accessed at will by the receiver.

The main advantages of this arrangement are that there is minimum technical overhead for the LAN administrator or remote user, other than a modem and access to a telephone and that communication is sent and received at the convenience of all participants. The disadvantage is that access to host LAN services, if it exists at all, is limited and slow.

Right now, Internet access technology and service providers enjoy a booming market. The promise of easy, global access between LANs and PCs is a powerful lure that may lead to the development of revolutionary products for remote LAN access. It is worth your time to pay close attention to developments in this field, but be cautious. Brand-new digital technologies often have problems, and it is often a good idea to wait for a new technology to prove itself in the real world before rushing in with your scarce purchasing dollars. In addition, by the time a new technology is established, the price has usually fallen. To learn more about the relationship between the Internet and LANs, refer to Chapters 14–16.

Bandwidth

*B*andwidth is a term you will hear frequently when discussing network data traffic, especially when discussing remote and LAN-to-LAN communications. Traditionally, bandwidth is measured as the difference between the lowest and highest frequencies an electronic communication device can carry. For example, telephones carry a frequency range of 300-3300Hz; therefore, a telephone can be said to have a bandwidth of 3000Hz. In a networking context, bandwidth is jargon used to describe the maximum amount of data that can be transmitted simultaneously, using different frequencies, on your network or between LANs and remote sites.

Data moving between all the connections to a network is called *data traffic*. The more data traffic that can be transmitted along your network data pathways, the wider your network's bandwidth. Much network technology (and remote connection technology in particular), is devoted to reducing unnecessary data traffic and conserving your network's precious bandwidth. There are several ways of accomplishing this, including local processing, dial on demand, and dynamic bandwidth.

Local Processing

Local processing can occur at either the workstation, the remote site, or the network server level. At the workstation level, the workstation accesses data from the network server, performs all processes locally, and returns modified data to the server. Network resources are used only to access and return data. At the remote-site level, the remote connection is used only to transmit data to and from the remote PC, where all processing takes place.

At the server level, the LAN workstation (or remote PC controlling the LAN workstation or PC directly connected via a remote access server) transmits instructions to the network server to perform processes, and the server transmits the result of those processes back to the workstation. Because a remote link has a much narrower bandwidth than the LAN, the LAN handles all remote requests for processing as locally as possible.

Dial on Demand

This bandwidth-conserving method takes the concept of remote local processing one step further. Dial-on-demand software senses when a remote PC is engaged in extended processing and ends the telephone connection, which can speed up processing on both ends. When the remote PC needs to access the LAN once again, the dial-on-demand software senses this as well and reestablishes the connection automatically. Although some time is lost in continually re-dialing the host LAN, the elimination of the need to maintain a telephone connection during periods of extended local processing can speed up overall processing times on both ends.

Dynamic Bandwidth

Dynamic bandwidth is an optimization technology for ISDN remote-access connections. In this method, the remote node server monitors the rate of transfer for various types of data along the connection. When data is dense (for example, during graphics information transmissions) and the designated speed of transfer falls below a predetermined level, a second communication channel is opened to accommodate more data and speed up the transfer rate. When data density levels return to normal (for example, during transmissions of simple e-mail messages) the two-channel data transfer is no longer required, and the second channel shuts down to conserve transmission overhead.

Making the Connection

The decentralization of the work force surrounding centralized data offers competitive advantages to businesses. Some of these advantages include: direct client services on site, order processing direct to vendor by client, short production and development cycles, faster responses to marketplace changes, and direct access to distant markets.

In addition, employers can be more flexible when hiring, and employees can benefit by a decreased emphasis on physical location as a condition of employment. Greatly reducing the number of commuters would help to lower (somewhat) our dependence on oil and help to reduce smog. But decentralizing the workforce will also reduce the person-to-person contact that most human beings desire and find beneficial. It remains to be seen what other social advantages and problems may crop up as a result of these new styles of doing business.

Where to Go from Here

The possibility of significant economic advantages for businesses make remote access worth looking into. You may find that remote access is a good investment in your business's competitiveness and market penetration.

Nonetheless, proceed slowly, and keep a careful eye on your budget. The most cost-effective means of employee access may be through a modem and remote-control software, if an employee requires only occasional access and security is not paramount. For more complex, long-term, or high-security applications, consider the remote access server approach. Direct access connections move you closer to implementing a Wide Area Network (WAN) with its added complexity and high cost.

Finally, if you are interested in providing remote access to customers, your best bet may be the Internet. The costs of implementing this technology is falling, and Internet development is getting easier. You will learn more about Internet access in Chapters 14–16.

In the next chapter, we will look at the software that ties your entire network together: the *network operating system* (NOS).

For Further Reading

- Jordon, Larry, and Bruce Churchill. *Communications & Networking for the PC*. New Riders, 1994.

- Clark, Martin P. *Networking & Telecommunications Design and Operation*. John Wiley & Sons, 1997.

- Held, Gilbert and George E. Friend. *Understanding Data Communications,* 5th ed. Sams, 1996.

CASE STUDY

GAB's employees sometimes visit clients at their offices for on-site meetings. On occasion they have expressed wishes that they could access data at the home office while on site with clients. However, this is not such a frequent concern that GAB's owner is willing to invest thousands of dollars into a direct-access solution. A remote-control solution, on the other hand, with its rigid requirement that a top machine, does not offer the flexibility the company needs.

GAB's owner talks it over with the office manager and agrees that once the network is up and running, they will look into adding a remote access server, to allow employees in the field to access centralized data on the network. Knowing that this feature is important now may help them narrow down their upcoming choice of network operating system and application software. However, since they are still in the planning stages for a brand-new network, they agree it is important to have the network up and running smoothly before investing in remote access technology.

PART

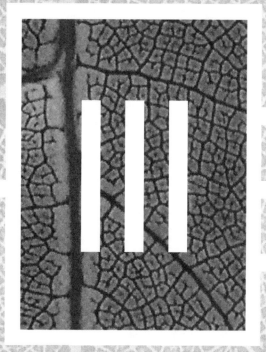

III

NETWORK SOFTWARE

CHAPTER

8

Network Operating Systems

All desktop computer systems require an operating system in order to work. The operating system is software that provides a platform of low-level services shared by various applications. An application (for example, a database management program) calls upon the operating system continuously for the common tasks (sending data to the monitor, updating files on disk, receiving input from the keyboard and mouse, and so on) that support its processing.

A network operating system (NOS) does everything a stand-alone operating system does, and more, in a much more complex environment. Some network operating systems work on top of a foundation operating system; for example, LANtastic works on top of DOS. Others, such as NetWare, are independent operating systems in their own right. In addition to the usual lower-level computing tasks, a network operating system is responsible for all of the following:

- Directing data traffic throughout the network

- Allowing and preventing access to data based on security requirements

- Preventing access to data files while they are being processed

- Managing the flow of data between a variety of different (and sometimes otherwise incompatible) workstations

- Managing requests for printer services

- Managing communication and messages between network users

- Managing connections between the network and remote sites

In addition, the network operating system must make its services as transparent as possible to each user; when a user must access NOS services, the network should present as intuitive an interface as possible, translating complex digital tasks into simple instructions using words and pictures that are readily understandable to non-technical human beings. Depending on what it is doing at any given moment, an NOS can function as a digital traffic cop, international ambassador, interpreter, teacher, pupil, file clerk, secretary, janitor, repairman, or watchdog.

There are several different network operating systems available, and the ones discussed here support the hardware configurations we have discussed in previous chapters. Some are more complex and have more features than others. Your choice of an operating system for your network will be based on the best combination of features you can afford. This chapter looks at the most common NOSs currently available and offers you an overview of what they can accomplish.

Networks in a Box

If you are new to networks or are installing one for the first time, look into the possibility of obtaining a complete starter kit from the operating system manufacturer. All major operating system vendors offer some type of start-up kit; these kits include two or more NICs, standard lengths of cable, and all necessary software. In addition to the convenience, you can be assured of compatibility between your software and hardware.

LANtastic

LANtastic is a classic operating system for peer-to-peer networks. It is manufactured by the Artisoft corporation, which also manufactures network hardware. LANtastic's advantages are ease of setup, relatively low memory requirements, good security for a peer-to-peer system, and fairly low cost.

LANtastic can run with minimal hardware. You can make a LANtastic workstation out of any IBM PC or compatible with at least 640KB RAM (and using either DOS 3.1 or later, or Microsoft Windows). LANtastic can run using most standard Ethernet NICs, or you can choose Artisoft's own proprietary cards that boost the network's performance.

The LANtastic operating system is NetBIOS-compatible, meaning that it sits on top of DOS (or any other NetBIOS-compatible operating system) and makes use of certain file and data-flow services belonging to the underlying system, in order to manage its network operations. (Think of LANtastic as a network running on top of a more basic operating system.) For more information on NetBIOS, see Chapter 3.

Once you have the adapter cards installed and connected, you can install the network system software at each machine on the network using LANtastic's automated installation program. During the installation procedure, you can designate each workstation as one of two types:

Server   This type of workstation can send and receive data across the network. Server workstations have data that must be accessed by other workstations on the network. A server can also receive data from other workstations.

Client   This type of workstation can only receive data from server workstations. Other workstations on the network will not be able to access this workstations's data.

Once LANtastic is installed, other workstations are identified on each local workstation using DOS-like drive letters. This procedure is very easy to understand if the user is familiar with basic DOS commands, and because drive letters are used, most DOS-based software can access the data directly. LANtastic also supports a basic e-mail system for sending messages between workstations.

LANtastic offers a number of optional security features for controlling access to data throughout its peer-to-peer system. LANtastic controls access rights to files using *access control lists* on each workstation. You can adjust access rights to files, directories, disks, printer ports, and other workstations, any of which can be designated as having a specific right of access:

Search only The user can look up files in directories but cannot access the files' contents.

Read only The user can read the files but cannot make changes.

Create only The user can create new files or directories but cannot overwrite or delete existing ones.

Delete only The user is allowed to delete only designated data files and data directories.

Change attributes only The user can modify file attributes (for example, designating a file as a hidden or system file).

Execute program files The user may launch specific application software.

Full access The user can access designated files and directories without restrictions.

Why Choose LANtastic?

LANtastic is an inexpensive solution for workgroups that need to share data in a free-flowing environment that nevertheless requires some basic security. You can purchase additional utilities that make it possible to connect a LANtastic workgroup to a larger NetWare network. A LANtastic network can handle more users than most other peer-to-peer systems. It is a good choice when cost and simplicity issues outweigh power and foolproof security.

Who Gets Access

Access rights to nodes on a network are based on two underlying security issues: keeping unauthorized people away from data and preventing errors that can occur when several people access the same data.

For example, users in an order-entry department would need full access rights to order-entry files so that they could create and modify records of customer orders. On the other hand, the shipping department would be given read-only access to the same files because their business need would be only to review them if there were a question regarding order fulfillment. Other workstations in the business with connections to the outside world (for example, workstations connected to a modem for access from the field) might be denied even read-only access, to prevent competitors from slipping in and acquiring sensitive information about customers.

Windows for Workgroups

In Windows for Workgroups, Microsoft Corporation has integrated a set of peer-to-peer network services and network-aware applications within what amounts to an expanded version of Windows 3.1. The advantages of Windows for Workgroups are the ease and efficiency it offers to first-time networkers already familiar with the Windows operating system.

Windows for Workgroups requires the same hardware that Windows 3.1 requires to run in Enhanced Mode: a PC with at least an 80386 (or compatible) CPU, running DOS version 3.1 or later. In addition, each workstation should be equipped with the following:

- 4MB RAM (3MB is possible, but not recommended). A larger amount of RAM is a good idea, as it will increase performance. 8MB to 16MB is common—even more in very demanding situations.

- A minimum of 13.5MB of hard disk space (or 8.5MB if you are installing over stand-alone Windows). This is just for the operating system; other software will require additional space.

- One floppy disk drive.

- Windows-compatible displays and printer drivers.

Using Windows for Workgroups

After installing your network cards and cables, install the operating system on each workstation, using Windows for Workgroups' automated Install program. If you are installing over an existing copy of Windows 3.1, Windows for Workgroups will attempt to use your current Windows configuration settings. Windows will allow you to do either a fully automated (express) setup, or an interactive (custom) installation that allows you to fine-tune your system at installation time.

During the installation procedure, you must assign a unique name (up to 15 characters long) to each workgroup and workstation. You must tell Windows what types of network communications hardware you have installed on each workstation and how it is configured. You must also identify your shared printers and the local ports to which they are connected. When the installation process is complete, Windows 3.1 restarts as Windows for Workgroups.

Once fully installed, Windows for Workgroups offers a useful set of new Windows utilities:

New File Manager The WFW File Manager includes a customizable toolbar and a dialog box for connecting logical drive letters to network workstations and file directories. You can also assign *alias* names to nested subdirectories. For example, if you wanted to access files on directory \ACCOUNTS\INVOICES\BACKORD\PAYABLE, you could shorten the name to Payables, or whatever name you like. Directory aliasing makes it much easier to access files in complicated file directory schemes.

New Print Manager   This Windows utility includes a toolbar in Windows for Workgroups. It also has a larger, easier-to-read display.

New Control Panel   The Control Panel contains a network icon, which you can use to manage names of workgroups and PCs and adjust the amount of time spent on local applications before allowing data to flow across the network. You can also make configuration changes to cards and drivers that allow such changes at the software level.

Windows for Workgroups also offers some useful network-aware applications:

Microsoft Mail   This application allows workgroup members to send and receive messages through a central database that resides on one member's machine.

Schedule+   This application is a calendar and time scheduler for workgroups. It facilitates appointments and meetings and allows team members to determine each other's whereabouts.

ClipBook   This application is like the Windows notepad, but its contents are accessible to everyone in the workgroup.

Chat   This application allows real-time messaging between workgroup members. Outgoing messages are displayed in an upper window and responses are displayed in a lower window.

WinMeter   This program charts the balance of time spent between local and network services. You can use this information to make adjustments at the Control Panel and optimize your workstation's performance.

NetWatcher   This utility displays an overview of network activity. For example, you could use NetWatcher to discover that one shared printer was being used far more often than another.

Windows for Workgroups, following a peer-to-peer standard, also identifies network drives using drive letters, permitting you and your

Windows applications to access them as local drives. You can access shared printers and other hardware with familiar Windows interface commands and use them as locally connected devices. Windows for Workgroups allows read-only and read-write access to files and directories, with optional password protection.

It is possible to connect Windows for Workgroups to a NetWare server, but doing so requires patience and the right set of communications drivers. This is a job best left to an experienced technician. It should come as no surprise that connections to Windows NT and NT Server are much more straightforward than NetWare connections.

Why Choose Windows for Workgroups?

Windows for Workgroups is a good solution for users who are committed to the Windows environment, who want the convenience of a familiar interface with good connections to other Windows-based systems and software, and who don't require a lot of file security. Some stand-alone users have switched to this operating system, just to use the improved versions of File Manager and Print Manager.

Windows 95

Microsoft Corporation has also integrated peer-to-peer network services within its latest version of the Windows operating system. The advantage of Windows 95 is its integration of basic peer-to-peer capabilities into an independent operating system, without the purchase of additional software.

Windows 95 does have significantly large hardware requirements:

- A PC with at least an 80386 (or compatible) CPU, with an 80486 or better recommended.

- 8MB RAM (not a realistic minimum; 12–16MB RAM is the more practical minimum; even more in very demanding situations).

- Approximately 100MB of hard disk space for a fully-featured implementation; other software will require additional space.

- One floppy disk or CD-ROM drive.

- Windows-compatible displays and printer drivers.

Using Windows 95

After installing your network cards and cables, if your network cards are plug-and-play compatible (check this out with your vendor before you buy), install the operating system on each workstation using Windows 95's automated Install program. Windows 95 will see your adapters and install the appropriate drivers. Otherwise, you can open up a DOS window and run whatever DOS-based configuration software is required by the card you have purchased. Then, click on the Add New Hardware icon in the Control Panel and specify what network cards and drivers you have.

Double-click on the Network icon in the control panel and bind any necessary protocols to your network adapter card. (Most peer-to-peer network cards will use either NetBEUI or IPX/SPX.)

While you are using the Network Control Panel, be sure to add File and Print sharing services for each workstation on the network, if they aren't implemented already. Be sure to give each machine a unique network name but the same workgroup name.

Windows 95's simple peer-to-peer networking allows you to share resources, such as other machines' disk drives and printers, right away. However, to take advantage of more sophisticated networking features, consider using Windows 95–based machines as clients in larger networking systems. For more information on Windows 95 as a client workstation, see Chapter 9.

Why Choose Windows 95?

Windows 95 is a good solution for users who need only file and resource sharing capabilities in a peer-to-peer context, who want a low-cost, low-maintenance solution, and who don't require much in the way of network security.

OS/2 and Warp 4

IBM's answer to Windows, OS/2, enjoys a reputation as a very robust and reliable operating system, which has inspired enthusiastic devotion from its users. Its earliest version lacked built-in networking features, beyond a rich and elegant set of Internet-access features called the Internet Access Kit. IBM added local-area networking features to later releases, called OS/2 Warp Connect, and finally Warp 4.

Early versions of OS/2 obtained networking capabilities using add-on software. For example, Artisoft released a 32-bit version of LANtastic for OS/2, which gave early versions of OS/2 peer-to-peer networking features similar to DOS-based LANtastic, while allowing users to take advantage of OS/2's smoother graphical interface and more powerful internal architecture.

Like its Windows competitors, OS/2 Warp 4 supports peer-to-peer networking, sharing applications, data files, and printers using standard NICs and network cables. In addition, Warp 4 supports peer-to-peer connections using the PC's parallel ports, for faster transfers of data between workstations.

To establish an OS/2 presence in the client/server world, IBM combined OS/2 Version 3 and another of its products, LAN Server Version 4.0, into a product called Warp Server 4. This product is interesting in that it integrates into the operating system several important network services like system management, communications, backup/recovery, and remote access—services that require add-on software in other operating systems such as NetWare or Windows NT. IBM has also developed Internet Connection Secure Server (ICSS), a tool for building OS/2-based intranets and Web sites.

Why Choose OS/2 and Warp 4

One of OS/2's main strengths is its ability to allow DOS and Windows applications to coexist. For example, OS/2 can recognize and use DOS drivers while switching between Windows and DOS applications, Windows cannot. Warp Server is a good choice if you are already a loyal OS/2 user and are looking for smoother integration between DOS and Windows applications on your network. It is also a stable platform for its own Internet and intranet software. One caveat, however: OS/2 does not enjoy the widespread market acceptance of Windows NT, Windows 95, or NetWare. Because of this, IBM may show a less aggressive commitment to continuing upgrades or adding new features.

Macintosh NOS

Apple Computer integrates networking services with its Macintosh operating system. Once your Macintoshes are up and running and the cables are connected, your network operating system is ready to go. The system requires Macintosh machines; more powerful models, as you would expect, offer more efficient network service.

The integration of network services with the operating system is smooth and reliable. You access the Control Panel to designate local printers and directories as shared and specify what access levels are permitted. Access levels are similar to those offered by LANtastic.

To access shared services, use the Finder. The Finder will display all shared resources, including any found on AppleShare servers. You select services from what is displayed and access them like locally connected devices.

Macintosh networks offer a convenient process called interapplication communication (IAC), which means that applications can access data from other applications dynamically. For example, a word processor can search an IAC-compatible database for a name and address and bring it directly into the document. This kind of dynamic linking can take place across the network.

Another nice feature is the Publish/Subscribe system. Using this utility a user can "publish" a message (make it available to other users on the network), and it will be instantly available to all "subscribers" (those users who have opted for immediate display of "published" messages). This makes for convenient sharing of up-to-the-minute information.

Why Choose Macintosh?

Macintosh is the obvious solution for users who have all-Mac systems and want to take advantage of Mac's legendary ease-of-use. Also, the security system is more fully featured than those of most other peer-to-peer systems, making the Mac more attractive as a peer-to-peer system for sensitive data.

Why Combine?

It may seem like overkill to connect a peer-to-peer system to a larger, client/server type network. Why not just plug all the workstations into the large network? The answer is based on the workgroup concept. Within a workgroup, users want fast access to locally-shared resources and quick communications, group scheduling, and the like. At the same time, the workgroup needs access to the corporate-wide information on the file server. It makes sense to connect the members of the workgroup together for direct communications and not tie up the server with what is essentially local data traffic. Then, to get at the corporate-level information, one or more of the workgroup member's workstations can connect to the enterprise. This assumes, of course, that you have room for such conveniences in your budget.

Banyan VINES and UNIX

VINES (VIrtual NEtwork System) is a file-server based network operating system designed as an extension of UNIX System V or SCO UNIX. It was developed by Banyan Incorporated in 1984. Banyan's intention was to use the acceptance of UNIX in the large corporate computing marketplace as a platform to launch VINES as a networking standard. They succeeded not only in distributing their product widely, but in influencing the development of file server systems in general.

VINES can be used to operate very large UNIX-based networks spread out over large geographic areas and at the same time to present remote services as if they were local to the workstation. The concept of localizing remote services, introduced with VINES's *StreetTalk* technology, has now been incorporated into all major network operating systems.

StreetTalk is the commercial name for a feature called *global directory services*, which helps integrate the complex UNIX networking system running on more than one server. From the user's point of view, the VINES multiserver network appears as a single, unified system. Individual users do not need to know which server provides which services, nor do they need to log onto multiple servers to access those services. Instead, the user logs onto the network and requests services by accessing the global directory, and the operating system keeps track of which server provides the requested services. In very large networks, this greatly simplifies the day-to-day work of both the users and the network administrator.

NOTE   VINES requires workstations and servers running either UNIX System V or SCO UNIX as a base operating system. When installed, VINES takes over the base operating system and controls its functions.

You can connect workstations from many different vendors into a VINES network. It supports clients running DOS, Windows, OS/2, and Macintosh, as well as UNIX workstations. However, Banyan recommends that you use only workstations certified as VINES-compatible. Some individual manufacturers may have introduced components into their machines that will cause problems on the VINES network.

For more information on whether a particular machine is compatible, contact the vendor or Banyan Systems Incorporated at (800) 828-2404.

Using VINES

VINES consists of dozens of utility programs that control its various network operations. The utilities that control connections to the network are installed on each client workstation, while those that control shared services are installed on the network server. When you start a VINES client workstation, you must run the Ban command to load the NIC controller software and system connection software (for example, VINES Redirector and VINES NetBIOS).

After the connection has been made, you run the Login program which prompts you for your user name and password. After VINES verifies your login name, it searches for your *user profile*. The user profile is a set of information that has been previously set up by the system administrator. It determines which shared network services (directories of data files and remote services, like printing and e-mail) are available to you.

At this point, you can access the network services you need by calling upon them by name. Using its StreetTalk system, VINES gives each node on the network a three-part name that identifies the location of the node within the network's directory structure. Each node is named according to its type (workstation, printer, server, and so on), the workgroup to which it belongs, and the location of the workgroup in the network's directory. The three parts of the name are separated by @ characters. The StreetTalk name looks like this:

```
node@workgroup@location
```

For example, a remote printer can be named `LaserPrinter @Accounting@LosAngeles`. The first part of the name, *LaserPrinter*, is the identifier of the node (in this case, a printer). The second part of the name, *Accounting*, indicates the workgroup to which the object belongs (the Accounting Department). The third part of the name, *LosAngeles*, indicates the location of the workgroup (the Los Angeles business office).

Another example, for a more localized network, would be `BobThomas @Programming@FirstFloor`. In this case the node is a workstation, logged onto the network under the name *BobThomas*. The workstation is part of the programming workgroup, located on the first floor of an office building.

You can also omit parts of a name, and VINES assumes you intend to access your own workgroup or location. In other words, if you are accessing a node in the same location as yours, you can omit the location in the node name. Likewise, if you are accessing a node in the same workgroup as your own, you need not include the workgroup in the node name.

VINES networks can have dozens of node names, and complicated names like these can be difficult to remember. StreetTalk includes a feature called *Street Talk Directory Assistance* (STDA), which you can access to see lists of node names on the network. The system administrator controls the names that can be included in the directory assistance list.

VINES Security

Security on a VINES network is thorough and sophisticated. Virtually every connection can be controlled by the system administrator (SA).

The first level of security is the user password. The SA can configure the operating system to accept only certain types of passwords (for example, only passwords of a specific minimum length). The SA can also prevent users from changing their own passwords or can force them to change their passwords periodically.

Login procedures are subject to security controls as well. Logins can be restricted to specific times of the day, and connections can be sustained for preset lengths of time. The system can limit some logins to specific network locations; for example, a user named *Bob Thomas* could log in from Programming on the first floor but not from Accounting on the fourth floor.

The user is also subject to security limitations after logging in. Files and directories are controlled by access rights, settings that allow only certain permissible operations. For example, PC workstations can be granted one or more of the following access rights:

Search　The user can view the names of files and directories. This is the most restricted access right. Other rights are not granted without this one.

Read Only　The user is allowed to view the contents of files but cannot make changes to them.

Execute　The user is allowed to run executable files (in other words, run applications).

Write Directories　The user is allowed to create and change the attributes of files and directories and change the contents of files. The user with this access right may also create new files and directories.

Write Files　The user is allowed to change the contents of files only.

Delete　The user is allowed to delete subdirectories and files.

Control　The user is allowed full access to the system. This right is usually reserved for the system administrator. The user with control rights can make changes to the access rights of other users on the system.

As mentioned earlier, access rights are put in place to reduce the chances of errors across the network. Many users in your business may need to view data, but only a few may actually need to make changes to it. For more information on security, see Chapter 12.

Files and directories are also subject to security features called *attributes*. File attributes control how a file can be handled by anyone on the system. On DOS-compatible workstations, these attributes are in addition to the normal DOS file attributes:

No Delete   Prevents a file from being erased.

No Rename   Prevents all users from renaming the file.

Shared   Allows different users to access the data file simultaneously. This is a risky attribute for files that are not read-only, because when two or more users can write to a file, its contents can become corrupted.

Executable   Allows executable files to be run, but not copied or written to. They can be renamed or deleted.

Finally, it is possible for the SA to grant users one of three levels of printer access rights:

User   This is the lowest level; it allows the users to control only their own printing jobs.

Operator   This level allows the user to change the order of print jobs that are pending, stop jobs that are printing, change the print format parameters, and start new print jobs. In effect, a user with operator status functions as a print queue manager.

Administrator   This level allows the user complete access to the print queues. An administrator can assign hardware to a particular queue, set up printing filters to automate control of the printer, and delete print jobs from the printing queue.

Why Choose VINES?

VINES is a good solution for experienced users who need a powerful client/server network and are comfortable with the intricacies of its UNIX base. It is useful when you need to set up a very large network, need extensive security, and want all users to have a consistent view of the whole system.

NetWare/IntranetWare

NetWare is a large client/server system developed by Novell, Inc. Currently, about half of the PC-based file server systems run using NetWare.

There are three different versions of NetWare in use at this time, versions 2, 3, and 4. Version 2 is no longer sold, although many networks are still running this version. NetWare 3 remains in the marketplace because it is well established and widely supported by hardware and software vendors; it is also less expensive than version 4.

Each new version of NetWare introduced a number of advancements, new features, and improvements over the previous version. NetWare Version 4.11, also called IntranetWare, includes special features for administering network access to the Internet and integrating the network with Web-based technologies. For more information on intranets, refer to Chapters 14–16.

NetWare's Version 4.*x* is much larger, more feature-laden, and more complicated than previous versions. It includes significant changes in its file system and introduces global directory services.

NetWare is loaded on top of the DOS operating system, but once up and running, it takes over the entire network. DOS can continue to exist below NetWare (shoved into the basement, so to speak), and if you close the NetWare operating system, you can return to the DOS prompt. NetWare includes a command, Remove Dos, that you can invoke once it is up and running; this command deletes the DOS operating system from RAM, freeing up additional memory for NetWare.

NetWare's file system is proprietary and optimized for the networking environment. It has many unique features that can improve a network's overall performance, speed, and reliability.

PC-based NetWare versions 3 and 4 require the following minimum hardware for workstation and server nodes:

- Intel 80386-compatible processor, or better

- 4MB RAM for Version 3, 8MB RAM for Version 4

- A minimum of 80MB of hard disk space

These requirements are minimums, and they don't account for performance or the overall usefulness of your NetWare network. Workstations may get by if they aren't running any really demanding applications, but for servers, 32–64MB RAM and 1–4 gigabytes (trillions of bytes) of hard disk space are more practical requirements. NetWare can support up to 4 gigabytes of RAM and 32 gigabytes of hard disk space.

NetWare also supports a wide range of network adapter cards and cabling systems. Your choice of specific network interface hardware for NetWare will be based on the kinds of performance and budget considerations discussed in previous chapters of this book.

Using NetWare

NetWare uses many different utility programs to control its various operations. When you start a client workstation, you must first load the software driver for the network interface card that you are using, followed by an important piece of software called the NetWare Shell. All workstation requests for network services are handled by the NetWare Shell. If you want to run NetWare using Windows, you must also load additional driver software for Windows.

When the NetWare Shell loads, it polls the network for the first server it can find, which becomes the default server for that session. Once you are connected to a server, you can run NetWare's Login program. This program prompts you for your user name and password, and (assuming that you enter them correctly) executes a *login script*, which (if it exists) is a series of commands that set up network environment parameters for all workstations logging in. Among other configuration commands, this script can establish a link to a specific server other than the default.

The login script is followed by the *user login script*, another series of commands that set up custom parameters applying only to the individual workstation. If the user login script for a workstation is not present, NetWare looks for a *default user script* to run. This script exists on the file server and can contain generic workstation configuration commands that apply to everyone, or to any workstation that logs in to that particular server.

Finally, in version 4, a third script can be run, behind the login script but before the user login script. This is the *profile script*, which sets up network parameters for a predefined group of users. This script is set up by the NetWare Administrator.

NetWare relies on a modular architecture. The network designer can choose specific network services to include in the operating system. For example, the designer can choose to include special programs, called NetWare Loadable Modules, or NLMs, that run in the background on the NetWare server, in order to be available at all time the network is running. NLMs can be used to control the server's hard disks and interface boards, support non-DOS file names, or provide applications on the server to users. In addition to NLMs, NetWare places at the designer's disposal a set of small programs called *Virtual Loadable Modules*, or VLMs. A VLM is essentially a utility program that specializes in performing a narrowly-defined network service (for example, a network management and resource tracking system, a database driver, an e-mail system, and so on). NLMs and VLMs conserve memory by allowing the NOS to load only those services NetWare actually needs to run on your system. VLMs have another significant advantage: They can be written by third-party developers, which makes it possible to customize your NetWare network along lines not necessarily envisioned by Novell.

NetWare Directory Services

In Version 4.*x* of NetWare, Novell introduced a special feature called Novell Directory Services (NDS), a system for organizing network locations into a hierarchy. This hierarchical structure is often referred to as a *tree* structure because of its branchlike nature. Figure 8.1 shows a simple NDS tree.

Network Directory Services begin with a *root directory*, which contains any number of *objects*. There are two types of object: a *container* object and a *leaf* object. A container object holds other objects; for example, a country, an organization, or a workgroup within an organization. A leaf object identifies a single node on the network such as a workstation, file server, workgroup, or user name.

To locate an object on the network, you can identify it using its complete directory name. An object's complete name includes the various

FIGURE 8.1

A diagram of NetWare NDS

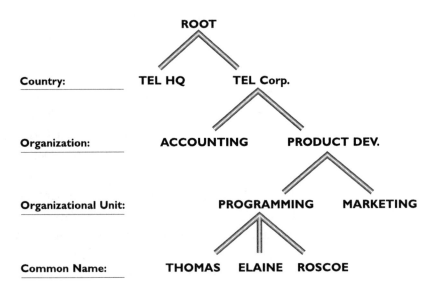

branches in the directory that are connected to it, starting with the object name and moving up to the root. The branch names are separated by periods (also called *dots*):

```
COMMON NAME.ORGANIZATIONAL UNIT.ORGANIZATION.COUNTRY
```

For example, using the directory tree in Figure 8.1, the complete name of user Bob Thomas would be:

```
THOMAS.PROGRAMMING.PRODUCT DEV.TEL CORP
```

The purpose of NDS is to identify network locations based on function and physical location rather than network addresses. Although the Directory can get quite complicated on very large networks, it is still much easier to look for information about other users and shared hardware using recognizable names, workgroups, and organizational units. To assist users in navigating NDS, NetWare includes utilities for searching NDS and looking up lists of names based on NDS object specifications.

NetWare Security

NetWare security is implemented at every level throughout the system. You can set levels of security that are customizable and that form-fit every user on your network.

The System Administrator

The system administrator can configure the operating system to require a password from selected users at login time. The SA can also configure NetWare to do any of the following:

- Accept only passwords of a defined length

- Prevent users from sharing the same password

- Force password changes at defined intervals

■ Put limits on the times of day when a user can log in, the calendar period during which logins are valid, or the amount of time the user is allowed to remain on the network.

The User

The user, once past the login level, still cannot roam the network scot-free. The user may be made subject to one or more of the following *file access rights*:

Supervisory   Grants complete access to the network data files, and the right to assign other file access rights to other users.

Access Control   Allows the user to grant other rights, except Supervisor.

Scan   Allows the user to display the contents of files and directories.

Read Only   Allows the user to view the contents of files but not to make changes to them.

Create   Allows the user to make new files and directories.

Modify   Allows the user to change the name of a file or directory but does not allow access to its contents.

Write   Allows the user to change the contents of files and directories.

Erase   Allows the user to delete files.

Files and Directories

NetWare also establishes attributes for files (in addition to the usual DOS file attributes—read/write, system, hidden, and archive). The following file attributes apply to both directories and files and limit what any user can do with them:

Delete Inhibit   This absolutely prevents file/directory deletion, even by users with the right to erase files.

Rename Inhibit   This prevents name changes to files and directories, even by users with the right to modify files.

Purge   Completely removes a file or directory from disk when deleted. Without this attribute, a deleted file remains on disk but is subject to being overwritten by new data. (Until the deleted file without this attribute is overwritten, it can be restored using NetWare's File Restore command.)

The following attributes apply to files only:

Execute Only   Prevents copying and erasure of executable files.

Indexed   Places file name in NetWare's directory index for faster access.

Shared   File can be accessed by more than one user. (Dangerous unless the file is read-only. As mentioned earlier, two users attempting to write to the same file at the same time can corrupt the file.)

The following additional attributes are available in NetWare 4 and apply to files:

Compressed   The file is stored in compressed format.

Can't Compress   The file was subject to compression but could not be compressed (usually because it's too small to begin with).

Migrated   An infrequently-accessed file has been moved to a backup storage area.

The following NetWare 4 attributes apply to both files and directories:

Normal   No NetWare 4 attributes set.

Immediate Compress   Compresses files (or the entire directory) when saving to disk, to conserve disk space.

Don't Compress   Saves files in uncompressed format.

Don't Migrate   Keeps a seldom-accessed file or directory on the hard disk—does not automatically move it to a backup storage system.

File Transaction Tracking

NetWare can protect data from system crashes during write operations using its *Transaction Tracking System* (TTS). This system is handled at the file server level. Certain files stored on the file server can be flagged as *transactional* files. When NetWare senses that such a file is about to be overwritten, it marks the current file as a backup and writes the entire updated file to the disk in a new location. When the copy process is completed, NetWare deletes the backup file.

TTS can be used to recover files that would otherwise have been lost if a power interruption occurred during the write operation. In that event, the untouched backup file would remain on the hard disk, flagged as a backup. Upon restoration of normal operations, NetWare can sense the existence of this backup file, understand that the write operation was aborted, and restore the backup automatically. TTS is NetWare's "insurance policy" when dealing with critical, time-sensitive files that must be protected between backup times; for example, you may not be able to risk the loss of some critical or time-sensitive legal, investment, or tax information. TTS prevents this type of data loss, which results from events that are beyond your control.

System Fault Tolerance

As a further security mechanism, NetWare uses special disk-storage techniques to prevent data damage due to hard disk failure. These mechanisms are collectively called *System Fault Tolerance*, or *SFT*.

NetWare provides two levels of system fault tolerance (plus a third in NetWare 4). SFT Level One performs an operation called *read-after-write verification*, to account for the possibility of bad sectors that may appear on the hard disk over time as the result of normal wear and tear.

SFT Level One is a complicated read/write/compare mechanism. In simple terms, NetWare does the following:

1. Before NetWare begins a write operation, it stores the data in a special comparison buffer in memory.

2. NetWare then writes the data to disk.

3. After writing, it reads the data back into a second memory buffer.

4. It then compares the two buffers.

If the comparison matches, the buffers are flushed and only the verified disk copy remains. If the comparison does not match, the sectors are marked as bad, and NetWare tries writing the data again at another location on the hard disk. It repeats the process until the data has been saved successfully.

SFT Level Two provides support for *disk mirroring* or *disk duplexing*. Disk mirroring is a process by which duplicate hard disks are run off the same controller and data is copied to both disks simultaneously. If one disk fails completely, the other disk can serve as a backup, immediately taking over and allowing your network to function normally until you can replace the bad disk. In addition, because the same data is stored in two places, NetWare can take advantage of this to speed up access. (For more information about this process, see Chapter 6.) Disk duplexing works the same way, but the duplicate hard disks are attached to separate controllers. This system guards against data loss resulting from controller failure in addition to disk failure.

SFT Level Three provides support for *mirrored file servers*. In this system, the data is stored on a primary file server and immediately transferred at high speed to a secondary file server. NetWare can also use the secondary file server to access data and boost performance. This system guards against disk, controller, and file server damage. (In case of massive disaster that destroys all your file servers at once, you're on your own—but then again, so is everybody else, probably.)

Why Choose NetWare?

NetWare can handle extremely demanding client/server networks, and because it is in widespread use, virtually all vendors support its features. Because of its complexity, however, you must have a well-trained, experienced network administrator to maintain it.

Windows NT Server

Windows NT Server is a Windows-based client/server operating system developed by Microsoft Corporation. It is positioned in the marketplace as a direct competitor to Novell's NetWare. As such, Windows NT Server looks to provide the same levels of security, features, and robust performance as NetWare, with the added convenience of a fully integrated Windows interface.

Windows NT Server can be run on file servers using advanced Intel processors (at least an 80486 is recommended) or DEC Alpha RISC processors. It is designed to interact with its companion client product, Windows NT Workstation, but it can interact with other platforms as well: MS-DOS (using Microsoft LAN Manager), OS/2, Windows 3.1, Windows for Workgroups, and Windows 95. Client software is discussed in greater detail in the next chapter.

Windows NT Server supports virtually all network adapter cards and cabling systems. You can choose your own based on personal evaluation and performance and budget considerations, or you can purchase Windows NT Server in kits with network interface cards and cables included.

NT Server Protocols

NT supports four protocols. Of these, TCP/IP has been discussed in detail in Chapter 2. The other three protocols are:

NWLink   This protocol is compatible with NetWare's IPX/SPX protocol, and provides compatibility with Novell's NetWare.

NetBIOS Extended User Interface (NetBEUI)   This is a small but very fast protocol that is suitable for self-contained networks (where all nodes establish direct links with the server).

Data Control   This protocol is provided to establish communications with mainframe computers (which also must support Data Control) and peripheral hardware (for example, a network-aware shared printer with an internal NIC) that is connected directly to the network cable.

Using Windows NT Server

Windows NT Server is a fully integrated system. Installation on the file server is automated; you run it by inserting an installation disk and booting the server. During installation, NT creates a special database called the *Registry*, containing information that you enter about the server system and clients who have logged on. The registry controls the overall configuration of the network and its clients.

If you are installing Windows NT Workstation clients, you can install the client software over the network from the server or from other workstations, a convenience when installing many workstations spread out over a wide area.

Client data is centralized in the NT system. Each client is given a *user account*, which gives the user access to network services. The network administrator has centralized control over client accounts and can restrict access to specific services for security purposes. User accounts include the following information:

User Name   The unique log-in name for each user.

Password   The user's access password.

Full Name   The user's true, full name.

Logon Hours   Times during which the user is permitted access.

Logon Workstations   Workstation names from which the user is permitted access.

Expiration Date   The date on which the account is deactivated (user no longer permitted access).

User Directory   Private directory on the server for the user.

Logon Script   A batch file of operating system commands that executes when the user logs on.

Account Type   Either global or local. A global account gives the user normal access to the network. A local account gives the user access to the single local domain. (See the later section on Windows NT domains.)

In addition to the user account, each client has a *user profile* that is stored on the server. This profile contains configuration settings and preferences for the user's workstation. Because the user profile is stored on the server, the user can log in from different workstations and still see a familiar working environment.

Windows NT Server Organization

Windows NT Server is organized into *domains* and *trust relationships*. A domain is simply a server, or group of servers, that process a set of client accounts. When a group of servers share client account information, one server is designated as a *primary domain server*, and all changes to client account information are handled by this server. The other servers function as *backup servers* that store copies of the primary server's account database.

A trust relationship is a communication link between two domains. When a trust relationship is established, the first domain (called the *trusting* domain) allows access by users in the second domain (called the *trusted* domain). This type of communication allows users to access different domains without requiring that they set up separate accounts in each one. At the same time, because these communication links are controlled by the network administrator, security can be maintained.

Trust relationships can be established between domains so that only one has access to the other, or so that both have access to each other (in effect, two trust relationships between a pair of domains). You can also establish trust relationships between several domains in a series. However, trust relationships are not passed through domains. In other words, each relationship must be established separately between two domains. Different kinds of trust relationships are diagrammed in Figure 8.2.

In a small network, there is only one server to which all clients are linked. There is no need for trust relationships because only one domain exists. In larger and more complicated networks, however, the concept of domain and trust relationship can be used to develop highly organized models of data sharing and secure access. For example, in networks with several domains, you can establish different types of relationships:

many-to-one	Multiple domains have access to a single master domain but not to each other.
many-to-some	Multiple domains have access to a number of master domains.
many-to-many	Multiple domains have two-way access to each other (no master domain).

Windows NT Server Security

Windows NT Server maintains security by means of password access to the network and user access rights to network services. On the network-access level, the network administrator has all the usual controls over password usage: for example, minimum and maximum length of passwords and frequency with which passwords must be changed.

FIGURE 8.2

Trust relationships among
Windows NT Server
domains. The arrows
indicate which domain
(trusted) has access to
the other (trusting).

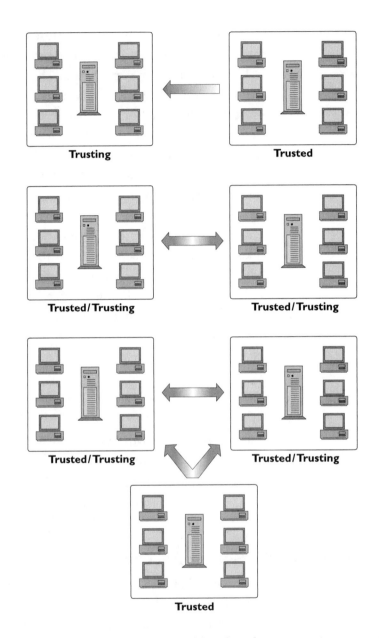

User-level security is implemented by classifying users in categories
based on the network services they are permitted to access and the
degree to which they are allowed to manipulate data files. The network

administrator (or administrators—there can be as many as you deem necessary) has the power to control file and directory access and the power to modify files, for each category of user. Following are examples of common NT user categories:

Administrators have control over network organization; for example, managing all client accounts, client access to files, backup procedures; security assignments, and so on.

Server Operators control server functions. For example, back up files, control file sharing, control print services.

Account Operators create and modify client accounts (but not server operator or administrator accounts) and user profiles.

Print Operators manage print services only.

Backup Operators manage backup procedures only.

Power Users log on as clients, but have reading, writing, or modifying access rights to files on the server as granted by the system administrator.

Users log onto the system to access network services and applications and have more limited server access rights than power users.

Network access rights are granted on the domain level. A right granted on one server in a domain is extended to all servers in that domain but not to servers in other domains. Access rights must be set separately for each domain to which a user has access.

Why Choose NT Server?

Windows NT Server is a good choice if you need an operating system with power and features comparable to NetWare but with a smoother integration with the familiar Windows interface. Windows NT Server also offers a well-integrated, centralized management package that can be used to ease the management problems associated with large, multiserver networks, as well as networks that must support different communication protocols. It is also competitively priced for its array of features.

Where to Go from Here

Your choice of operating system is largely a function of how information is normally communicated in your business. Assuming that your business is well organized and the lines of communication are clear, the operating system should model the way information flows in your existing real-world system. For example, if your business depends on access to centralized data, a client/server system such as NetWare or Windows NT might be most appropriate. If you have less need for centralized access and a greater need to move files back and forth between users, a peer-to-peer system might be preferable.

On the other hand, perhaps your real-world information and communication system may need revising. If it is subject to systemic bottlenecks because your business communication rules aren't clear, you may need to take a step back and establish clearer information rules before deciding on which computer network to install. It is axiomatic that a computer does not replace an organizational model, it merely amplifies it. Be sure that you are amplifying an understandable and efficient real-world system.

Now that we've looked at some operating system software, the next chapter will describe the other aspect of the client/server model: client software.

For Further Reading

- Cougias, Dorian, with Tom Dell and Tom Hessel. *Managing Appletalk Networks*. Ap Professional, 1997.

- Cowart, Robert. *Mastering Windows 3.11 Internet Edition.* Sybex, 1997.

- Cowart, Robert. *Mastering Windows 95 Internet Edition.* Sybex, 1997.

- Dyson, Peter. *Mastering OS/2 Warp.* Sybex, 1995.

- Gaskin, James. *The Complete Guide to NetWare 4.11/ IntranetWare.* Sybex, 1996.

- Laubach, Edwin G. *Networking with Banyan VINES.* Windcrest, 1992.

- Minasi, Mark. *Windows NT 4 Complete.* Sybex, 1997.

- Stoltz, Kevin. *Inside LANtastic.* New Riders, 1994.

CASE STUDY

GAB's staff begin the process of selecting their network operating system by revisiting their original set of networking goals. The features that were of most concern to them were:

- Reliable backups

- Efficient administration

- Shared resources, especially printing

- Secure access to information

- Efficient communications and scheduling

- Growth into a full-fledged intranet

GAB has already decided that a client/server architecture will be the best choice for achieving the goals they have laid out, so peer-to-peer operating systems can be set aside right away.

Whenever possible, GAB hopes to continue using (albeit with major upgrades) their current hardware. This hardware is Intel-based, running DOS and Windows. A UNIX-based system would require considerable adjustment to integrate; and, in comparison with other operating systems available, a UNIX-based system doesn't offer enough special features for GAB's specific needs.

This leaves GAB with a choice between NetWare and Windows NT. Both systems are robust and full-featured. Both systems allow for growth into intranets. Both systems have features that permit complex levels of secure access to data and support

for communications and scheduling. Both systems will require skilled and experienced administration. NetWare has an edge in its ability to handle GAB's older DOS-based software while still allowing a reasonable upgrade path for new applications. Windows NT, on the other hand, has an edge in its smoother integration of intranet protocols, for growth into a full-fledged intranet. Windows NT will require more hardware processing power (specifically, larger amounts of RAM) at the workstation level than NetWare. GAB would do well at this point to revisit their proposed hardware requirements and be certain that their proposed workstations will support the operating system they eventually choose.

Taking into account GAB's special needs for security and communications and reviewing each system's features in this regard, GAB's staff conclude that NetWare will offer a more powerful platform, but will be more complex to install and maintain than Windows NT.

GAB's staff arrange to see demonstrations of each system. This is important because their decision will be largely subjective, based on the comfort level the staff feels with the two systems' interfaces. Those staff members who are used to older, DOS-style applications are more likely to be comfortable with NetWare. Those who have grown used to Windows interfaces are more likely to be attracted to Windows NT.

In the end, the Windows contingent wins. It appears that GAB will achieve its networking goals more easily with a native Windows system, even when taking into account the enormous flexibility and raw power of NetWare.

C H A P T E R

9

Client Software

local area network isn't always put into place as an integrated, turnkey solution. Many businesses turn to networking technology as a means to connect and integrate a variety of different client workstations (DOS, Windows, OS/2, for example) that have landed on different users' desks over time. For this reason, modern file server systems support a variety of client platforms. This chapter describes common client software and compares how they go about the process of making a connection to server-based networks.

DOS Clients

Industry experts were surprised that DOS lasted as long as it did, hanging on for dear life as the operating system of choice for IBM-compatible stand-alone computers. The users who continue to stick with it do so because it is an inexpensive, reliable, familiar, and fast operating system. Those features outweighed its nearly nonexistent native user interface and cryptic command structure. It's worth noting that Windows has played a role in extending the life of DOS, by adding a graphical interface and shielding the user from its idiosyncratic line commands. Windows puts a graphical layer and specialized application platform on top of DOS, which still runs, more or less quietly, underneath. This dual operating system configuration is thorough enough to give users a friendly gateway to applications.

Although DOS's desktop domination has faded, machines using it will be around for several years to come. Some users of these machines will want to connect to networks.

DOS Clients on NetWare

Connecting a DOS client to a NetWare server requires installation of protocol drivers and NetWare shells that handle communication between the local client DOS and NetWare. In older versions of Net-Ware, the connection was made using two executable files, IPX.COM and NETX.EXE. IPX.COM was custom-configured for the particular workstation's NIC by the system administrator. NETX.EXE was the NetWare redirector; it received user commands and determined whether to direct them to the local operating system or the network.

NetWare 3 and 4 have a more flexible and powerful connection scheme, based on a standard called the Open Datalink Interface. Under this specification, the network interface card must be equipped with a special software driver, called a Multiple Link Interface Driver (MLID). MLID drivers accept different kinds of data protocols; for example, AppleTalk, TCP/IP, and NetWare's IPX. When the driver receives data, it passes it on to a link support utility, which identifies the protocol type and passes the packet to a protocol stack. The protocol stack translates the data so that the NetWare redirector can understand it and react appropriately.

When you initiate the NetWare connection, these processes are loaded into the client workstation's memory by means of executable files, in the following order:

1. LSL.COM, the link support utility

2. The MLID-compliant NIC software driver (supplied with the NIC)

3. Protocol Stack utilities (for example, IPXODI.COM to support NetWare IPX, TCPIP.EXE to support TCP/IP protocol)

After the ODI connection is set up, you can load the NetWare re-director, VLM.EXE. This program, like NETX.EXE, directs data flow between the workstation and the network. However, this version of the redirector is more modular and flexible than NETX.EXE. Specific network services can be loaded into the redirector on an as-needed basis, thus conserving memory. These services are stored in files called *virtual loadable modules*, or VLMs. VLMs perform services such as verifying data accuracy, providing compatibility with older versions of NetWare, and handling file and print services.

NetWare DOS client configuration is a richly detailed topic, well beyond the scope of this book. For more information, refer to *The CNA Study Guide*, by David James Clarke, IV and *The CNA Study Guide for NetWare 4*, by Michael Moncur and James Chellis, with James Chavez, both published by Sybex. These books cover configuration issues in depth.

DOS Clients on Windows NT

Windows NT supports DOS clients running Microsoft's LAN Manager (or fully-compatible) software. To make the connection to a Windows NT network, use LAN Manager's NET USE command. For example, a DOS client could use the following command to access Windows NT's \ACCOUNT\INVOICES directory and see it on the client workstation as drive letter I:

```
net use I: \\account\invoices
```

There are restrictions on how a DOS client will view Windows NT file names. Windows NT supports long file names, up to 255 characters. As DOS users know all too well, DOS can only read file names that are up to eight characters long with an optional three-character extension. Windows NT automatically translates long names into shorter names that comply with DOS's restrictions. When you create an NT long name, NT shortens the name using specific rules, in the following order:

1. All spaces are removed from the long name.

2. Illegal DOS characters (for example, ? : = \ |, among others) are changed to underscores in the long name.

3. If the resulting name is less than six characters long, skip to step 6.

4. If a period exists within the first six characters of the name, the name is truncated to include just the characters before the period.

5. If the name is longer than six characters, it is shortened to six characters.

6. NT then adds a tilde (~) and a single-digit number to the truncated name, to create a unique eight-character name. (For example, SAMPLE~1, SAMPLE~2, and so on.)

7. If NT requires a two-digit number to create a unique name, only the first five characters of the truncated name are used, followed by a tilde and two-digit number.

8. If any periods exist in the original long name, the last period and the first three characters following the period are appended to the DOS-compatible name. (These characters are also subject to the translation rules in steps 1 and 2.)

Windows NT network users should also use caution when assigning alias names to shared NT files and directories. DOS clients can see only those NT alias names that conform to its own 8/3 character-naming conventions. This means that, even though NT supports alias names up to 12 characters in length, you should use only DOS-compatible alias names for shared NT directories that are to be accessible to DOS clients.

Windows Clients

All currently-available versions of Windows (Windows 3.1, Windows for Workgroups, Windows NT, and Windows 95) support connections to the most popular file-server networks. They differ in the number of features they offer once the network connection is made.

Windows 3.1

Windows 3.1 is supplied with drivers that support a number of popular networks: NetWare, LAN Manager, LANtastic, and VINES, among others. However, your network vendor may have supplied a Windows network driver that is more fully-featured and reliable than the default Windows driver. It is prudent to check for such an updated driver before setting up the network driver that comes with Windows 3.1. For example, all versions of NetWare include Windows drivers that should be installed before making the network connection.

To make a client connection using Windows 3.1, you must first make Windows network-aware using Windows Setup. From Setup's Options menu, pick Change System Settings and open the Network drop-down list to choose the correct network driver from those supported. If you're using a vendor-supplied driver, its diskette should be in your A: or B: drive. Pick "Other Network" from the list and, when prompted, enter the appropriate drive letter. After you pick the driver, Windows copies the driver file to its System directory, and restarts itself with its new configuration.

Once Windows 3.1 is set up to recognize your network, you can establish a network connection using the File Manager. First, pick Network Connections from File Manager's Disk menu. In most cases you will see a dialog box with prompts to enter the network drive and your user password. Pick the Connect button to establish the connection.

Once the connection is made, you can access network drives and directories using the File Manager. You can also define Windows program items using network drives; however, this process is a little smoother if you connect to the network before you set up a new program item.

Windows for Workgroups, or Windows 3.11

Windows for Workgroups (WFW) works similarly to Windows 3.1, but in addition has network connections built in for peer-to-peer access (as discussed in Chapter 8), and support for connections to other server-based networks such as NetWare and Windows NT. If the controlling software driver furnished with your network adapter card supports the changing of network configuration settings from within Windows for Workgroups, you can use a feature called Smart Setup to configure network settings, such as setting an exact percentage of computer time for shared and local programs.

Setting up the connection works as described above in the Windows 3.1 section: You use commands and dialog boxes in the File Manager to point to server drives and directories, subject to security-based access limitations, if any.

Windows for Workgroups includes two useful network applications that are not found in Windows 3.1:

Microsoft Mail This application allows messages of any type to be sent between connected workstations, provided they have Microsoft Mail installed. (You will need a separately-sold upgrade to this product if you want to send messages to other e-mail systems.) This message system works in the background so that you can send and receive messages while working on some other application. It can alert you to messages you have received and file messages you wish to save. Microsoft Mail also allows you to "chat" electronically with other users.

Microsoft Schedule+ This application enables you to define your schedule, make appointments, and set meetings among users. You can view the appointments of other users and they can view yours, except for those defined as "private." If you want to set up a meeting, you can list users who will attend, and you can search for available time slots from their schedules. When an available time is found, you can set up a Request Meeting form to be sent to the proposed attendees, who can respond using either Schedule+ or Microsoft Mail.

The advantages of Windows for Workgroups over Windows 3.1 are its integrated ability to access server networks and remain a member of a peer-to-peer workgroup, plus the mail, messaging, and scheduling applications that are included.

Windows NT Workstation

Windows NT Workstation is optimized for connection to Windows NT Server. Each NT client can participate either in an NT Server domain or in a separate workgroup. (Refer to Chapter 8 for more information on NT domains.) Connection to the network can be handled in typical Windows fashion, by accessing File Manager at the workstation, or the connection can be established remotely from another installed Windows NT Workstation over the network.

When a user logs on to the Windows NT Server, a logon screen prompts for the user's name, password, and domain. If the user has an account on an NT Server domain, the user enters that name of that domain. Windows NT Server checks the logon information against the user database on the domain server, and if the data matches, the login is completed.

The user can also log onto the network independent of a domain, entering the name of the local client workstation. Windows NT Workstation then checks the login information against a local database of access rights, and if a match is found, allows the login for local client resources only.

Whenever a user logs in, Windows NT Workstation looks for a *logon script*, which is a batch file containing operating system commands. If NT Workstation files the logon script, its contents are executed automatically.

The Windows NT Workstation environment is controlled by means of a *user profile*, a file containing client configuration data; for example, program items and groups, window sizes and locations, screen colors, and printer connections.

Windows NT Workstation accesses files and directories according to rights established by the network administrator. Directories available to different users are called *shared directories*. A shared directory is given an alias name, by which different users can access it. The directory alias can be the same name as the directory, but it is not required.

In this way, a complicated directory name like C:\ACCOUNTING\ PAYABLES\INVOICING can be aliased as simply Invoices.

Windows NT Workstation permits integrated access to NT Server's powerful networking utilities:

Windows NT Backup is an application that provides centralized management of one or more tape backup drives across the network. You can use Windows NT Backup to back up data on servers or other workstations; but it will not recognize Windows 3.1 or MS-DOS workstations remotely, and to maintain security, it will not back up the Registry or event log files except at the domain server.

Event Viewer is used to read NT Server's *event logs*, special files that record logons, file and application access, and errors. There are three types of event logs: The system log records logons, file accesses and hardware/software errors; application logs record application usage; and security logs record errors and events that may be related to breaches of internal security settings.

Server Manager monitors current system activity (who is logged on and what network resources have been opened for access).

Performance Monitor displays performance statistics for various technical aspects of the system; for example, number of data packets transmitted per second, wait time for processes, and percentage of processor being utilized. Such statistics are useful when diagnosing network performance problems.

Windows 95

Windows 95, the latest version of Windows, includes several useful networking client features and supports connections to NetWare 3 and 4, OS/2 LAN Server, and Windows NT Server. If you like, you can also link a group of Windows 95 users as a small peer-to-peer network using most manufacturers' NICs and cables.

Configuring and Connecting

To configure the Windows 95 client, you access the Network Connections dialog box from the Control Panel. You then define the network type, supported protocols, user name and password, and network-specific security information (if any). Also, you can define your local workstation as a client or a server (including a dial-up server, with password protection, for remote access).

Windows 95 stores configuration information in a special database called the Registry. The Registry replaces the initialization files used in previous versions of Windows and allows for an easier means of updating configuration information using the operating system interface.

If you connect as a NetWare client, the Windows 95 NetWare client software can execute your NetWare login script—but it will not load memory-resident NetWare applications except from a separate batch file. Windows 95 clients can share local disk drives and printers with NetWare clients, using utilities that reside on the Windows client only. However, you can choose only one or the other (files or printers), not both at once.

Networking Features

Although functionally similar to Windows for Workgroups and Windows NT, Windows 95 has some unique networking features that make it an interesting alternative to those other Windows versions. For example, Windows 95 supports 32-bit, protected-mode versions of TCP/IP, NetBEUI, and IPX/SPX protocols, which are faster and use less system memory than the 16-bit versions in Windows for Workgroups. Although Windows NT and Windows for Workgroups both have Microsoft Mail and Schedule+, Windows 95 lumps a variety of messaging programs together as the Microsoft Exchange. The Exchange permits you to have a single mailbox for e-mail, fax, data files, and connections to commercial on-line mail services, such as CompuServe, or to an Internet mail provider.

In addition to the Control Panel, there are three other networking utilities in Windows 95:

Network Explorer is an expanded version of the old File Manager, which allows you to access and modify files on the network server, assuming that the network's security features allow you the appropriate access rights.

Network Neighborhood is a display of available servers, domains, workgroups, and files. You access it through the Network Explorer. Using Network Neighborhood, you can map a local drive letter to a server directory or attach directly to the server drive. Neighborhood also allows you to browse server resources—for example, file names and print queues—but in read-only mode.

Briefcase is a file transfer and compression utility for copying files between the workstation and floppy disks or portable PCs. File transfers between the desktop and portable PCs require a parallel or serial cable connection.

Security

File security in Windows 95 is limited. You can assign passwords to client directories or printers. If you want to assign more flexible access rights, or restricted rights to individual files, you can set them up using the security design of your attached file server (Windows NT or NetWare).

Windows 95 offers four useful network management utilities for system administrators:

Netwatch allows you to connect to a server and monitor connections to that server: who is connected and what files they have open. System administrators can disconnect users remotely.

System Monitor allows you to track a client's performance and use of resources, either at the workstation or across the network. You can choose different display formats for the analysis: bar graph, line graph, or numeric chart.

Registry Editor allows you to access and make changes to users' system settings in the Windows 95 Registry.

System Policy Editor allows you to set each user's interface and network resource rights. For example, you can prevent certain users from accessing certain printers or from setting up their workstation as a server.

OS/2 Clients

OS/2 has been slow to attract support from developers of broad-based desktop applications. Its earlier versions, up through OS/2 Warp 3, lacked significant local-area networking functions.

The latest version, called *OS/2 Warp 4*, includes drivers and utilities for the most popular server-based and peer-to-peer networks. Warp 4 includes file requesters and redirectors that will allow direct connections to NetWare 3 and 4 and support for IPX, NetBIOS, plus enhanced TCP/IP protocols that will permit concurrent access to both network services and the Internet.

Warp 4 also includes *LAN Distance* software to support dial-in remote access. Messaging services are provided by including Lotus Development Corporation's *Notes Express*, a messaging system with functions similar to Microsoft Mail.

Additional Warp 4 networking utilities, designed for larger corporate customers, can be purchased separately as a suite of applications called the *OS/2 Extend Pack*. These utilities include connections to mainframes, system performance monitors, remote software installation, and remote node configuration.

Warp 4 can run Windows applications as native programs (in other words, without requiring a copy of Windows itself). However, to do this, you must make a separate purchase of add-on Windows applications drivers called the Win-OS/2 libraries.

Macintosh Clients

If you are using Macintosh computers as clients in Macintosh environments, the AppleTalk network is built right in; you simply make the hardware connections and go. Refer to Chapter 8 for more information about networking the Mac and to Chapter 3 for more information about AppleTalk.

If you want to connect Macintosh machines as clients in networks that are not Macintosh-based, be aware that the necessary software drivers and connectivity tools will be the responsibility of your host NOS. For example, if you want to connect a Mac machine to a NetWare system, you will need an add-on product, NetWare for Macintosh (a set of NetWare loadable modules and a client desktop accessory that together support the connection between NetWare's protocols and AppleTalk).

In addition, you should make certain that there are available Macintosh versions of your network's applications. For example, Lotus Notes, WordPerfect, and AutoCAD offer versions for the Macintosh. These applications can share data files with other workstations on the mixed network while running under the local operating system.

This is not intended as a dismissal of the idea of connecting Mac clients to non-Mac networks; it's a fine idea. However, if you know in advance that you intend to put Macintosh machines on a non-Macintosh network, take the time to be certain that that the necessary software and drivers are available for your host NOS.

Where to Go from Here

In many cases, your choice of client software will be a function of the network you are using; for example, you'll have an easier time running copies of Windows NT Workstation on a Windows NT Server system. However, if you are just starting out, it is useful to pay close attention to client software options because the client interface is what your network users will be working with every day. It makes sense to choose a network partly on the basis of how appealing the users find the features of the recommended client interface. Because these choices are so subjective, by all means visit vendors for first-hand demonstrations of these applications and their interfaces.

It is fairly common that as networks grow, different client platforms will join the network. This aspect of networking is always a challenge for system administrators. However, network operating system software continues to evolve and become more powerful, integrating support for a wider variety of client platforms, making this a bit less of a headache than it used to be.

At this point, you have become acquainted with some of the standard hardware and software that makes up a networked system. Many network operating system software includes some applications, like integrated messaging. The next chapter will take a more detailed look at network applications, the actual business-task software you use from day to day.

For Further Reading

- Clarke, David James, IV. *The CNA Study Guide.* 2d ed. Sybex, 1995.

- Cowart, Robert. *Mastering Windows 3.11 Internet Edition.* Sybex, 1997.

- Dyson, Peter. *Mastering OS/2 Warp.* Sybex, 1995.

- McClelland, Deke. *Macintosh System 7.1: Everything You Need to Know.* 2d ed. Sybex, 1993.

- Minasi, Mark. *The Expert Guide to Windows 95.* Sybex, 1996.

- Minasi, Mark, and Patrick T. Campbell. *Mastering Windows NT Workstation 4.* Sybex, 1996.

- Moncur, Micheal, and James Chellis, with James Chavez. *The CNA Study Guide for Netware 4.* Sybex, 1996.

CASE STUDY

GAB currently has stand-alone workstations running Windows 3.1, Windows 95, and even DOS. GAB, having researched Windows NT's capabilities, knows that it is possible to run all these systems as clients on a Windows NT network.

However, GAB's staff is sophisticated enough to recognize that a standard client operating system will make day-to-day network administration easier. GAB recognizes that the workstations running all versions of Windows are ready to integrate with a minimum of trouble; still, GAB staff decides to upgrade to Windows NT Workstation as the client system for the sake of smoother integration. The Windows 3.1 users will have to adjust to a different style of interface, but the Windows 95 users will have little, if any, adjustment to make.

The DOS users have a more difficult road ahead. GAB elects to connect two DOS machines to the Windows NT network, using NT's standard Network Client Drivers (version 3.0) for MS-DOS. They will want to be sure that their network administrator is familiar with these drivers and has experience installing and supporting them. This compromise will allow those DOS-based employees to continue working in their familiar DOS environment while having access to Windows' network services. GAB fervently hopes that, as time goes by, those DOS-based employees can see for themselves the advantages of upgrading to a more fully integrated client system, simply by observing the performance of others on the network.

In addition, GAB is already considering ways to develop an intranet as part of their networking solution. One of the advantages of intranet capability is that specific client platforms are less important; an intranet will comfortably accommodate a wide variety of client platforms. (You will learn more about intranets in Chapters 15 and 16.)

The goal of a fully standardized system is lofty, and given the highly individual needs of real human beings, not necessarily ideal. Fortunately, GAB is making sure that their network will be flexible enough to support different styles of working.

CHAPTER

10

Network Applications

ost of the software discussed in this book so far has been *system* software, the software that controls computers.

Application software is the software you use to get things done: writing letters and memos, reporting income and expenses, drawing pictures, printing paychecks, designing skyscrapers, balancing the bank account.

It is outside the scope of this book to evaluate individual software applications. There are simply too many. Software companies upgrade their products with such frequency that information on individual products (in book form, at least) quickly becomes out of date. Finally, it is not this book's intention to imply any recommendations for any specific product.

This chapter discusses three types of applications that have come into existence because of networks. For each of these, this chapter describes features that make these applications useful and describes what you should be looking for when making comparisons between various product offerings. This chapter also makes some observations about application software in general.

Stand-Alone Applications on the Network

In theory, an application that runs on a stand-alone desktop computer should run on the same computer connected to a network. In practice, stand-alone applications present some risks when running on a network because they are not programmed to comply with the network's rules for shared access to data. It is up to you and your network operating system to enforce those rules and prevent the stand-alone application from inadvertently corrupting shared files.

You are better off running applications that are *network-aware*, meaning that they are programmed to recognize shared-access file systems and respect your network's rules for keeping shared data safe and sound.

Types of Desktop Applications

Although there are a great many competing applications being marketed out there, business software falls into five broad categories of purpose: database, spreadsheet, word processing, communications, and graphics:

Database   Includes applications for accounting, inventory, personnel, statistics, order entry, shipping and receiving records; in general terms, the kind of data that used to be stored in file cabinets.

Spreadsheet   Includes applications for making analysis, comparisons, and projections. Modern spreadsheets offer document-formatting capabilities to enhance their final output. While many small businesses use spreadsheets to maintain simple databases, this approach is inefficient and is not recommended.

Word processing   Includes applications for both writing and document formatting, from simple in-house memos to glossy advertising brochures.

Communications   Includes applications for sending and receiving digital messages of all types; for example, e-mail systems, groupware, and Internet access.

Graphics   Includes applications for communicating ideas using pictures: Computer-Aided Drafting and Design (CADD), charts and graphs, presentation slides, scanning, photo editing, sketch drawing.

Some applications combine these categories: A project-management application may combine a database of tasks with a graphic output showing how task schedules overlap. In another example, a spreadsheet is actually a specialized form of a database, using a row-and-column format for its user interface.

Many network-aware applications are stand-alone applications that are enhanced with additional features that provide secure multi-user access to their data files. As such, they do not differ, in a functional sense, from their stand-alone cousins. The three types of applications discussed here are those that rely on network services for their native functionality: the distributed database manager, electronic messaging, and groupware.

Databases

There are a large number of networked database products on the market, but they all have the same fundamental purpose: to provide a centralized repository of data, allowing multiple users to access it, update it, and produce meaningful information based on it, all the while protecting it from accidental corruption and enforcing your business rules for keeping it accurate and reliable. That's a large job for a software program, and many programs require the ongoing support of a skilled database manager.

The integrity of the database is vital to the survival of many large and small businesses today. A Database Management System (DBMS) is an application that organizes data into a structured framework and uses that framework to provide access to the data and a vehicle for processing (modifying) it.

The Structure of a Data Table

A database framework organizes raw data into a hierarchy of relationships. At the lowest level of this hierarchy, the data is broken down into fundamental building blocks, called *fields*. A field defines an aspect of the data that is common to all instances of it; for example, a Last Name field would contain persons' last names, and a First Name field would contain their first names.

Fields are combined into *records*. A very simple record might consist of first and last name fields, and each record would then contain the full name of a person.

A set of such records is called a *table* (or in some systems, a *datafile* or *file*). A phone book is a real-world example of a table. For each listing in the phone book, there are three fields: one for names, another for addresses, and another for phone numbers. One set of fields—a person's name, address, and phone number—forms a record. The records are alphabetized into a list and bound together to make up the table/phone book.

By breaking up data into fields and records, a DBMS can access and sort the data very quickly. For example, a DBMS can sort a mailing list alphabetically using the Last Name and First Name fields and sort it in ZIP code order by using a ZIP code field.

Relational and Flat-File Databases

A DBMS that uses only a single table is called a *flat-file* database. But a DBMS can go further: Several tables can be related to each other and the DBMS can access them in a synchronized way to create highly detailed analyses and meaningful relationships between their various fields (or subsets of fields). In other words, the DBMS takes raw data and forms relationships that turn it into useful information. This ability to synchronize relationships between tables is far easier for a computer than a human being.

To visualize how a computer works with related tables in a database, imagine a company that ships a variety of products to customers. The company maintains a table of customers, including a customer ID number, name, and shipping addresses. If the company had to add a field to the customer table each time a customer ordered a product, the table would quickly become bloated, full of fields that not all customer records would necessarily need.

Instead, product numbers, names, and prices are stored in a separate inventory table. When a customer orders products, just the product numbers, along with the customer's ID number, are copied into a third table, a shipping/invoicing table. This third table is very small because only the relevant ID numbers are duplicated. The shipping/invoicing table can be sorted on the customer's ID number and invoice number, to keep all the ordered items together. The details about the customer and the products remain in their respective customer and inventory tables.

The DBMS can print shipping orders and invoices based on the small table, using the ID numbers to look up the details about customers and products. While this process would be tedious for human beings, it is easy for a computer. The relational database saves disk space, especially as shipping and invoicing records accumulate. The shipping/invoicing table, with its three fields, is much easier for a computer to sort and maintain than a single table with many fields. Figure 10.1 shows a relational database model.

The multiple-file, relational database model can be applied to many different types of business record keeping. For example, you can relate a mailing list to a set of demographic categories; a single student to multiple records of classes taken and grades received; a single accounting code to multiple instances of expenses and income; and so on.

Databases on a Network

A Networked Database Management System (NDBMS) is an application that synchronizes multiple users' access to centralized databases. There are two basic forms of networked databases:

Peer level NDBMS   In a peer-to-peer network, each user accesses the database records directly, using the NDBMS software to read and assemble the information and to make changes to the data as required. The system is simpler than client/server, but it produces

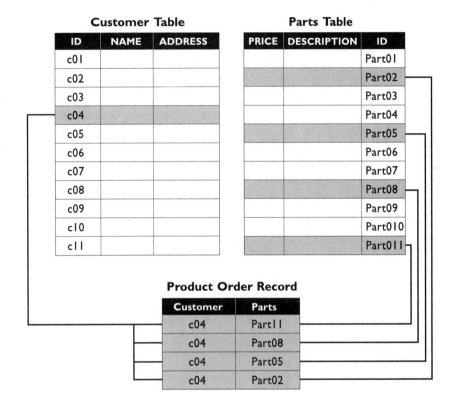

FIGURE 10.1

A simplified relational database. Here, a table of customer records is related to a table of products. Each product order record is in turn related to the records of customers and inventory items. Data duplication is minimized. The database management system maintains the relationships and can assemble the referenced data into meaningful information.

large amounts of data traffic across the network and can be slow. Also, great care must be taken to enforce rules of access so that data is not corrupted as multiple users tie directly into the stored tables. Examples include popular database products like dBASE and Paradox, which include language-level commands that implement access rules for shared datafiles and records within them.

Client/server NDBMS   In a client/server network, users do not access the records directly. Instead, they pass instructions to the file server, which performs operations on the stored data and passes the results of those operations back to the user. This process is more complicated, and thus more difficult to implement and maintain, but it is also faster and more efficient. Because data is handled by separate servers, the process of access and modification can take place locally at the server level, reducing network data traffic and speeding up the process overall. Also, the databases on the servers can deploy their own safeguards that keep multiple users from simultaneously accessing the same records and accidentally corrupting them. Examples include products like Access, Oracle, and SyBASE.

To further complicate matters, related tables can be stored at various locations throughout the network. Consider an accounting table stored on a workstation hard disk in the accounting department, which keeps records of customer payments against invoices, the details for which are stored in a separate table stored on a hard disk in the shipping/receiving department. The networked DBMS is responsible for accessing and relating information in tables that can be far-flung throughout the enterprise. Fortunately, many database product vendors provide utilities for accessing such *distributed databases*.

One important tool for accessing information in distributed databases is a language called SQL (Structured Query Language). This language is a standard for networked databases and is supported by most, if not all, client/server database products. It is a rich and robust language, and you can sample how it works in Chapter 14.

Data Locking

If more than one user were allowed to change the same data at the same time, only the last user to save the data would actually record the changes. The previous user's changes would be overwritten. This would cause data to become unreliable. To prevent this, an NDBMS needs a system for preventing changes made to data by more than one user at a time. If only one user can access the data, then subsequent users will see what changes have been made to date and make correct decisions about further modifications.

Locking is a term used to describe a standard system for preventing simultaneous access to data by more than one user. Databases can lock fields, records, or entire tables.

To enable locking, the fields, records, and tables in a networked database are equipped with headers that can store an either/or symbol (often expressed as a 1 or 0; or a logical True or False) that indicates whether a field, record, or file has been accessed. When any user accesses the field, record, or file, this header code is set to True and the data is considered "locked for the duration." Once the lock has been set, other users are prevented from accessing the data until the original user saves the modifications and releases the "lock."

The system is simple enough and works well enough most of the time, but there can be problems if the network malfunctions (a power failure or hard disk crash, for example). If the locking codes are not reset normally, data can become permanently locked. This is why most networks allow the system administrator the ability to access the data whenever necessary and remove erroneous lock codes.

Data Table File Formats

So far we have been talking about the logical arrangement of data in a relational database; that is, data broken down into fields, records, and sets of related tables. This concept is well established in the desktop database market. However, different database product developers choose to implement different file formats for their tables. Each vendor, as you might expect, touts their own file format as the best for fast and easy access to data, as well as suitability for use on a network. Some common database file formats are: Oracle, SyBASE, Paradox, Access, and xBASE-dialect files (which includes dBASE, FoxPRO, and Clipper).

It is fairly common for users to want to share tables, and if these tables are in different formats, the data may be unusable. Fortunately, many products come with utilities that translate tables from one format into another. When you are evaluating the merits of a particular database product, one important criterion to keep in mind is how well the product can translate its file format into others' formats.

Working with the Database

The usefulness of your database depends on two important skills described below: *network database design* and *network database programming*.

Designing the Network Database

We touched on the basic principles of database design when we described the simple order-entry database in the previous section of this chapter. In a nutshell, database design is the process of deciding what kinds of fields to include in your tables, which fields to use to sort the records, how to access the records and display their contents, on what basis to relate different tables to each other, and how you will store these tables on your network. The goal of database design is to make the best use of disk space, keep network traffic to a minimum, and thereby speed up the process of adding, deleting, modifying, and reporting the data.

Because your business records are bound to have certain unique qualities, a DBMS must allow you to define whatever fields you need, to arrange them in records to your liking, and to set any number of relationships between tables based on whatever criteria suit you.

Database design is a broad subject, and an in-depth discussion is beyond the scope of this book. Fortunately, if you are new to databases and want to learn, there are plenty of training venues available just about everywhere—try calling your local vendors and computer stores; ask them about training resources in your area. The vendors themselves may run training sessions of their own, usually at moderate cost. There are also plenty of consultants and on site trainers who will be happy to do the job for you—at a price, of course.

Programming the Database

Most database products offer a number of preprogrammed utilities that permit you to access and process the data in specific, fairly fundamental ways. These utilities often come in the form of sample programs using the database's control language; others might be executable programs designed to automate the process of creating tables or changing their structure. You may be able to get along by using those utility programs, supplied by the manufacturer as "standard equipment." It is also quite possible that you will have unique needs—based on personal preference, requirements of those with whom you do business, or unique aspects of the information you use, that will be beyond the scope of those generic utilities that come "out of the box."

A useful database product therefore includes some form of a programming language that allows you to manipulate the data in a more customized fashion. Some of these languages are little more than *macro languages*; in other words, a method for stringing built-in functions together so that the DBMS can execute them in order, in effect automating the steps of a particular task.

Other database languages rival high-level programming languages, complete with functions that allow you to access your computer's storage devices and RAM at the level of individual bits. (In other words, they give you the power to wreak total havoc if that's what you want.) The more powerful database products can be programmed to perform highly complex processes, and in the hands of a skilled programmer they can easily justify their cost. But programming, like database design, takes time to learn—an investment that is sometimes difficult to justify in a world where deadlines have come to be measured in days, if not in hours or minutes.

Many business people settle for a compromise, a blend of canned utilities that come with the product, third-party add-on programs that amplify the power of the database, and perhaps some in-house programming by a dedicated employee.

Electronic Messaging

Electronic messaging is a process that has expanded rapidly, from its beginnings as simple text messages passed from one workstation to another, to an application that combines secretarial, mailing, translation, formatting, and storage service for communications across your network, or between different networks, or around the world.

Programming without Code

As you might expect, database product developers are hard at work trying to simplify their DBMS languages, thereby adding to their commercial appeal. The job is daunting. Databases that use *graphical user interfaces* (GUIs) require specialized programming that adds complexity to the language for the sake of making things easier for the end-user. DBMS product developers also compete on the basis of power and features. More power and more features in the product mean more functionality (and vocabulary and syntax) that must be added to the language.

Lately, the trend in programming is toward special design utilities that permit the programmer to assemble user interfaces by arranging predefined *interface objects* (such as windows, pushbuttons, and drop-down menus) on the screen. The programmer links these interface objects to specific data processes (modifying the contents of a file, producing a report, and so on). When the programmer is finished arranging and linking, a built-in utility analyzes the screen information and writes code to produce the interface and the linked processes.

This kind of programming is called *object-oriented* because it is based on the concept of specific screen objects (windows, buttons, menus, and the like) linked to data processes that the end-user can access by pointing with a mouse or pressing special keyboard combinations. The results can be spectacular, but the development time in the beginning stages will be slow.

In object-oriented programming, the goal of the programmer is to produce an end-user interface for those who will manipulate the database. This interface, if programmed expertly, will be easy for end-users to understand and use and will shield those users from the arcane and difficult details of direct database manipulation.

However, while on-screen object-oriented programming is a great leap forward, it does not altogether eliminate the need to learn the vocabulary and syntax of the database programming language. Often the programmer will find that some direct manipulation of the program code is necessary to produce exactly the desired results. But great progress has been made in this area; and simplified, object-oriented database languages have great market potential.

In Chapter 8, you looked at simple message systems that some vendors of network operating systems provide with their products. These systems are useful for sending messages across a single installed network, but to access a larger base of recipients, a more complex product may be necessary.

A fully-featured electronic messaging application (for example, Novell's MHS, or Microsoft's MAPI) is based on a central database that contains electronic addresses of message senders and recipients (sometimes called a *post office*). A good messaging application also includes sets of instructions for formatting complex messages—messages that may contain not only text, but control-information that formats the text with character fonts, integrates picture displays, and broadcasts sound. The messaging application must include instructions for collecting, storing, and retrieving these messages—at any time from any user running any type of workstation over any type of connection allowed by the network.

Messaging Standards

If a user sends a message across a local network to another user running the same message system, the process is relatively simple. But if you want to send a message to a user running a different messaging program, some translation may be necessary. Because of the complexity involved in having many different systems send and receive messages in many different formats, the issue of standards arises once again.

Any number of vendors may attempt to develop and market their idea of a superior messaging system, using proprietary systems for sending, receiving, and storing messages. It would be impossible for all vendors to provide support for all other vendors' messaging specifications. Instead, vendors have tried to support a limited set of standard specifications, translating messages between their own message system and the accepted standards.

There are a few message formats that have evolved into *de facto* standards, and most messaging products include support for them. These include Lotus's cc:MAIL, Novell's Message Handling System (MHS), and Microsoft Mail. In addition, there are shared standards for message storage and retrieval systems, including Novell's Standard Message Format (SMF), Microsoft's Messaging Application Programmer's Interface (MAPI), and Lotus's Vendor Independent Messaging (VIM).

X.400

The messaging standard with the greatest international impact is called X.400. This standard was developed by the International Consultative Committee of Telephony and Telegraphy, a body of international experts headquartered in France. X.400 is a monumental specification. It attempts to lay down standards for all electronic messaging systems in the world.

Large-scale messaging services (such as CompuServe and America OnLine) use the X.400 specification. If you send a message to an electronic address over one of these services, the service converts the message to comply with the X.400 specifications and then sends it on to its destination, where it is converted again, into the message format the receiving program uses to make the message understandable to the receiving party.

Message Addresses

In order to send a message, you must specify a destination, or *address*. This address can be simple or quite complex, depending on the destination and how remote it is. Within a messaging database, the address can be simple: bobthom would be enough of an address for a message to Bob Thomas's workstation on the same local network (with "bobthom" as its identifying name).

To send a message to another messaging database (for example, on a separate network with a connection to yours), the addresses would consist of a user name in the remote messaging database plus the messaging database's identifying name. For example, a messaging database on my network is identified as "TEL." Someone using another messaging database on the network could send a message to me addressed as: bobthom@TEL.

There are many possible addressing formats with varying degrees of complexity, allowing you to send messages to destinations just about anywhere. To send a message to me over the Internet, try bobthom@telis.org.

Digital Dialog

The process of sending and receiving messages has evolved quickly into highly automated systems. For example, very little of the editing of this book was done on paper. Manuscripts, revisions, additions, and editorial comments were exchanged using a messaging system that connected author and editors, living many miles apart.

Memos, in the form of plain text files, were linked with binary-based document files. Once a package of information was complete, the message system was invoked and an automatic "address book" linked message with destination information. The address book feature allowed author and editors to exchange messages using familiar names rather than arcane addressing schemes. When a file was completed and sent, the recipient could expect to receive it in a matter of several minutes (or sometimes an hour or two, if the system was loaded with other messages).

In addition to saving paper, the messaging system allowed the editing and publishing process to proceed more efficiently; the digital dialog cut hours off the project that would have been spent printing repeated revisions of the text, as well as days that might have been spent waiting for traditional delivery services to send paper manuscripts back and forth.

The final result is the paper-based document you hold, born of a digital dialog.

Easy Messaging Systems

If your business communication needs can be met simply by exchanging text-based messages with colleagues, two simple options are available: on-line services and freemail.

On-line services, such as CompuServe and America OnLine, support e-mail services both within their own network and elsewhere via the Internet. These online services make money by charging for features that go well beyond e-mail, so look carefully at what they have to offer before you sign up.

A less expensive option is *freemail*, a service offered by a number of vendors that permits you to exchange simple e-mail messages on the Internet for free. One of the pioneers in offering this type of service is Juno (http://www.juno.com). A freemail vendor will supply you with the necessary software to set up an e-mail address and access to the Internet for sending and receiving messages at no cost. The catch is, these vendors usually provide only bare-bones messaging services, lacking fancy text-editing features and the ability to attach binary files to messages as are usually available from fee-based providers. Also, the freemail software is equipped to accept Internet-based advertising, which scrolls across your screen as you type, send, and read your messages. The freemail vendor wants as many free users as possible, to attract paying customers for advertising sales.

If you prefer to access the Internet directly for messaging, most Internet service providers will make the process fairly easy and straightforward, for a monthly subscription fee. Most of these vendors supply free software (or at least shareware) that allows you to use the Internet as your messaging system. You will learn more about the Internet and its relationship to local area networks in Chapter 14.

Messaging System Functions

What should a message system do for you? The following features can be considered a minimum standard for a full-featured message system:

Composition   The product should include a basic text-editing mechanism plus a system for importing into your messages additional documents created using other word-processing and text-editing software. In addition, because much communication centers around exchanging data files, the message system should provide a means of attaching binary files to messages so that text messages related to the binary information can be sent together with the file as a single message. More complicated systems can include support for messages sent in *rich-text format*, which allows you to embed pictures, sound and animated graphics within the body of your message.

Addressing The system should store frequently-used addresses, access them by means of a user directory, and offer optional reply-receipt services when the message is picked up by the recipient. A good messaging product should include *directory aliasing*, a feature that allows you to store complex electronic addresses under more readable names. For example, you can use a directory of alias names to send a message to "Bob Thomas," which is far easier to remember and recognize than a complex e-mail address such as `bobthom@telis.campus.mci.net`.

Mailbox The system should store incoming messages, display them in any order, and offer a mechanism for immediate reply. Sequences of back-and-forth messages (*e-conversations*) should be stored as such and replayed in order when necessary.

Forwarding The system should include, when desired, the ability to forward messages received at the local address to an alternate address (good for people who travel from one network to another).

Status reports The system should be able to display the results of sending, receiving, forwarding, and replying. (Did the message go through? If not, why not? Was it picked up at the destination?)

Translation The system should support mechanisms for handling messages between different vendor's messaging products (usually by support—either direct or through translation—for a common standard).

Filing The system should allow for filing or disposal of messages as required and default storage and disposal systems if no specific instructions are given (for example, unless otherwise instructed, the system may delete messages after a given number of days).

Background processing The system should run smoothly while the user performs other tasks. It should include an alarm system for messages tagged as urgent and be able to display urgent messages while other applications are running.

Messages Plus

Messages can include all kinds of slick, non-text–based information. For example, messages can include *raster images,* instructions to your computer to display pictures on the screen by arranging colored light points, called pixels, within a specified area. Messages can also include *embedded sound files,* stored digital representations of recorded sounds, or custom sounds created using specialized software.

The combination of text, graphics, and sound is called *multimedia,* not long ago a hot topic throughout the industry but lately revolving around new software applications for home use, such as games and entertainment software.

If your message system supports these features and you need them in your business operations, fine; but if you don't need them, consider a less expensive system that does not support them. The critical issue is whether the system actually expedites and facilitates real business communication between employees and work teams, makes money, or saves money.

Groupware

Groupware is special software that allows members of a work team to coordinate their activities and communications around specific shared projects. Groupware encompasses features of electronic messaging, but it does more—facilitating collaborative processes such as group conferencing, storing and updating shared information, and managing the schedules of workgroup members. It must do this regardless of the size of the enterprise, the actual locations of the group members, or the scheduling of project tasks.

To handle these sometimes conflicting goals, groupware creates an environment within the network built on a highly flexible database that stores and organizes rigidly structured information (fields and tables) together with more loosely structured information (notes, text, messages).

In addition, groupware must be flexible in how it deploys this information throughout the enterprise. For consistency's sake, it would be best if shared information were kept in a single, centralized location. But in far-flung, wide area networks, where workgroup members can be located anywhere in the world, accessing data from a single location is slow and inefficient. Groupware employs a technology called *automated replication* to make continual updates to copies of a project database located on local servers at points throughout the enterprise. The replication and distribution process is managed by a groupware project manager, whose job it is to configure the groupware system so data is distributed as fast and efficiently as possible.

Groupware products provide the following specific kinds of services:

Scheduling   This is a distinguishing feature of groupware. All members of a work group have access to public-access portions of their schedules, and work group members can review each other's schedules, request appointments, or arrange meetings of the entire group or select members of the group.

E-mail   Usually incorporated into groupware products as a basic electronic messaging service, this feature tracks sequences of messages and allows you to replay them. It also sends and tracks the flow of shared data.

Shared databases   This feature allows group members to store and retrieve project data as needs require in a centralized location. The database functions as a kind of bulletin board and history book containing project-related information.

Workflow transfer   Simply put, this feature allows individual group members to work on a particular aspect of a project and pass the result along to other users as necessary, supporting the transfer of data between different applications.

Updating distributed information   Groupware can keep track of shared information located throughout the enterprise. If one member of the workgroup updates a particular piece of information, groupware makes sure that the changes are replicated everywhere that information appears.

Here's a simple example of how groupware might work: Suppose a customer sends your company an e-mail message asking for help solving a problem. Your groupware application logs the incoming message and forwards it to the member of the customer service team who normally deals with this particular customer. In addition, groupware stores a copy of the incoming message in the customer's service file, alerts supervisory personnel if required, and automatically generates a confirmation to the customer that the message has been received. The service representative reads the message and conducts a search of company-wide service records to see if solutions to similar problems have already been recorded there. After determining a possible solution to the customer's problem, the service representative posts a message to other service team members asking them for input on developing a solution for the customer. Groupware keeps track of the ongoing dialog and maintains records of how the solution is eventually hammered out. Next, the customer service representative formats the agreed-upon solution (using illustrations drawn from the service records, step-by-step instructions, or whatever may be required) such that the customer can clearly understand the solution. Finally, the service representative sends the reply message back to the customer, and groupware stores the entire process for use by the service team should a similar problem arise any time in the future.

Examples of groupware products are:

Groupwise (Novell)   This groupware tool is built on an e-mail and messaging system, designed to run on Novell NetWare. It incorporates a calendar, task management tools, conferencing, message threads, Internet access, and remote-site access.

Lotus Domino/Notes (Lotus Development Corp.)   Domino handles groupware functions (collaboration, scheduling, messaging) at the server level. Domino also includes Web authoring, Internet deployment, and application development tools for client/server networks. Lotus Notes/Client is the workstation-level application for accessing Domino features.

Microsoft Exchange/Outlook 97 (Microsoft Corp.)   Microsoft's groupware product is designed to run on Windows NT. Exchange 97 is the server-level tool for managing groupware functions such as messaging, collaboration, scheduling, and applications development. Outlook 97 replaces standard Microsoft Exchange Client and Schedule+ and integrates with Exchange 97 to manage user calendars, journals, contacts, and task management.

Even a simple scheduling system like Schedule+ will be a boon in business where a simple meeting takes forever to set up because everyone is out of their office running hither and yon. Fast communications and instant access to individuals' appointments and calendars make meetings far easier to arrange and keep everyone informed regarding when and where meetings will take place.

Office Suites

In recent years, the major software vendors have the created the *suite*, a package that includes several of a vendor's business applications (most often a word processor, a spreadsheet, some kind of graphics or presentation package, and a database management system) bundled together and sold as a unit. The suite takes advantage of the ability of modern operating systems to move data between different applications running on a single workstation or at various nodes along a network. Suites include special features that translate data from one application's format into another. For example, a word processor can extract and format data from a spreadsheet, which in turn received that data from a database, and merge the final result with a graphic created using a graphics/presentation application.

Because software suites come from the same vendor, they offer the user a consistent interface design across several applications. This helps reduce learning time and facilitates overall understanding of what the various applications do. Also, suites make it easier to standardize fundamental business processes around a single vendor's software. Of course, the vendors use suites as an attempt to convince you to buy only their software, rather than encourage you to mix and match different applications from other vendors based on special features you might find more desirable.

Examples of Office Suites are:

ClarisWorks (Claris Canada)   Includes word processing, database, spreadsheet, drawing tools, organizer (Macintosh only), and FaxWorks (Windows only).

Corel Office (Corel)   Includes Web publishing, spreadsheet, word processing, database, presentation graphics, and calendar.

Microsoft Works (Microsoft)   Includes word processing, spreadsheet, database, drawing, and communications tools.

Office 97 (Microsoft)   Includes spreadsheet, word processing, presentation graphics, and scheduling. Database is available as an added option.

SmartSuite 97 (Lotus)   Includes spreadsheet, word processing, database, presentation graphics, and scheduling.

Where to Go from Here

This chapter has covered a specific category of application—those that are specially designed to take advantage of networks. Undoubtedly you will use other applications on your network, such as word processors, spreadsheets, graphic image processors, and programming languages. How do you go about selecting which of these are the best for your network?

There are dozens of network-aware applications written to perform all manner of business tasks, and the process of choosing the correct one may seem daunting at first.

In fact, the process of selecting application software has become fairly standard, and vendors have adapted themselves to it. You begin by collecting printed information from software dealers and manufacturers. Next, whenever possible, acquire demonstration versions or have your dealer demonstrate the software you are considering.

Computer magazines regularly publish reviews and comparisons of competing software products. The problem is often one of timing: The reviews don't usually appear just at the time when you are evaluating software. However, your public library has an important resource that can help you locate software reviews, the *Index to Periodicals*. You can use this index to identify which issues of computer magazines have reviews of software that you are considering. If the issue isn't in the library, most magazine publishers have back-issue services through which you can purchase old issues for a reasonable fee. Check the reader services section of a current issue for back-issue ordering information. This is an underutilized and very valuable resource.

Most importantly, whenever you can, talk to people who use the product, getting them to open up about its flaws as well as strengths. This is not always easy; there exists an all-too-human tendency to downplay mistakes. Few users will say to a stranger, "This product's a dog; I never should have bought it, but now I'm stuck with it because there's no more money in the software budget for a replacement." But a lot of us have had similar thoughts on occasion.

Investigate the possibility of user groups in your area, or if you have a modem, consider on-line services such as CompuServe or America OnLine; or, if you have an Internet connection, try using a search engine such as Alta Vista (which can be found at URL http:// www.altavista.com) or Yahoo (http://www.yahoo.com) to find on-line information about software products, obtain technical support, or contact user newsgroups. The on-line world is a rich source of support forums for an extensive variety of applications. In addition, people can be more forthcoming when on-line, and it's easy to get a diverse range of opinions.

Take your time; you are buying not only for yourself but also for the other users on your network. With patience and gentle persistence, you will find the right applications for your business.

In the next chapter, you will look at how your network and its applications are integrated into a smooth-running system—the network design.

For Further Reading

There are hundreds of books available that cover just about any software application on the market. Below are some titles from the Sybex catalog for groupware and office suites. They include good information on running these types of applications on networks:

- Dannenberg, Nancy B. *Mastering ClarisWorks for the Mac.* Sybex, 1994.

- Brown, Kenyon, Kyle Brown, Francois Koutchouk, and Kevin Brown. *Mastering Lotus Notes 4.5 and Domino.* 2d ed. Sybex, 1997.

- Gerber, Barry. *Mastering Microsoft Exchange Server 5.* 2d ed. Sybex, 1997.

- Moseley, Lonnie E. and David M. Boodey. *Mastering Microsoft Office Professional for Windows 95.* Sybex, 1995.

- Cowart, Robert. *Mastering Microsoft Works for Windows 95.* Sybex, 1995.

- Eddy, Sandra E. *Mastering Lotus SmartSuite 97 for Windows 95.* Sybex, 1996.

CASE STUDY

With regard to applications, GAB's network administrator must accomplish the following goals:

- Identify which existing applications, if any, are already network-aware, which will exist on the network without problems, and which will cause problems on the network.

- Upgrade or replace those applications that can cause problems on the network.

- Reconfigure those applications that are network-aware to operate most effectively on the new network operating system.

- Configure the operating system and (where possible) those benign non-network applications to eliminate problems that might arise from running non–network-aware applications on the system. For example, GAB will configure the operating system so only one user at a time may write to non–network-aware datafiles. While inconvenient, this will insure the integrity of the data used by those older applications.

- In general, keep applications and data in separate directories. Give users read-only rights to executable files in application directories, and full rights to files in data directories.

- Limit users access to secure and confidential files on an as-needed basis.

GAB must also raise their awareness of software licensing. In general, each user on the network must have a license from the software vendor to use the software. In the past, GAB's licensing took care of itself because the company was scrupulous enough to purchase a separate copy of each software program used on each stand-alone computer. Now that users can access network-aware applications from a server, GAB must be more careful, in order to avoid possible liability and business losses that could result from non-compliance with network licensing agreements. The network administrator agrees to evaluate various network-management software packages that monitor applications in use by employees, to determine how many users access each network-aware application concurrently. The minimum number of licenses will be purchased at the beginning, with additional licenses added as need be, based on the NA's ongoing audit of software usage and licensing compliance.

PART

IV

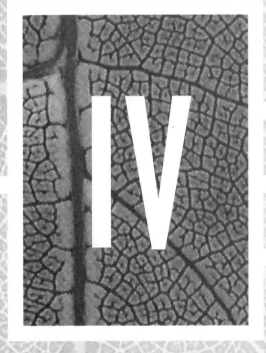

NETWORK MANAGEMENT

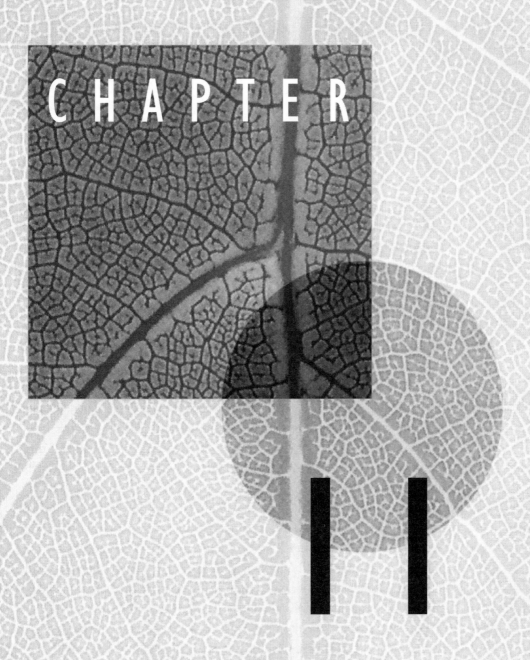

CHAPTER

11

Planning the Network

Previous chapters have introduced you to the various hardware and software components that make up a local area network. It is important to understand these technologies, in order to inform your decisions about the type of network that might be best for your business. However, a successful network is as much the result of good planning as of good selection of hardware and software. This chapter will introduce you to the steps required to plan and design your network.

Every business has certain unique characteristics. The everyday logistics of running your business are based on careful planning of business rules. The rules you plan evolve over time into further levels of refinement, depending on the type of business you are in as well as various human issues, such as personnel management and customer relations.

Some people mistakenly believe that the acquisition of computer technology will automatically turn a poorly organized business into a well organized one. (Advertisers are notorious for capitalizing on this dangerous notion.) Actually, computers are likely to make a well-organized business better, but they can also make a badly organized business even worse, and connecting computers into a network amplifies this effect. Remember that a local area network increases both the amount of data you will handle and the speed at which you will handle it. At the same time, it leaves responsibility for the quality of that data entirely in your hands.

For this reason, you should be willing to spend a lot of time analyzing how you do business and how information flows into and through your business before making any final decisions regarding network hardware and software. If you plan your network in this context, you stand a better chance of creating a useful, problem-free system.

The planning process for your local area network has two aspects worth highlighting.

- First, the process affords you the opportunity to reevaluate the manner in which your business currently manages information. It also allows you to make immediate adjustments to that management scheme, adjustments that can save or earn money and that you can implement with or without the assistance of computers.

- The second aspect of the planning process is more what you might expect: It clarifies your needs for network hardware, software, and configuration in the context of your business problems, solutions, and goals.

As the process unfolds, you may find yourself moving back and forth between these two aspects—choosing a network type and making refinements to your business rules, and then making changes to your network proposal based on changes you made in your business.

For example, if you are currently in a non-computerized or non-networked environment, installing a network can raise significant questions with regard to the physical plant: Will existing electrical outlets become overloaded? Can you save money by moving employee desks around? What changes to the physical plant might affect the network design?

Networks can produce significant changes in the ways you do business. For example, installing an e-mail system can have enormous impact, raising serious interpersonal (and sometimes legal) issues with regard to access rights, privacy, and e-mail etiquette. All these issues are best addressed earlier rather than later.

The network planning process may seem tedious and time-consuming, especially if you perceive an acute need to implement your new system as quickly as possible. Nevertheless, good planning is as important to the usefulness and reliability of your system as the hardware and software you intend to purchase; do not neglect it.

The Planning Process

Planning your network is accomplished in a series of steps, each of which is described in this chapter. You may find, depending on the type of business you are in, that some steps have more importance than others. You will have to reckon with each along the way though, so be prepared to spend at least some time with each.

WARNING Murphy's Law applies especially well to networking. One of the many corollaries to Murphy's Law is worth mentioning here: *Every project takes longer than you expect.* There is actually a reason projects almost always take longer than planned: No one can anticipate surprises (if we anticipated them, they would not be surprises). So, why not plan equal amounts of time to deal with both the planned processes and the surprises? If you expect the unexpected, chances are you will start sooner, move forward more carefully, and have time to prevent surprises from becoming crises. I know, I know; this is far easier said than done, but you're planning a local area network here. I had to warn you.

This chapter describes an eight-step planning process for networks. The steps, explained in detail in the following sections, are:

- Needs analysis

- Site analysis

- Equipment matching

- Configuration plan

- Server directory structure

- Configuration lists

- Installation schedule

- System log

Bear in mind that this description is not intended to be a forced march through some rigid formula; instead, be prepared to shift back and forth through the process as your network plan takes shape. Some of these steps influence each other, and it is not unusual to revise previous decisions based on discoveries made later.

Also remember that this chapter describes a general network planning process, which could apply to just about any reader. Your business may have unique aspects that are not accounted for here. Feel free, therefore, to approach the process described here as you might any textbook sample business plan—use it as a foundation framework only; alter it and customize it to whatever extent your unique situation requires.

Needs Analysis

Because you are reading this book, it's safe to say that you have already identified one or two organizational issues in your business that you believe a network can effectively address. For example, you may want to centralize your data to improve its accuracy throughout your enterprise, or you may wish to share expensive peripherals, or automate workgroup scheduling and communications.

The first step in developing a needs analysis is identifying and writing down your business problems. In this context, a business problem is not some kind of puzzle to be solved. It is a situation that either costs too much for you to allow to continue or is a block to additional income that you perceive could be flowing into the business. In other words, your effective needs analysis should revolve around saving or making money. There are any number of ways a network (or for that matter, a computer) can help you do business faster or more profitably, but this does not necessarily mean that you can quantify those gains in terms of money saved or earned. Still, it is a good idea to be on the lookout for circumstances in which the addition of technology can be related to your bottom line. For example, you may be able to show that network communications between the order-entry and shipping departments can increase shipping volume. You can then build incentives into the ordering process that encourage customers to order larger quantities of merchandise. Although the relationship between networking and increased orders may not be immediately apparent, it is nonetheless real. Throughout the planning process, strive to avoid even the appearance of introducing new technology for its own sake.

Some business bottlenecks are frighteningly complex. It is always a good idea to break a large complicated problem down into a set of smaller problems. For example, you might notice that the shipping department takes two days to get a package out the door and that this is unacceptably slow because the competition ships on the same day. Stated in this general way, there is no way to know what kinds of solutions are appropriate; "we must ship our orders faster" is too general a solution to be of any use.

However, suppose the problem is that your business rules require the order entry department to record all incoming orders and verify the client's credit before sending the order to shipping. Back when the business was small, order entry and shipping were in the same room, and it wasn't a problem. You've grown bigger now, and order entry is in another room down the hall. The delay occurs because someone in order entry has to pick up the confirmed orders and send them down the hall to shipping (using paper, or floppy disk, or whatever). This movement is taking place near the end of order entry's work day, so shipping is always sending orders out the day after your business receives them.

In addition to breaking down the problem into quantifiable smaller problems, you now have a basis for proposing a solution: Allow shipping to receive a verified order nearly instantly by sending order confirmations to shipping through the network.

Following are some examples of other common business problems that you may be able to address by networking:

Need for data centralization If many users address the same data, errors can creep in unless that data is stored in central locations that all users access. This applies not only to business records like customer information, shipping, inventory, and accounting records; it can also apply to internal information like boilerplate language and business memos. This type of information is less prone to error when stored, accessed, and updated from a shared source. Fewer errors mean less time wasted correcting them, better customer and employee relations, and greater productivity.

Need for automation   You can automate work flow by sending files across a network. This makes the flow of information faster and less prone to error. As mentioned before, reducing errors can save your business money. Speed is important but less so than accuracy and reliability. If a speeded-up work flow means that you can handle more information, and if this increase in volume translates to greater profits, then you can use "more speed" as a justifiable reason to network.

Need for communication   Often, you can increase production by making communication easier, both between employees and between employee and customer. Communication, when viewed as a means to save or make money, is a competitiveness issue. For example, if you can service customers more promptly than the other guy, you have a distinct competitive advantage.

Need for security   No amount of insurance can adequately compensate you for a significant data loss. If your business cannot survive a large-scale loss of data, you may want to use a network to automate the backup procedures; for example, an automated routine can kick in every night and make certain that the day's records are safe from accidental deletions. (See Chapter 12 for further discussion of security, data backups, and other network management issues.)

The next step in developing a needs analysis is to translate your business problems into goals. For example, if you cannot afford a separate high-speed color pen plotter for each stand-alone computer in your business, your goal becomes "implement a system for sharing a single, high-speed color pen plotter."

Restating a problem as a goal gives you an opportunity to quantify the results. For example, you could say that "sharing a single pen plotter will save us thousands of dollars, compared to the cost of purchasing multiple copies of the same device for each desktop."

Similarly, you can establish a goal of "centralizing the order entry and shipping records." You can justify this goal by stating, "This will save us half the cost of our current system (storing paper-based records in a single place rather than two) by consolidating the information on a server disk and allow us to cut our shipping turnaround time from two days to one day. It will promote additional sales for ourselves on the basis of improved, faster customer service."

The important thing to remember about this step is to write down whatever may be preventing your business from being as profitable as possible and to restate those problems as goals. After that, consider whether a computer network is the appropriate tool for implementing those goals.

Site Analysis

A network has to be installed in a suitable location. The best way to determine your site's suitability for networking is to draw out a site plan. In the case of large networks—the kind that can be spread out all over a building or between buildings—the site plan can be complex, even incorporated into the architectural renderings. In the case of small local networks, the site plan need only be a simple floor plan.

A good site plan is a drawing that includes the following information:

- The dimensions of the work spaces for each employee on the proposed network (important for determining the installation of the network workstations and servers)

- The locations of electrical outlets, including the devices that are currently using them (important for determining the electrical load distribution throughout the proposed network)

- The location of all immovable objects (support posts, dividing walls, or built-in wall cabinetry, for example)

- The current location of all furniture and other movable objects such as cubicle dividers (important for determining overall network layout, as well as assigning convenient locations for shared devices)

- The current location of all computer equipment (for example, current desktop PCs, also peripheral devices such as printers)

- The locations of doors and windows (important for installing cable)

- The location of ventilation ducts and air conditioning systems (important because computer equipment generates heat and proper ventilation is critical)

- The current electrical wiring scheme (important because you may need to add shielding to prevent existing electrical wiring from interfering with network cabling)

- Other businesses with which you may share your office building (because you may need to make arrangements with your neighboring companies when installing cable under floors, behind walls, or above ceilings)

A sample site plan is shown in Figure 11.1.

Before you install a lot of additional electrical equipment in your building, ask your building supervisor or local fire official for a copy of local fire regulation codes. Depending on your particular location, you may have to modify your design or upgrade your building to stay within the fire codes.

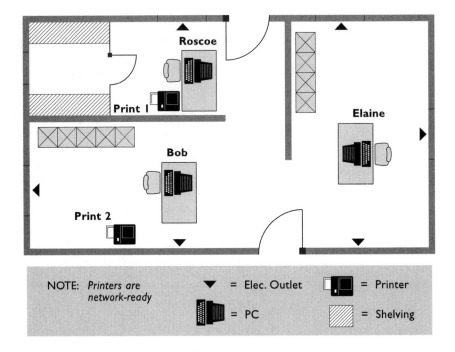

It can be especially useful to draw your site plan to some kind of
scale. This does not have to be a strict architectural drawing, but if you
apply a consistent scale to your plan, you can use it to make reasonably
accurate estimates of the length of cable runs, thus avoiding the stren-
uous (and occasionally embarrassing) process of running around your
plant (over doorways, under desks) with measuring tape. To make your
life a little easier, consider investing in one of the many inexpensive
software programs that are available for do-it-yourself home remod-
elers. These products, for very little money, create scaled floor plans
quickly and easily.

Making an Inventory of Your Equipment

Notice that, as you draw up your site plan, you are also creating an
inventory of existing business equipment. This inventory is extremely
useful because it will allow you to identify which equipment has enough

capability to be incorporated into the proposed network, with or without some degree of modification, and which equipment is likely to become obsolete once the network is installed. This kind of information can reduce your start-up costs and get maximum value from your existing equipment.

Depending on your network, you may be able to extend the life of some of your older workstations by using them as print servers. They may have sufficient memory and hard disk space to handle incoming print jobs intelligently and direct those jobs to printers that are not network-ready. Other older workstations may be able to handle remote access via modem.

As you inventory each piece of your current equipment, you should create a list of each item's features. This information will be immensely valuable throughout the networking process. For example, the feature list for a stand-alone desktop computer would include such information as:

- Processor (for example, Intel 80486DX, 100mhz)

- RAM size and configuration (for example, 32MB, 16MB SIMMs)

- Hard disk (for example, Connor 1.2GB)

- Monitor (for example Hitachi 15" VGA)

- Floppy Disks if any (for example, one 3.5", 1.44MB)

- CD-ROM (for example, Toshiba internal 8X)

Also, because you will be incorporating this information into your network system log (as discussed later in this chapter), it would be a good idea to make note of all serial numbers and warranty information for any device that carries an unexpired warranty. You (or your network administrator) may well need this information in the future.

Equipment Matching

Once you have completed your needs analysis and site analysis, you are ready to begin the process of matching the kinds of equipment you need to the goals you have identified. If you have pre-existing equipment that you intend to incorporate into your network, or if your business requires that you adhere to specific technology standards (say, for example, you are required to purchase only Macintosh- or IBM-compatible workstations and printers, to fit as easily as possible into an existing setup), your choices may be limited enough that this step practically takes care of itself. On the other hand, if you are starting completely from scratch, your job is harder; although you have an opportunity to create a system that is a more precise match with your proposed solutions, you also have a larger field of possibilities from which to choose. At this stage, the information in the previous chapters can help you narrow the spectrum of choices. If you still aren't sure, a qualified consultant can help you clarify your options. (Refer to Appendix A for tips on choosing a networking consultant.)

Software as Your Consultant

Software is available now to help design and validate networks. For example, NetSuite (http://www.netsuite.com) allows you to build a network from scratch and produce bills of materials and work orders. The software validates your design as you go along and warns you of mistakes (such as exceeding distance limitations or attempting to connect a PC to a hub without the proper connectors).

Equipment matching will overlap somewhat with the next step in the process, the configuration plan. The configuration plan will be affected to some extent by whatever equipment you select, as will your selection of equipment be influenced by your planned network configuration. Keep everything flexible until you have worked out a good balance of configuration and equipment.

You can also clarify your options by taking your needs analysis and site plan to several vendors, soliciting their recommendations for hardware and software that meets your needs.

Some vendors might be shocked by your level of preparation, even at this stage; many are used to clients who walk in the door with only a vague understanding of how a network will help them. Use this to your advantage. Of course, tell them you are comparison shopping. Encourage them to make competitive bids and get everything they promise in writing.

The recommendations from vendors should be specific, identifying the brands and versions of hardware and software they propose and also specifying prices, including proposed installation and maintenance services. Also, be certain that the vendor addresses any compatibility issues regarding your current equipment. Be sure to elicit a guarantee from the vendor that all the new and existing hardware you intend to use—especially NICs—is compatible with the exact version of any proposed network operating system.

Take the time to consider the amount of electrical load any proposed system will require. This issue can be especially urgent if you are installing your network in an older building. Ask your vendor for electrical specifications for the equipment you are considering and try to make a reasonable estimate of power consumption for your existing equipment. Consult your building's owner or builder for electrical specifications, or if necessary, you can hire an electrician to analyze the power capacity and consumption at your site. Do this if you have any doubts whatsoever about your site's power capacity. An overloaded circuit is a fire hazard and a legal liability, not to mention a golden opportunity to dispatch your spanking-new network into sudden oblivion.

In addition, be sure to talk with your vendor about cabling issues. Using your site plan, you should be able to make reasonably good estimates of how you intend to run the cable throughout your site and how long cable segments will be. A good vendor should be able to tell you if your choices are constrained by cabling requirements.

Use a comparison chart similar to the one shown in Figure 11.2 to list the recommendations of the various vendors you contact. It is extremely helpful to establish a simplified overview of the various recommended products and their prices. In addition, preparing the chart will give you an opportunity to find out how much you know about the proposals. You can call the vendors back with additional questions as you complete the comparison chart.

Configuration Plan

Your network configuration plan is based on your site plan and includes the newly added and relocated equipment. Most importantly, you can use the site plan to draw up your cable runs and determine what cable lengths you will need to connect your network. Figure 11.3 shows how the site plan is modified into a configuration plan.

Cable safety is an important issue. When you draw up your configuration plan, make note of places where cable might be exposed. Do whatever you can to hide cable, out of sight (because dangling cables are just plain ugly) but especially out from underfoot. Tripping over cable leads to significant loss of productivity because of expensive injuries, cooked adapter cards, and workstations flying off desktops, among other unpleasantnesses. If you have to run a cable across an area that is subject to foot traffic, install a cable cover over it. A cable cover is a piece of hard rubber that looks something like a speed bump. It's very hard to trip over, impossible not to notice, and will prove that you really are safety-minded, should you ever need to prove that.

F I G U R E I I.2

A sample comparison
chart for establishing an
overview of competing
proposals

	Vendor A			Vendor B			Vendor C		
	Quantity	Model	Price	Quantity	Model	Price	Quantity	Model	Price
Server:									
Workstation:									
NIC:									
Cabling:									
Kits:									
NOS:									
Apps:									
Connection Hardware:									
Accessories:									
Total Cost:									

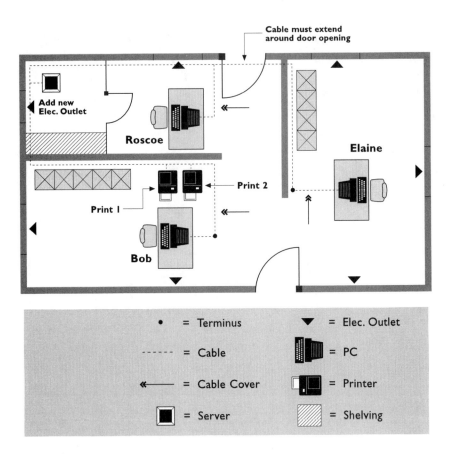

FIGURE 11.3

The sample site plan is modified to include cabling and relocated equipment.

Server Directory Structure

A server directory structure is a set of named logical addresses on your server's hard disk that organizes related disk files into logical groups and makes them easier to find. The directory structure begins with a root directory, which normally holds other directories, which in turn can hold disk files or still more directories, and so on, to whatever depth of organization your system requires. Figure 11.4 shows a fairly typical network directory structure. It is a good idea to set up an initial server directory scheme during your network's planning stages.

The structure of the directories on your servers' hard disks is largely a personal issue. You do have to stay within some fairly broad requirements regarding the directory structure for your network operating

F I G U R E   I I .4

A typical network
directory structure, such
as might be found in a
NetWare file server

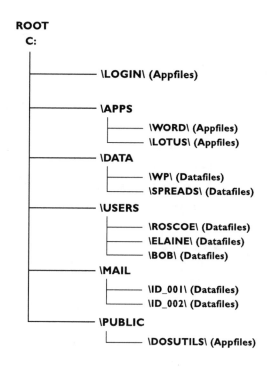

system's files, but beyond that, you can set up virtually any directory scheme you like. However, the experience of many network users has shown that some directory structures are more efficient than others. The following general guidelines—and they are only guidelines, not hard-and-fast laws—can help you organize your server's files into an efficient directory structure.

There are certain types of files that can be found on a great many servers. These include:

- Network operating system files

- Client system files

- Application files

- User data files

- Shared data files

- E-mail files

Your directory structure should accommodate all of these types.

A modern network operating system comes complete with an automated installation process that will ask you questions about your system and how you intend to use it and then set up a default directory structure for its operating system files. Unless you have a compelling need to do so, do not make changes to this automated setup. Much of your network's operation will depend on locating the correct operating system files when the time comes, and if you have improperly deviated from your operating system's default directory structure, you can bring the system to a resounding halt.

Certain directory names have become common in the network world, and if you use them properly and keep an accurate system log, other concerned individuals (for example, third-party technical support) will be able to make sense of how your network files are organized. Here are some examples of common directory names:

APPS   A fairly standard directory name for software applications that are to be run across the network or accessed remotely and run locally. Typically, the APPS directory contains no files but instead contains more directories, each one holding a separate application and its related system files. These applications are frequently installed by means of automated installation software, which create additional directories below that of the individual application name. If you have no compelling reason to switch the application system files and change the application's directory structure, leave it alone.

DATA   This directory normally holds other directories, containing data files that are unique to a particular application. For example, there could be a subdirectory named WP within the DATA directory, holding document files for a particular word processing program. Another subdirectory, named SPREADS, can hold spreadsheets.

LOGIN   This directory, which appears in NetWare (among other network operating systems), is the directory that the client first logs into when accessing the network system. Once the user has made the initial connection, he or she can traverse the directory structure at will, provided he or she has sufficient access rights.

MAIL   This directory holds a database of messages sent and received on the network's communications or e-mail system.

PUBLIC   As the name implies, this directory holds files and other directories that can be accessed from just about anywhere on the network. For example, under PUBLIC, you may want to create a subdirectory that holds utilities for a particular operating system used on various client workstations. By storing the utilities in this location, you make them accessible to anyone on the network who needs it.

USERS   This is a common directory name for data files that are the exclusive property of individual users on the network. The USER directory frequently contains no files but instead contains private directories for users of the system.

As a rule when organizing directories, remember that the closer you are to the root directory, the closer your are to the system-wide organization. In other words, the first level below the root directory is going to be occupied mostly by other directories, which apply to the system as a whole (APPS, USERS). The next level below that will apply to categories within the system-level directories (APPS\WP, USERS\ROSCOE). The next level below that will apply to specifics within each category (APPS\WP\WINWORD). And below that, to files, or still more directories, increasing levels of hair-splitting and possibly diminishing returns.

Bad directory structures are possible. Here are some general principles regarding what to avoid:

Directories that are too shallow   You could conceivably create all your file directories one level below the root. While easy to set up, this structure is woefully inefficient because the network and your users have to battle through a long list of unrelated directories in order to find any given one.

Directories that are too deep   It's not a good idea to go overboard nesting subdirectories below one another. No one wants to log onto a long series of directories like \USERS\ELAINE\WP\MEMOS\ INTEROFF to find Elaine's interoffice memos. With the exception of directory structures that are created by automated software installation routines, try to keep your subdirectories nested no deeper than three or four levels.

Duplicate user names   Although it is possible to have a user directory named USERS\ROSCOE and another directory named APPS\ WORD\ROSCOE, this kind of design usually points to bad organization. If two or more directories reference the same user, try to redesign the structure so that all user datafiles are arranged under a single user directory. Figure 11.5 illustrates this problem and one possible solution.

Directory names should make their contents apparent; for example, APPS could suggest a directory containing application files, but a cryptic name like TSD001_C suggests very little. Above all, bear in mind when creating your subdirectory structure that your most efficient solution is likely to be the one that is as shallow and simple as you can make it.

FIGURE 11.5

An example of a bad directory structure and one possible way to correct it. The advantage of the second structure is that all of Roscoe's or Elaine's different data files can be found by logging onto a single USERS subdirectory. This is usually a more efficient means of organizing user files.

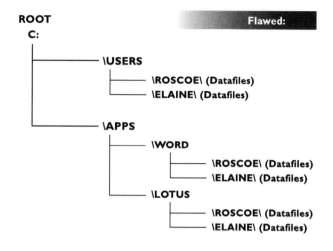

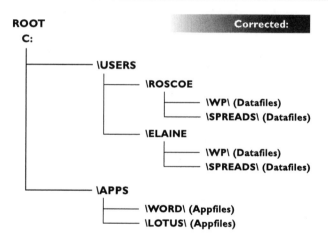

Configuration Lists

After you have drawn up your configuration plan, you will draw up a few important lists. You should make these lists carefully because the information will go into your network system log:

Machine name list You will give each workstation and server on the network a unique name. The choice of name is usually easy to make. Usually machines are named for the user or their function within the network. Keep in mind that machine names are not passwords and generally are not part of the security system. So, for example, if the machine on the programming desk is being used by Elaine, either "Elaine" or "Programming" would be appropriate names. The list of machine names should also include each machine's location and function: Is the machine a client only, a server only, or both client and server? If it is a server, what responsibilities does it have? For example, it may be a file server (if so, which files?), print server (which printers?), or backup storage (for whom?).

Server directory list   This is a listing of the directory structure for each server on the network. In its simplest form, this list could be a simple printout of the directory tree. Many network operating systems have utilities for producing this printout. A hard copy of the directory structure can come in handy, for example, in case of server failure. A hard copy of the system setup can speed up the rebuilding process.

Server users list   It can be useful to draw up a list, for each server, of machine names with access to that server. Besides the machine names, the list should include such information as the login schedule (days and times when access is permitted); access rights; login expiration date, if any; and password-renewal schedule.

Printer list   This list should include configuration information for each printer on the network. Include the name of the printer, its communication port on the print server (for example, LPT1: or COM1:), baud rate (if applicable), and its default configuration. This list can save time and guesswork if you need to replace the printer for any reason. The names you give to workstations and other networks nodes can help document your system, especially if, sometime in the future, you need to call in a third party or hire a replacement administrator. A name like "Accounting" (naming-by-function) or "Jim C" (naming-by-employee) is more descriptive and illuminating than a name like "Section 8" or "G12." A third party looking at your network scheme will appreciate all the help you can give them.

Bear in mind that, even though this process of assembling lists and documenting your network design is tedious, the information you record now can be a lifesaver when problems crop up. Take the time to record any information, even if it seems trivial—it's better to have it and not need it than to need it and not have it.

Installation Schedule

Networks take time to install and, as Murphy's Corollary states, usually more time than planned. Still, creating an installation schedule (and posting it well in advance and for everyone to see) is important because it allows you an opportunity to get an overview of the process of physically installing the network into your business. You can go over the schedule with co-workers and create a timetable that can anticipate conflicts with work that must be done, conflicts with deadlines, and the like. In addition, an installation schedule will help your co-workers breathe a little easier because they can prepare for the planned disruptions, while looking forward to a scheduled end of the process.

Plan the installation over weekends. This is a good practice because it minimizes user disruption.

By all means, and if at all possible, elicit the advice of someone who has installed a system like yours before, and allow extra time for the unexpected. Here are the installation steps you should allow time for:

1. **Equipment purchase** Be ready for shipping delays. If all your equipment does not arrive on schedule, it is probably better to

move the entire installation schedule back until all the necessary equipment arrives. In practical terms, you want to avoid a long stretch of downtime during which the network is partially installed and you must wait for a crucial part (a printer, for example, or a segment of cable) to arrive.

When equipment arrives, check it thoroughly for signs of damage, and check the equipment in the carton against the packing list. Do not assume that the packing list is accurate; if there is a mistake, rectify it now to avoid warranty problems in the future. It's not a bad idea to take the equipment out of the box and power it up, just to make sure it can at least do that much before you install it.

2. **Read the manuals**   Arrgh! All this neat stuff to play with, and you have to read a bunch of books. Sorry, life's like that sometimes. At least read the portions of the manuals that deal with installation and configuration options. Computer equipment changes quickly, and you may find that the configuration you had anticipated has been updated.

3. **Prepare the site**   This means moving furniture, taking out obsolete equipment, installing new electrical outlets, and the like. (Maybe you have a co-worker who can help out with this while you're reading all those manuals.)

4. **Back up your data**   Also, be sure to test your backup by restoring a few non-critical files (or files that you create just for this purpose). If you can safely restore some sample files, you have some assurance that the backup is good. This is a dull step but a vitally important one. The last thing you need is an unexpected glitch that destroys files and catches you without a backup. Think of it as installation insurance. No one has ever felt bad because they made an unused backup.

5. **Set up the hardware** Now at last you can begin to work with all that new equipment. The most important thing to remember about this phase of the process is to take your time. Careless handling at this stage can ruin a network. Specifically, double-check all switch settings and jumper pin settings (if any), even if you are using the default settings that are supposed to be already set on the shipping product.

6. **Install the software** This could easily be the most time-consuming phase of the project. Again, take your time and double-check all configuration settings. Mistakes are common at this stage; take them in stride and make the necessary corrections. Don't allow your focus to be undermined by pressure to complete the project. Send onlookers and kibitzers away with a confident smile and a polite but firm reminder that they must have work of their own to complete.

7. **Test, test, test** Chances are you can't do too much testing. Especially test the printer services. Network problems and delays are often related to printing. The goal is to find and eliminate system bugs before the first user logs on. In the real world, this is nearly impossible because users have personal work habits and idiosyncrasies that will reveal problems you never anticipated. However, the next step can help.

8. **Training** There are two levels of training. On the first level, you must acquaint users with the network's features and supervise their initial practice until they are comfortable with what is expected of them. On the second level, you should train them in procedures to follow if problems occur. As with every other stage of this process, you should allow plenty of time and schedule additional time if your users request it.

Get the Users on Your Side

Remember that training is a two-fold process. You must do more than acquaint your users with their system's features. You must also enlist them as allies in your troubleshooting efforts.

This part of the training process is extremely important. One key to quick problem-solving is psychological preparation of your users. Inform them from the beginning that problems are not unusual in the early stages of the network's operation (say this even if, in your heart of hearts, you believe you've got the system set up perfectly). Emphasize to your users that they should avoid, if at all possible, high-pressure situations during this transition period, as those are the times when problems are most likely to appear.

It can be extremely frustrating and anxiety-provoking for a user to experience a workstation shutdown and not have any idea what to do about it, beyond uttering a sometimes-embarrassing cry for help. The object of this aspect of training is to give your users permission to experience problems and report them promptly without fear of losing face, regardless of the problem's actual cause.

Train your users to follow a definite procedure for reporting problems to you, and make sure each user is familiar with it and can find it if a problem occurs. Make this procedure quick and easy. A user's response to technical problems can be as basic as referring to a simple problem report form, such as the one shown in Figure 11.6, as they talk to you on the telephone.

The existence of a planned response to problems is often more important than the procedure itself. When confronted with an unexplainable problem, the user is more likely to remain calm and communicative if there is a simple, definite plan of action to fall back upon, one that the user feels is easy to follow.

The System Log

Previous sections of this chapter have referred to the *system log*. A system log can be as simple as sheets of paper in a file folder or as

F I G U R E I I.6

A simple problem report form. The information on the form can be helpful, but an additional purpose of the form is to give the user a sense of recourse in a stressful situation.

PROBLEM REPORT

Date _____

Machine Name _____

Reported by _____

Application in Use _____
(When error occurred)

Other Apps in RAM _____
(if known)

_____

_____

Problem Description ------------------------------------
Please be as specific as you can regarding the sequence of steps
that caused the problem and the exact results.
If any messages were displayed, include them in the space below:

_____

_____

_____

_____

_____

Error Messages _____
(or Error Code Numbers)

_____

_____

_____

complicated as an entire file cabinet, depending on the size and complexity of your network.

The system log is, in effect, your network's documentation. The purpose of the system log is to provide you with a detailed history of all your network's hardware, software, and configuration features. It is your most valuable resource when troubleshooting problems.

The only way to keep an accurate system log is to start at the very beginning, writing down any and all system information as your design and install your system. There is very little likelihood that you will find the time to go back and document the revisions, upgrades, and other changes made to a system that has been up and running for some time.

If you are the system manager for your network, do not neglect this important part of your job. Here are some of the items you may wish to include in your system log:

Hardware warranties   Keep a separate section for warranty agreements for your hardware. Sort them by type: monitors, network interface cards, hard disks, and so on. If the equipment is part of a workstation or server, add the machine name to the warranty and file it according to the machine name.

Equipment information   For each piece of hardware attached to each machine, store the serial number, make, configuration settings, vendor name, and telephone number.

Current setup diary   Store the current directory structure and operating system configuration details in a separate section. Be sure to include the date the configuration was installed. Add new, updated configuration information in front of the old. Keep the old configurations on file.

Backup plan   Good network management includes a detailed backup plan, which will be discussed in more detail in the next chapter. Your backup plan should be dated, written down, and stored in the system log. Add new dated updates to the backup plan as necessary, but keep the old plans for reference.

Backup logs   You should keep a record of when backups are done, plus who is responsible for doing them and verifying their integrity. If your backup procedure is automated, the server responsible for backups can print a report, which you can file here.

Error/downtime logs   Keep a record of each time there is network downtime, why it occurred, and what action corrected the problem.

You can use your computer to assist you in maintaining your system log. A little flat-file database can be handy, or if your budget can cover it, you can purchase one of the many fully-featured network management software programs available. However you create it, do not keep your system log stored exclusively on a hard disk. You should have an up-to-date log printed on paper and filed securely, just in case the network goes down and the hard-disk version is inaccessible.

Where to Go from Here

All this planning and writing and filling out of forms is tedious work. If your network is very small (say, a peer-to-peer network with only three or four workstations), it may seem unnecessary. However, it is always necessary. Networks have a tendency to grow more complicated over time. Hardware can fail. Vendors can keep bad records and have short memories when it comes to warranties and promises they made in the heat of trying to make a sale. Some part of your written log, sooner or later, will save you time and money. The only question is how much.

In the next chapter, we move on from this discussion of the system log to a discussion of network management in general.

For Further Reading

- Campbell, Patrick T. *Networking the Small Office.* Sybex, 1995.

- Dyson, Peter. *The Network Press Dictionary of Networking.* 2d ed. Sybex, 1995.

- Miller, Michael Joseph. *Managing an Inherited NetWare Network.* Sybex, 1995.

CASE STUDY

GAB is well into their planning and design process. They have completed their needs analysis (Chapter 1); equipment matching (Chapter 4); and configuration plan (Chapters 2 and 3). Since they have opted for a dedicated file server, a small office is modified for that purpose. They install new shelving, remove the carpet, and add a heavy-duty lock on the door.

They will work with their cable installer to create their site analysis for cabling. GAB located blueprints for their building and used these to mark the cable layout. Cable and card installation was scheduled for Saturdays, to minimize disruption of employees' workdays. In addition to the time set aside to install and configure the operating system, GAB schedules time to train the employees on the basics of working on the network. As much as possible, the network administrator will attempt to keep the interfaces familiar, and work in more-advanced features over time. However, employees must receive training right away regarding access rights, file systems, and the meaning of common messages displayed by the network.

CHAPTER

12

Managing the System Day-to-Day

Almost everyone who uses a computer must spend some time on management duties. For example, stand-alone PC users are responsible for making sure that their data is properly backed up in the event the PC (or the power company) fails them. In addition, users manage their stand-alone PCs whenever they install software, configure an application, optimize their system's memory usage, or attempt to "tweak" the system for better performance.

As you can surmise from the previous chapters, network management is more complex and demanding than managing a stand-alone PC. Network managers must acquire a large amount of technical knowledge and must also have human-relations skills to succeed at the job. If the network is large enough, the management responsibilities may be divided between members of a management team; still, whether these duties are carried out by a single person or a team, a computer network is only as good as those who manage it.

Good network managers carry out the following fundamental responsibilities with regard to the network. They must:

- Understand the system

- Maintain backups

- Maintain security

- Maintain the system log

- Manage printing

- Monitor all network functions for maximum efficiency

- Evaluate and maintain applications

- Keep abreast of changes and updates in the industry

This chapter describes these aspects of a network manager's job.

Understanding the System

If you are responsible for hiring the network manager, do so if you can at the beginning of the network planning process, before choosing the network you want to install. The involvement of the manager in all phases of initial planning will help installation and configuration go that much more smoothly. The knowledge acquired during the planning process provides your manager with an invaluable base of information to help with the troubleshooting and upgrade processes that generally occur over the life of your network.

If you are planning to hire a new manager for an existing network, expect that the new manager will need a significant amount of time to become acquainted with your system. Do not assume that previous experience with a similar system means that a new manager can step in without missing a beat. Every network has unique features and idiosyncrasies and a unique set of users. To understand your system, a good manager requires two things: knowledge of its technical features (which comes from formal training) and knowledge of its real-world performance (which comes only from day-to-day practice). Putting it another way, the longer the manager works with your system, the more valuable he or she becomes.

For example, one of the trickier aspects of network management is installing application software on your network so that it runs with maximum efficiency. In many cases, the manager will want to place a copy of an application on the hard disk of each workstation that will run the application. This is not the most efficient storage method, but each workstation can then access and run the application locally, reducing network traffic and increasing performance efficiency. This can be the case with traditionally stand-alone applications such as word processors and spreadsheets, where frequent access to the application's software files across the network would hamper the network's overall performance and thus, your business's productivity. However, suppose that a particular application is not likely to be accessed by more than one user at a time; or that the sum of its files is too large for a given legacy (older model) workstation's hard disk; or that it is of a type that can be loaded completely into a workstation's memory and then run all day from there (like some simpler spreadsheet software). In these cases, the manager may elect to keep it on the server and let the individual user run it across the network.

With regards to some types of network-specific applications, the manager may find it to be more efficient, perhaps even required, to store the application on the server. This can be the case with applications such as SQL database server software, which works directly with a shared database on the server and transmits the results of its processing to the workstation. There is simply no increased performance to be gained from running this kind of software locally. Yet, a front-end database (an application that formats the results of an SQL query) may or may not run most efficiently from a local hard disk; the manager may simply have to test different configurations to find out how best to run it on a given system.

You can take the above examples as a basis for a general rule on network software (stand-alone style applications tend to work best locally, and network-specific applications tend to work best from the server), but exceptions abound. You must be prepared to make necessary changes and improvements to your system and gain valuable experience.

With regard to data files, the subject can get even thornier, as individual user preferences and work styles influence how data files are to be stored on the network. As before, a consistent rule is hard to come by, but you may be able to start with this: Whenever possible, store client/server data files on the server, to make backups more efficient and backup routines more reliable. However, encourage users to make separate backups of their most critical files.

On peer-to-peer systems, data file integrity can be a more complex issue. If there is little need for sharing centralized data files, such as may be the case on many peer-to-peer systems, you may consider allowing individual users to take local responsibility for the integrity of their own data files and use a specialized node for storing backups. As mentioned before, be prepared to make changes to your system as needs evolve, you gain more experience, and you learn what is desirable and possible.

Backing Up the Data

Making reliable data backups is arguably the most important job a network administrator has. You can replace hardware and software, you can move to a new location, you can hire new employees, your company can start over with a new manager if it must. But if you lose your data and have no backup, you are either out of business or starting over from scratch.

Data on a network tends to be massive. It is either stored in a centralized server or distributed among multiple servers throughout the network. In either case, the process of making reliable backups is far more complicated than it was in the days of stand-alone desktop PCs, where individual users took responsibility for making their own backups.

A network manager has to make careful decisions about what to back up, when to back it up, and where to store the backed-up data. This section provides some general guidelines for making those decisions.

Most local area networks use an automated system to make backups at regularly scheduled intervals. It makes sense to use an automated system because of the large amounts of data that are typically stored on networks, the added convenience of programming backups to occur during off-peak times when data traffic is minimal, and the freedom to impose a disciplined backup schedule on the computer rather than on yourself.

There are several types of automated backup systems. For example, Chapter 6 described a particularly rigid form of data backup: RAID systems, which make backup copies of the data on separate hard disks as it is being created or modified. Other networks use dedicated servers to retrieve and store backup data.

Software vendors, recognizing our anxiety over data loss and our demand for reliable backups, have responded with dozens of programs for automating backups of data distributed across networks. Examples of such programs are Backup Exec for Windows NT (Arcada software) and Norton Backup (Symantec). These are just examples, not recommendations. You should evaluate as many different backup software and hardware systems as you can before making a final selection of an automated system that's right for you.

Tape cartridges are a common storage medium for backing up network data. To use a tape-based backup system, you install special tape-handling hardware in one or more servers; these devices use high-speed copying technology to reproduce data on the tapes from the server's disk. Tape backup systems come with software that you can program to log onto the computer after hours, perform the backup, and log off automatically.

After-hours backups are convenient, but you should take care that your automated tape backup system has access to your network during times when it would be the most difficult for others to enter your building and acquire access to the servers. (When an automated backup is in process, a determined hacker would find it far easier to access the system.) You might have the backup procedure take place when trusted employees are still at hand to keep an eye on things. Assign limited read-only and copy-only rights to your automated backup system and make sure you program it to log off quickly when the backups are complete.

Tape is especially useful as a backup medium because the cartridges can be carried off-site and stored in a secure separate location, such as a bank safe-deposit box. Off-site storage is an effective and frequently employed strategy for insuring against loss from disasters such as broken plumbing or fires. If you live in a region where there is some risk of weather-related disasters (for example, phenomena such as hurricanes or tornadoes), you may want to employ a system whereby backups are regularly moved farther away, to lower-risk areas.

Tape backup systems can have their disadvantages, though; in particular, they can be somewhat rigid if you want to restore just one or two files. You may need to restore whole groups of files just to get the ones you want or muddle through a complex user interface to mark specific files for restoration. Nevertheless, for many users, the advantages (speed and built-in scheduling) outweigh the disadvantages (rigidity).

Whether or not you employ a tape backup system, individual users on the network would be wise to make personal backups of critical data files. Individual users can use floppy disks or, if large amounts of data are involved, high-capacity disks such as Iomega's ZIP drives. It is far easier to restore single files from these media. Consider creating batch files or scripts that start an application and, upon exiting, automatically make disk backups of new or revised data files from your subdirectory. Nothing like forcing good habits upon yourself.

What to Back Up

You need to back up application software files less often than data files. If you have master installation disks, make backups of these before installing the software. If you installed the software from a CD-ROM disk, or if the installation and configuration process was particularly complex, you may want to make a backup of the installed files off the hard disk to avoid having to re-install the application from scratch.

Back up the configuration files for application software separately. Make a new backup of the configuration files each time you update the configuration for any reason.

Once you have one or two good backups of your application software files, you need not continue to make them. This will save you time because software application files comprise a considerable amount of the data on your hard disks, and there is no need to back up files continually if they rarely change.

If you have a well-organized directory structure, you will store your data files in directories that are separate from your software application files. Automated backup software allows you to specify exactly which directories (and which files within those directories) you need to back up on a regular basis.

One strategy I've had success with is to place all repeatedly backed-up files in directories under a single \USERDATA directory and give \USERDATA a virtual drive letter. Users (and the backup software) see something like G:\BOB, even though on the server it's actually C:\USERDATA\BOB, or whatever. A directory structure can get complicated, but it's possible to hide the directory's complexities from the users.

In addition to everyday data files, you must also make regular backups of your network system data. Different networks manage their system data in different ways, but some examples of the types of system files you should back up include:

- Security files (such as access-rights information files)

- Directory structures

- Login script files

- User information files

- Workgroup information files

- Workstation configuration files

It is the manager's responsibility to understand the system well enough to make careful note of network-specific data files that must be backed up on a regular basis.

Do not back up your passwords. If you must, be certain they are encrypted. Passwords should be rigorously memorized, never written down, and never backed up. You'll learn more about passwords later in this chapter.

Once you have used your automated backup software to mark your critical data files, you are ready to make scheduled backups. You have taken your first steps toward data security. However, you must still determine your backup schedule.

When to Back Up

Data backup schedules answer a central question that the network manager must reckon with: How much data can your business afford to restore from scratch? Of course, no one wants to lose any data at all, but if a loss does strike, how much loss is too much—a day's worth? an hour's worth? The less you can afford to lose, the more time you will spend making and maintaining backup data.

Most experienced managers use some form of a staggered backup system. For example, they may back up data daily, then store the backup tapes after a specific period of time (a week to a month is fairly common). Using a series of backup tapes also provides an extra level of insurance: Should errors creep into the most recent backup, you could fall back on the next most recent, and with luck would lose only slightly more time making the older backup data current.

Some managers, in addition to daily backups, make complete backups at regular intervals (perhaps once a week, or once or twice a month). These backups are stored both for archival purposes and for emergency restorations when other backups are lost. They are permanent, never overwritten.

There is a curious irony with regard to backups: The most experienced and professional managers are fanatical about backups and keep multiple sets in one form or another. Also, because of their experience and professionalism, they tend to have fewer problems with their systems and have less need to actually use the backups they so fanatically maintain. Nevertheless, you should emulate those managers; they sleep better at night.

Types of Backups

There are three basic strategies for maintaining multiple backup sets:

Full backup   In a full backup, all your critical data is backed up. As you would expect, this has the disadvantage of taking the most time and requiring the largest amount of backup storage space. It has a distinct advantage, however, if you need to restore the data. All the most recent versions of your data files are conveniently stored together in a single, albeit large, package. At a minimum, you must make a full backup the first time you back up your data.

Incremental backup   This backup system reads file attributes to determine which files were added or modified since the last backup. Only the modified files are actually backed up. This is the fastest backup process, since it copies the fewest files, but restoration can be a chore. To get a failed system back to normal, you must restore your most recent full backup, followed by each incremental backup made since the full backup. If you have not made a full backup in a while, this type of restoration can be tedious.

Differential backup   This system falls in between the first two. It reads the data file date attributes and backs up only those files that were added or changed after the last *full* backup. This often takes a little longer than the incremental backup, but it makes restoration more predictable. To bring a failed system back to normal, you have to restore the last full backup, followed by the last differential backup.

It is impossible to overemphasize the importance of making regular and reliable backups. Once you have settled on a backup procedure, test it from time to time to make sure that the backups are both complete and reliable. If you are a network manager, you cannot afford surprises when it comes to the quality of your backup data. Simply making the backup isn't enough; it is your responsibility to be absolutely sure that the backup can be used to restore the data if that becomes necessary. (For additional information regarding backups, refer to "Backup schedules" in the following section.)

Maintaining the System Log

In the previous chapter, you learned about starting your system log during the network's planning process. This section examines the elements of a network system log in more detail. Bear in mind that your network may have special features not described here but which you should document in the system log nonetheless. In general, a good system log is your best evidence that you understand your system and your business's best insurance against system-wide failure or your temporary unavailability. (It would be a shame to have to come back early from your well-deserved vacation in Tahiti because some simple glitch popped up in the system while you were away.)

Many modern network operating systems come with worksheets and forms that you can fill out to maintain your system log. Take these forms seriously. They are time savers. You can find many automated network management software packages that help you maintain an up-to-date system log. However, do not assume that prepackaged forms and management software will take care of your system log completely. Certainly add your own information. The subtitle of your system log should be "No Surprises."

Here are some of the fundamental ingredients of a system log:

Hardware specifications   Keep lists of specifications for all your server and workstation hardware. These lists should include make and model names, serial numbers, internal network numbers, warranty information, as well as the names of the manufacturers, vendors, and installers. Include such hardware devices as disk drives, network interface cards, monitors, and printers and any peripheral devices such as modems. Also remember to store information about add-on equipment such as routers and transceivers. Finally, remember to keep files of your purchase records and payment receipts.

Boot files   Keep printouts of all your server and workstation boot files; for example AUTOEXEC.BAT and CONFIG.SYS, for DOS-based workstations and servers.

Directory structure   Keep dated printouts of the directory structure. Add a new printout each time you update the structure. Include volume and directory names, attributes, and access rights. Most network operating systems include a utility for producing a printout showing how directories are organized and nested below one another; for example, NetWare uses a command called LISTDIR to produce such a printout.

User profiles   At a minimum, keep a printout of each user's machine name, given name, groups to which they belong, login script, and access rights.

System login scripts   If your network uses a system login script, keep a dated copy on file. Keep a copy of default login scripts that users without individual scripts may need to use.

Configuration diary   These records represent a history of your server and workstation configuration changes. Be sure to include configuration records of installed hardware such as network interface cards. When you update a configuration, store a dated printout of the new version along with the old. It helps to keep a copy of previous configurations; you may find it necessary to go back to an old configuration someday.

Pay special attention to the configuration of workstation and server RAM. For example, make notes of how RAM has been allocated for such features as file cache buffers and memory-resident utilities. Also keep track of how various devices, such as printers and modems, use communications ports and internal interrupts. This information is especially useful for tracking down and troubleshooting network conflicts.

Software diary   Keep version numbers, licensing information, and locations of your installed software applications. Keep the names of valid users and of who originally installed the software. As you did with hardware, keep purchase, warranty, and payment records on file as well.

Hardware and software standards   Keep (and distribute) a list of standard hardware types and software applications that you have approved for use on your network. This amounts to a policy statement regarding the types of hardware and software for which you will furnish support. Users love to add their own personal items to their workstations (screen savers are a notorious example), and sometimes these items interfere with the network. If you have a support policy in place, you are in a better position to exert some small measure of control and expertise with regard to what the network will tolerate.

Backup schedules   Keep records of how data backups are made and what files are backed up. If you are using an automated backup system, your backup software may print a log of the files you backed up, when the backup took place, and if any errors occurred during the process. If you are backing up manually, keep a checklist showing when you made the backup and what type it was (full, incremental, or differential).

Printing configuration   Keep a record of printer configurations, names, internal network numbers, port and interrupts used, and printer queue information. Because printing often is a problem on a network, complete documentation regarding printers can be very important. Refer to the section on printing later in this chapter.

Error diary   Keep a history of errors, problems, and what solutions were applied. This can be increasingly valuable over time as a reference for solving similar problems that tend to crop up now and again.

Security procedures   Keep (and distribute) a written policy regarding procedures and access rights for new and current users. Include such things as when passwords must be changed and limitations on the types of passwords that you have configured the system to accept. Refer to the section on security later in this chapter for more details.

A good system log can save you time and money when problems arise. For example, you can use the system log to look up the commands for undoing some minor configuration change without endlessly searching through thick volumes of vendor-supplied documentation. A network log gives you the power to enforce security practices and to maintain hardware and software standards consistently, which will reduce users' anxieties—even if on occasion you have to deny them some cute little utility or game they just could not resist bringing in from home. You just may find that, in return for all the trouble you put into it, your network log saves your career someday.

Although you will store your system log in electronic form on the network, you should keep an always-up-to-date copy of your system log in printed form as well. That way, if the network is completely down, you can still have access to it.

> ### Remote Management
>
> Backups, system logs, controlling access, maintaining security—it's a big job, and as you might expect, software vendors are doing their level best to create applications that they tout as tools to simplify and streamline the job. Mostly, these tools enhance utilities that you already find supplied with your network operating system. The best of them allow you to diagnose and fix workstation and server problems across the network, rather than having to visit workstations in person. If your network is so large and complicated that you spend as much time traveling between workstations as you do actually servicing them, it's time to look into installing remote management software.
>
> Following are some examples of software programs that offer remote management tools. Bear in mind that these are simply examples, not recommendations. Check out as many different brands as possible before you buy (by visiting vendors for demonstrations or searching the Internet for information and demo downloads):
>
> - LANDesk Management Suite (Intel Corp.)
> - Norton Administrator for Networks (Symantec)
> - Systems Management Server (Microsoft)

Evaluating Applications

The workstation represents your network to your users. It is important that you keep the workstation interface as consistent and easy to use as possible. You can accomplish this by loading applications that are used by everyone, but allow for some degree of customization to individual user preferences. Modern, well-written applications for networks have these features built in, but it is your responsibility to evaluate software before it goes on your network, to be certain that it implements those features in a manner consistent with your network configuration and other applications you have already installed. Also, if you find that pressing needs for a specific application require you to adjust your users' interface, you will need to understand those adjustments well enough to explain them to your users and provide some training, thereby keeping your users interested in the network and productive while they are using it.

Of course, the network-readiness discussed here is not the only consideration in evaluating application software. The network manager also needs to consult with knowledgeable users and department managers about the performance and application features of the software being evaluated. Will it meet the users' needs as a word processor or spreadsheet or whatever?

Here are some features to look for when evaluating applications for possible installation on your network:

Compatibility   Most software vendors will assure you that their application is compatible with your network. Do not take these claims at face value, however. Some networks have features that may conflict with a software application. Obtain a guarantee from your vendor that, should the application prove incompatible with your network, you can return it within a reasonable time for a full refund.

Support for simultaneous users   Beware of installing applications that are designed for a stand-alone environment. Although you can usually get such applications to run on a network, you must take special care to configure your network to allow only one user at a time to operate these programs:

- You may have to install the application on a single user's subdirectory, or launch the application with a special script or batch file that changes other users' access rights to the data files while the application is in use and restores the original access rights when the user exits the application. These are fairly complicated configuration issues and difficult to set up and maintain.

- When you install stand-alone software on your network, you may be required to take special action with regard to licensing fees or pay a separate fee for each user of the application.

Directory organization An automated installation routine is standard for any modern software product, as is the ability to install the software in a default directory or to one of your own choosing. Still, you may encounter an application that will not allow you complete flexibility with regard to the directory locations for its files. Be certain that you can install the software in a directory configuration that will fit comfortably within your current directory structure. Otherwise, you may be introducing a complicated exception to your painstakingly planned directory structure, which may have an adverse impact on your network's overall ease of use. For example, it could complicate your automated backup procedures.

An Installer's Work Is Never Done

Even after you install a software application on your network and it appears to be running properly, keep an eye on its performance for a while. You may have to make some additional changes to the application's standard configuration in order to get reliable performance on your network. Some things to look out for are:

Setting file attributes After installation, check the file attributes for the application files you have just installed. Normally, you would mark application software files as shared and read-only, but there may be exceptions; for example, some applications need to make changes to some of their system files while they are running. Also, you will normally mark an application's data files as read/write, but you may want to mark some files as read-only, for example, files that contain default information you do not want the user to change.

Setting user rights   After installing, check to be certain that newly created directories have the appropriate access rights. Normally, Read and File Scan rights are enough for directories of application files, but a specific application may require a different directory setup. Also, you may have to configure an application to find its data files in different user directories, depending on the access workstation or the name of the user launching the application.

Changing workstation configuration   Automated installation routines sometimes make changes to workstation configuration files (for example, CONFIG.SYS and AUTOEXEC.BAT on DOS-based systems or WIN.INI and SYSTEM.INI in Windows-based systems). A good automated installation program will notify you of the changes it intends to make and give you the option of making them right away or creating copies of the configuration files for you to edit manually. (You can make copies of these files before you begin installing, just in case.) You must understand your system well enough to know how these automated configuration changes may impact your network's performance. The information in your system log can be a helpful reference during these times.

Temporary files   Many applications create temporary files on disk while they are running. If the application attempts to write these files to a directory where it does not have read/write access, it may lock up or fail without warning or error messages.

Security

Network security is a balancing act for the system manager. Data on local area networks can be distributed throughout the system on different servers, and users who legitimately need the data must have flexible access to it. On the other hand, flexible access for legitimate users is an obstacle to security. How can you keep the data accessible and keep it away from unauthorized users at the same time?

Breaches of network security can come from malicious sources (such as disgruntled employees, competitors stealing trade secrets, immature thrill-seeking hackers, or computer viruses), or your network data can be damaged because of simple mistakes. In practice, the latter problem is more common and harder to ward off than the former, because it is difficult to predict how someone might unintentionally corrupt data. This means that reliable data backups are just as much a security measure as anything you read about in this section.

There are two overall aspects to computer security: first, granting particular users permission to access the network on any level; and second, after allowing access to an authorized user, granting permission to access particular data in restricted ways. The first level of security involves programming your network to identify legitimate users and lock out those it does not recognize. The second level involves granting authorized users specific sets of *access rights* to files as well as attaching certain attributes to files that restrict what users may do with them.

One good way to test your network's security is to create a regular user account for yourself and then logon using that account and try to crack your own system. Can you, as a regular user, find security loopholes (for example, accessing and reading the system files)? If so, it's time to recheck your account setup.

Global Network Access Security

There are three ways your network can identify users and grant them permission to access it:

Permission based on who they are   This is the most secure system, because it identifies users based on unique physical attributes: Examples of who-you-are systems include fingerprint, palm print, and voiceprint readers, among other expensive and sophisticated identification devices. You can find examples of them near the entrances to restricted areas in airports.

Permission based on what they have   This is a frequently used system. It recognizes authorized users and grants access if they have a key to insert into a lock, or a magnetic card to slide through a card reader. The weakness of these devices is that they can be stolen or replicated.

Permission based on what they know   This is a common access system, but it has certain glaring weaknesses. Examples include secret passwords, lock combinations, or personal identification numbers (PINs). The most prominent weakness of this system is its requirement that the identifying knowledge (for example, a secret password) must be memorized. Passwords must be chosen carefully; the password must be at the same time unique, impossible to guess, and easy to remember. Passwords and lock combinations can be forgotten or, if written down somewhere, found and memorized by others, without leaving evidence that a theft has taken place.

WARNING   Password access is also subject to accidental abuse; for example, a legitimate user can log into the network and then walk away from the workstation without logging out, leaving the workstation vulnerable to anyone who happens along.

You can create a good security system using a combination of the second two levels of permission. Systems like these require that you combine some item the user must have (for example, a card with a magnetic stripe that you insert in a reader) with something the user must know (a password or PIN). Bank teller machines use this type of security system and have good results most of the time. If your network has extremely sensitive data that must be kept from unauthorized access, your vendor can supply you with magnetic card readers that will secure your workstations and servers in a manner similar to bank ATMs.

Another frequently-used level of security is to lock away the file server behind a physical barricade (in a locked room, for example).

Only those with the key to the room can get access to the server. Servers are often locked away because competent hackers can be very successful at bypassing network security systems if they are allowed direct physical access to the file server.

If locking a file server in a separate room is impractical or impossible (for example, if there is no good ventilation or air-conditioning in that storage closet), consider the simple expedient of using a machine with a security lock. This lock prevents access to the machine using the keyboard or other input device. A locked machine will at least force a determined hacker to carry a set of tools to open up the server and bypass the keyboard lock; with any luck it will slow down the whole process enough to discourage the would-be hacker altogether.

Many local area networks that do not have especially sensitive information will settle for a network access system based on passwords. You have read about how passwords are used in network operating systems (Chapter 8) and client software (Chapter 9). The following are principles for selecting, storing, using, and updating passwords to achieve maximum levels of security and effectiveness:

- Use passwords that are at least six characters long. (Eight characters, or even ten characters are exponentially even better.) The longer the password, the longer it takes to guess it. The longer it will take someone to break into your system, the less likely they will want to attempt it. For example, automatic password-guessing software can find a four-letter password in a matter of minutes; a five-letter password may take hours; a six letter password can take many hours, even days.

- Use passwords that combine letters, numbers, or symbols. These are much harder to guess than simple names or ordinary words. Even if you simply insert a single number somewhere within an ordinary eight-character password, you significantly complicate things for a hacker.

■ Most network operating systems can lock out a user altogether after a certain number of incorrect password attempts. Use this feature if you can. This will discourage someone who attempts to enter your system using automated password-guessing software.

■ Change passwords regularly. How regularly is a matter of how often it takes for you to feel comfortable. Change the password daily if your data is especially sensitive and likely to attract unauthorized access by talented hackers (an example of such data would be student grade records). You can change passwords less often if your data is less sensitive or not very valuable to unauthorized outsiders (for example, business records that do not involve trade secrets).

■ The users with the most extensive access rights and most power to make changes to the system (for example, the network supervisor) must change their passwords most often. Those with fewer access rights can change their passwords less often.

■ Although this may seem an extreme measure, you might want to update passwords for everyone in the system when an employee who is particularly computer-savvy—and particularly angry or malicious—leaves the company.

■ If you think you can get away with it, pick passwords for your users instead of allowing them to pick their own. They will not like it, but unsophisticated users tend to settle for easily-hacked passwords (phone numbers, family names, pets, and the like).

■ It's been said before in this book but it bears repeating here: Never store your password anywhere in written form or anywhere on the network unless encrypted by the system. Do not tell others your password or, if you must, change it shortly thereafter. In short, do not allow it to be appropriated by curious eyes and ears.

Access Rights

All networks allow you to establish access rights to the network data. They differ in their degree of sophistication and complexity. For example, NetWare has a complete and thorough system of access rights. It allows you to set up specific restrictions on what kinds of modifications are allowed to directories and the files they contain, by attaching a letter-coded attribute to files and directories. In addition, you can limit the file-creating and file-modifying abilities of certain types of users and limit those rights to specific files and directories as well. As a more detailed example, here are the common file access rights of NetWare users:

Right	Letter	Effect
Access Control	A	User can change others' access rights.
Create	C	User can create new files and directories.
Erase	E	User can delete files and directories.
File Scan	F	User can view the contents of file directories.
Modify	M	User can change file names and file attributes.
Read	R	User can only read contents of files.
Write	W	User can modify files.
Supervisor	S	Combines all rights listed above.

The system manager assigns these rights using utilities provided with the network operating system. They can be assigned in any combination, based on the supervisor's judgment of what is a reasonable set of rights for each user. (Some combinations would not make much sense. For example, assigning only A would give the user the ability to change others' access rights, while otherwise not being able to access the system. Assigning any rights in combination with S would be redundant.) Utilities that assign rights are secured, and access rights to them are usually limited to the system manager alone.

Depending on your network operating system and hardware, you may have other techniques at your disposal for securing your system. For example, some networks allow you to restrict access to certain regularly-scheduled periods of time, on a user-by-user basis. You could use a feature like this to keep individuals off the system after hours. Your network may allow you to force users to log out of the system at closing time. Your network may use workstations that do not have floppy disks, to prevent copying of files; or you may be able to configure your servers to boot only from a hard disk, thereby preventing someone from gaining access to the hard disk by booting from a floppy.

Your most important allies in your quest for perfect network security are your users. Impress upon them the importance of network security and seek their assistance in designing the sort of security system that you and they can feel comfortable using.

Firewalls

With the increasing demand for remote access to networks over the Internet, security becomes more complicated. You may want to make your Internet host site available twenty-four hours a day to Internet users. The object of firewall security is to allow public access to some parts of your system and prevent access to other parts. The software that accomplishes this task is called a *firewall*. Simply put, a firewall is a security system that selectively denies all access to designated portions of your network, based on how the network is accessed. For example, if someone were to access a workstation by modem, only designated files and directories would be visible. From the remote user's point of view, no other network features would exist. A local user at the same workstation, however, might be able to access more services (such as a printer, or additional file servers.)

Reliable, commercially available firewall software tends to be expensive (for example, Gauntlet, a firewall product from Trusted

Information Systems, requires on-site installation and training at high cost). Toolkits are available to build your own firewall systems, if you like. You can find one such toolkit on the Internet at `ftp://ftp.tis .com/pub/firewalls/toolkit`. Refer to Chapter 16 for more details on how firewalls work.

Printing

The paperless office remains an elusive ideal of enterprise computing. In the real world, a significant amount of the network manager's time will be spent maintaining the network's ability to produce printed information for users.

Network printers have become quite flexible. They can be attached to special *print servers*, workstations whose function is to receive data from other workstations and direct it to printers. Printers can be attached to workstations using one of the available *communication ports*.

A communication port is a hardware device, a receptacle into which you plug the printer cable. These receptacles have addresses that are recognized by the operating system. Ports with addresses LPT1, LPT2, and LPT3 handle *parallel* communications, data that is sent in 8-bit chunks. Ports COM1, COM2, COM3, and COM4 handle *serial* communications, data that is sent is a continuous stream of bits.

Any workstation can be a print server, as long as it has a communications port to which a printer's cable can be attached. The network manager configures the network operating system to recognize the workstation address and communications port as a local printing device and in certain cases may choose to assign specific access rights to that printer.

Many modern printers are *network-aware,* meaning that they come equipped with their own network interface cards and can be attached directly to the network cable. These printers act like network nodes; the network operating system can handle the printer server tasks and direct data to them as if they were other workstations on the network.

You can connect the printer to a communication port on the file server if you like. In this setup, the file server must allocate some of its processing time to act as a print server. Because this setup increases server overhead, it is only a possible configuration, not a preferred one.

The Print Queue

Network printers receive requests to print information from all over the network. Printer management revolves around the maintenance of the *print queue,* a utility that stores the print job requests and directs them to the print server in order.

Print queues are directories on the server's hard disk that store print jobs as data files to be sent to the printer. These data files contain both the information to be printed and instructions to the printer regarding how the information is to be formatted on the page.

In their simplest form, print queues simply hold onto the jobs and direct them to the printer in the order received. However, if you were to leave it simply at that, you would probably find yourself dealing with unfortunate printing bottlenecks: Imagine that you have to print a one-page letter and get it in the mail right away but that you cannot do so because the network printer is in the middle of printing a 500-page report. To avoid unpleasant situations like these, the network manager (or a designated print server manager) relies on software utilities to control the flow of print job information to print queues and from print queues to the various printers on the network.

The network manager uses a print queue management utility to access these print job files and direct them to specific printers on the network, to assign priority to one job over another, and to temporarily suspend a current print job and allow another to be printed. The network manager can automate the printing schedule, allowing print jobs to be stored and sent to the printer after hours, when there is no other network traffic on the system to slow down the printing process.

The network manager can also assign more than one print queue to a printer. This is done to allow high-priority documents to go to high-priority queues, while lower-priority documents go to lower-priority queues. The network manager or network operating system can monitor all the queues for a printer and allow those waiting in the high-priority queues first access to the printer, regardless of the order in which the print jobs were received from the network.

The network manager can also assign multiple printers to a single print queue. You might do this on networks where large amounts of data are printed and fast output is more important than any attempt to prioritize the print jobs. In this case, the print queue keeps track of printers that are idle and ready to receive data, and it directs waiting print jobs to the next available printer.

If you choose to assign multiple printers to a single print queue, be sure that all the assigned printers are of the same type and configuration. You must do this because a print queue normally has no intelligence of its own about which one of multiple printers might end up receiving information stored in the queue. Because the print job file contains formatting instructions, it's important that the receiving printer understand those instructions. If all the printers are the same model and configuration, the problem never arises.

Solving Common Printer Problems

Efficient printing is a challenge for most network managers, who can expect to spend some time troubleshooting problems. This section offers some suggestions on how to deal with printing problems.

Many printing problems are the result of faulty hardware. The first thing to check when a problem occurs is the printer cable. Printing cables can come loose and need only be tightened to restore the system to normal again. If a printer cable is cut or shows signs of damage, it should be replaced.

WARNING   Before you play with a printer cable, be sure to turn off the printer power. If you can, turn the printer server's power off as well. Pressing a loose cable back into place or even wiggling a printer cable with the power on can cause your network to suffer severe and permanent damage.

Sometimes a printer has simply gone off-line, or paper has jammed inside the printer in a spot that is hard to see. The printer may simply have run out of paper. Sometimes the simplest solutions are the easiest to overlook.

Another common cause of printing problems is a corrupted print queue. If necessary, use your network's print queue management utilities to clear all print jobs and send them again or, if necessary, delete the print queue altogether and reinstall it.

Check the print server's setup and be certain that the interrupts used by the printer port do not conflict with interrupts used by the network or other peripheral devices connected to the printer server. (For more information on system interrupts, refer to Chapter 4.) If you find an interrupt conflict, you must take the time to reconfigure your hardware.

If a printer fails to respond at all, check the printer configuration and be sure it is connected to the correct port and that the network is configured to recognize a printer at this port address.

If the printout is garbled, the user may be using an application that is configured to format documents for a different printer. Be sure that the application is using the correct printer driver and that the job is being sent to the correct printer.

Where to Go from Here

The networking industry is growing and maturing rapidly. Networks tend to grow larger and more complicated over time. Over the life of your system, you can expect that you will be called upon to upgrade and expand it several times. To maintain and upgrade your system at maximum efficiency, stay abreast of the developments in the field; your knowledge of the latest resources and techniques is a valuable asset for your business, your users, and yourself. Although this takes time, it is not difficult.

Good information is available from a number of periodicals that deal with LAN management issues. Of course, you should pay a visit to the computer-magazine section of your local bookstore or newsstand to find periodicals whose style and content appeal to you, and you should subscribe. For starters, here are two periodicals to look for that deal in depth with LAN management issues:

LAN Times, 151 East 1700 South, Suite 100, Provo, UT 84606, (801) 379-5850

Info World, 155 Bovet Road, Suite 800, San Mateo, CA 94402, (800) 227-8365

In the next chapter, we will look closely at the manager's biggest single responsibility: the network databases.

For Further Reading

- Chappell, Laura A., and Dan E. Hakes. *The Complete Guide to NetWare LAN Analysis*. 3d ed. Sybex, 1996.

- Jones, Douglas Wade. *Managing Small NetWare 4.11 Networks*. Sybex, 1996.

- Miller, Michael Joseph. *Managing an Inherited NetWare Network*. Sybex, 1995.

CASE STUDY

For GAB, managing the network will be a process of striking a balance between cost and efficiency. There is little doubt that they need to hire an experienced network administrator. Fortunately, their investment of time in planning and research will give them more than just a better set of hardware and software; they are now in a much better position to evaluate applicants for their network administrator job. GAB hopes to find someone who has experience working with Windows NT networks, accounting skills, and bookkeeping skills.

GAB will look for an administrator that can do the following:

- Develop, test, and maintain a reliable automated backup system
- Train users quickly
- Provide day-to-day user support
- Distribute network information to users
- Upgrade and maintain the network configuration
- Keep up-to-date records of all network hardware and software, workstation and server configurations, and system logs
- Audit network usage
- Help develop plans for the future growth of the network

CHAPTER

13

Client/Server Databases

As you've progressed through this book, you have learned that the most important reason networks exist is to provide shared access to data. It is important that you organize your shared data as efficiently as possible. If the data on your network is scattered about in a disorganized way, the network's performance suffers.

Ideally, shared data should be stored in a format that makes it quickly accessible to all users and allows those users to view and work with the data using different applications. While users are accessing that data in individual ways, they must be assured of its continual reliability and accuracy.

A computer can maintain data and keep it flexible, accessible, and reliable by storing it in a *database*. We've looked at databases briefly before: In Chapter 6, we looked at their relationship with file servers. In Chapter 10, we looked at them as network applications. This chapter focuses in a more detailed way on their organization and structure, the rules of information storage and access that are unique to relational databases and give them their central importance in the world of client/server networks.

We'll begin with a definition: A database is a set of raw data elements organized into tables of rows and columns, which define common features of the data and can be accessed and modified by one or more users to produce useful information.

There are plenty of examples of databases in the everyday world of work, many of them not found on computers. For example, a database can be:

- A Rolodex file

- An address book

- A desk calendar

- A case of floppy disks

- A pencil holder

- A file cabinet

- Some baseball cards stuffed in a shoebox

In each case above, an organizing entity contains items or information that are in some way related to each other. By grouping related items together, you make access to those items easier.

In the networking world, you have a situation in which several users are looking to access the same set of raw data. Each user has a particular purpose in mind when working with that data, and they will all access it in individual ways using unique applications. The purpose of a client/server database is to make the stored data available to different users at different times and for different purposes, while keeping its underlying organizational structure intact.

Advantages to Using Databases

You can store your business information just about any way you want, and businesses have discovered many different means of doing so. Some ways are clearly more efficient than others. Using a computerized database to store your business's information has certain obvious advantages.

Reducing Data Redundancy

Ideally, you will attempt to store each item of raw data in the database only once. When a data item is stored only once in the system, it can be modified quickly and reliably—rather than having to modify the same item of information that may be duplicated in several locations in different formats throughout your system, you need modify it only once in a single location. Then, any user or program can immediately access the updated data from different remote locations. It is up to the computer to make this access possible and to manipulate all the raw data items, assembling and reassembling them into meaningful information.

However, as a practical matter, some duplication of the raw data does occur within an enterprise-wide database. This duplication is allowed when the performance advantages outweigh the problems inherent in duplication. For example, it may be faster to access copies of certain subsets of data off of local servers rather than off of a single distant one because access via local servers can reduce data traffic across the network as a whole. (You can easily visualize this principle: Imagine what life would be like in a big city if it had only one supermarket rather than several.) Still, database designers spend as much time as possible trying to avoid data redundancy.

Access to a Common Storage Pool

One way in which a database manipulates its raw data is by presenting it in different formats, depending on how it is being used. A database may produce output that is text-based, such as a report of earnings and expenses, to format using a word processor. Or, it may produce output that is table-based, such as a budget comparison, for importing into a spreadsheet and performing what-if analysis. In both cases, the computer acts an intermediate mechanism to access the same data. The underlying repository of data is stored in a given logical structure and presented in different formats for the sake of the different users.

In addition, by maintaining data in a stored format that is independent of its displayed format, you have a degree of freedom to make changes to its underlying structure while making few, if any, changes to the presentation formats.

Enhanced Security

In Chapter 12, you saw how data can be secured from the system-wide level down through the individual datafile level. A database can take this security system further. Most shared database systems provide mechanisms that can control users' access to groups of records, columns, or even individual data elements within a table. These mechanisms are somewhat like the write-protecting mechanisms for rows and columns in spreadsheet programs, with the added ability to shield selected units of data from users' view altogether.

Simultaneous Access to Information

A database can allow more than one user to access different parts of its stored records simultaneously. Databases protect their data by implementing a system of *locks*. As you saw in Chapter 10, a lock is simply an electronic mark associated with a data element (or group of elements such as a record or series of records) that acts as a signal to alert other users that one user has accessed the data, has possession of it, and may be making changes to it. The computer prevents further changes to locked data until the first user has finished processing. When the user finishes, the database releases the lock and another user may have access to the data.

Normally the placing and releasing of locks is transparent to the user. The only time the user becomes aware of the system is when he or she attempts to access a locked record, at which point the computer displays a message to that effect and the database either denies access altogether or allows the user only to view the current data element without making changes. Chapter 14 takes a closer look at the SQL programming language's facilities for data locking.

Increased Data Reliability

A database product will include tools for creating and updating tables on your network's servers. Your chosen database will also include tools to help you keep the data in those tables as reliable and accurate as possible. Obviously, a database cannot prevent you from certain human mistakes, such as misspelling someone's name or street address, but there are some surprisingly powerful techniques at your disposal for maintaining the integrity of your data:

Constraints A database is normally equipped with tools that disallow obviously improper data entry; for example, not allowing letters in fields reserved for numbers only. Other constraints can be more sophisticated: allowing only a valid range of acceptable values, forcing data to be displayed in certain meaningful formats, or using custom-programmed functions to test the validity of data against your own business rules. (For example, you might want to add a function to your database that disallows ZIP codes that fall outside a given shipping region or disallows telephone numbers without proper area codes.)

Referential integrity A database also includes tools that check for the validity of the relationships between data elements. For example, suppose you were entering records of purchases by a customer. The database could check to see if there is a customer record on file, check to be sure that inventory items exist and are available for shipment, calculate the total cost of the order, apply rules regarding a customer's eligibility for credit, and add shipping instructions based on the quantity and nature of the items ordered.

Transaction processing A database can include tables whose sole purpose is to keep records of changes made to the stored data. These tables are called *transaction tables*.

- If a user makes (or discovers, after the fact) a serious error, or if a database instruction fails for any reason, the computer can step backward through the transaction table, reversing the changes that caused the mistake. This process is commonly called a *rollback*.

- On the other hand, if a series of instructions is carried to a successful completion, the database can be instructed to *commit* the changes, meaning to make them permanent such that a rollback of this series of instructions is no longer possible. This is done to prevent the transaction table from becoming overly large.

Automated Information Processing

Databases normally are equipped with various software tools for creating programs that allow as much fully automated data access and manipulation as possible. The consistent structure of the database allows access to the data using standard stored functions that can be combined to create very sophisticated information processing. The tasks of sorting, finding, and retrieving data, which formerly had to be programmed almost from scratch, can be accomplished by stringing together a database's stored procedures and objects, sharply reducing the time it would take to produce highly polished output.

Relational Databases

You learned in Chapter 10 that there are several different types of databases, including flat-file, hierarchical, object-oriented, and relational databases. The relational database is the most commonly used database in local area networks, and so we'll look at it in some detail here. A relational database is one that breaks data down into its most fundamental units, organizes those units into *tables*, and then forms associations between different tables.

A table consists of one or more *columns* (also known as *fields*) that define a common aspect of the stored data. For example, a table representing a mailing list would have columns that correspond to first and last names, street addresses, cities, states, and zip codes. A single set of stored data elements, one element for each column, combine to form a *row* (also called a *record*). Figure 13.1 illustrates such a table.

F I G U R E 13.1

A single database table.
A table such as this is also
an example of a flat-file
database, in which there
are no relations made to
any other table.

First Name	Last Name	Address	City	State	ZIP Code

It is possible (and actually fairly common) that some elements will remain blank in the table. Part of the fun of designing databases is coming up with tables that are as efficient as possible; database designers work hard at designing tables in which as many as possible of the row and column intersections will contain data.

Other Types of Databases

Besides the relational database model, there are other types of databases, which are generally not found in computer networks (in their pure form, at least). These other types of databases are listed below for your interest:

Flat-file databases   A flat-file database is simply a database composed of a single table. A simple mailing list, composed only of names and addresses, is an example of a flat-file database. So is a spreadsheet that does not link any of its cells to another spreadsheet. Flat-file databases are easy to work with and are generally very fast, but their usefulness is limited because they are inherently rather inflexible.

Hierarchical databases   A hierarchical database is a set of tables linked together in a series of one-directional relationships. An example of a hierarchical database would be a file directory structure in which a single root directory contains files and subdirectories that in turn contain other files and subdirectories, and so on.

Network databases   A network database is one in which the relationship between the tables is more free-flowing. For example, imagine a directory structure in which a single file or subdirectory can be referenced in more than one "parent" directory. Notice that in this context, the term "network" refers to the way two or more tables can "point" to each other, rather than to the kinds of computer networks that are the subject of this book. Network databases can be extremely complicated and difficult to maintain. A relational database is a tightly controlled type of network database; it keeps complexity to a minimum by enforcing strict rules regarding how relationships between data elements are established and maintained.

Object-oriented database   This more modern type of database is an extension of the relational database model. While the traditional database stores only data, the object-oriented database links instruction code with the data. This instruction code may execute when the user accesses the data. The instruction code linked to the data is called a *method*. A combination of data and method is called an *object*.

You will notice that there is some overlap in the definitions of these database types. For example, a hierarchical database can be used like a relational database; an object-oriented database can have relations between various tables. As computer-based databases evolve, the term *relational* seems to get less and less precise. As a practical businessperson, however, your first concern should be whether your database makes or saves you money, not whether it agrees with someone's definition of "relational."

In a relational database, several tables may be related to each other by using certain *key fields* to establish linkages between them.

For example, suppose you were to expand your mailing list into a membership list and wanted to keep track of periodic voluntary contributions made by your members. Each member could make any number of contributions. While you could add a contribution column to the original table and add a new record each time a member makes a new contribution, this would result in many duplications of name and address data each time a contribution was made.

A more efficient solution is to give each member a unique membership number and add a column for that number to the mailing list database. Then, you would create a second table consisting of membership numbers and contribution amounts, as illustrated in Figure 13.2. This system would allow any number of contribution records to be related to individual members while keeping duplication to a minimum.

In the example shown in Figure 13.2, the records in the contribution table derive solely from the records in the membership table. This is an example of a hierarchical database, in which every "child" contribution record must be related to a "parent" membership record to have meaning. This is also an example of a one-to-many relationship, in which a single membership record may be related to any number of contribution records. Although the database is not, strictly speaking, "relational," there are clear relationships between the records.

For an example of many-to-many relationships, consider a basic general ledger system for businesses. A general ledger is a series of numbered accounts that correspond to different areas of income and expense for the business. Each account number can be subdivided into

FIGURE 13.2

A membership table is related by means of a key field (the membership number) to a contribution table.

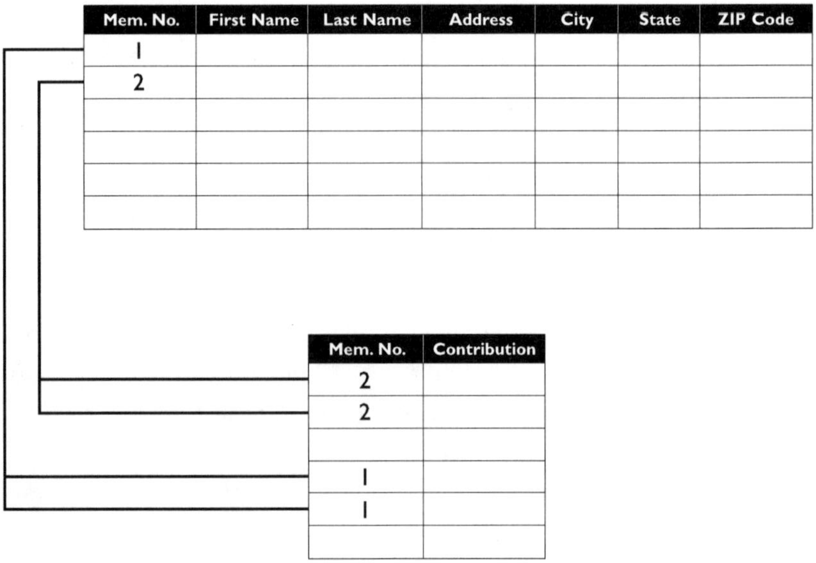

Mem. No.	First Name	Last Name	Address	City	State	ZIP Code
1						
2						

Mem. No.	Contribution
2	
2	
1	
1	

How Relational Is Relational?

Trying to establish a standard for the structure of a relational database, an IBM researcher named Edgar F. Codd defined a set of rules, numbered from zero to twelve, for designing a *relational database management system* (RDBMS). As time goes on, these rules are happily ignored by many vendors, who have found that they can increase sales of their product simply by touting their database software as "relational." Many people are unaware of these rules and still manage to produce useful databases.

On the other hand, remember that you will evaluate a relational database management system primarily by the results it gets and its capacity to maintain high-quality output over time. A database that can qualify as "relational" by Codd's rules probably has a better chance of doing that.

1. An RDBMS must use only relational techniques to manage stored information (in other words, no bending of the other rules).

2. All data elements in the RDBMS must be stored in tables of rows and columns.

3. Every data element can be explicitly referenced using its table name, column name, and the primary key field of its row.

4. An RDBMS must have a consistent means of identifying empty data elements. In other words, if the column-and-row intersection allotted for a data element is empty, there must be a unique and consistent way to identify that empty condition, other than simply zero for number-based data and blanks for character-based data.

5. An RDBMS must store its data in a standard format that allows the data to be accessed in standard ways. In other words, the RDBMS should not use a unique, proprietary storage system.

6. An RDBMS must allow the use of at least one controlling database language, which must use ordinary character strings as commands to define and modify tables, access the data, and secure its reliability. (An example is Structured Query Language—refer to Chapter 14 for more details.)

7. The database software must be able to update any view of the data whenever changes are made in the underlying data tables.

8. Command operands that query data should be applicable as well to those that modify data. In other words, the database access language must have a consistent syntax.

9. The underlying physical structure of the database must be flexible; that is, able to be changed without requiring changes to its controlling language.

10. Database tables must be similarly flexible; that is, changeable without requiring changes to the database language.

11. Only the controlling database language should be able to place limits on what types of data are permitted in columns and rows. In other words, application software, which may use the data, is not permitted to place constraints on the type of data stored in the underlying database.

12. The controlling database language must be able to access data distributed between any number of tables, in any set of separate physical locations, without forcing changes to software applications that use the data.

13. The database must prevent application software from bypassing the limits it places on what types of data it allows to be stored.

one or more departments, which allows for a more precise accounting of income and expenses. In addition, however, each department can be found under any number of account numbers. Figure 13.3 shows the table structure of a basic general ledger system.

In the example in Figure 13.3, there are three tables: One that holds account numbers, the type of account (income or expense), and a lengthy description of each; a second for account departments, also with a description of each; and a third table that joins account numbers and department numbers with amounts of income and expenses.

In this general ledger, lengthy descriptions can be applied to account and department numbers, but only the numbers themselves are repeated to create income and expense records. Income and expense records can be created in any order and any time during the day-to-day operations of the business. Later, the database can extract and combine specific records into a complete, formatted financial statement.

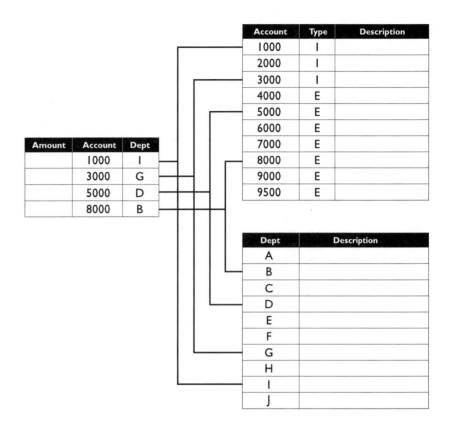

FIGURE 13.3

Tables in a basic
general ledger

Besides the ability to produce a variety of financial statements in different formats, this type of data organization permits you to isolate and analyze various aspects of your business's finances and make important financial decisions (for example, allocating budget figures to specific areas of expense) based on your own analysis of the financial information.

Designing Databases

Databases are by nature quite flexible and can apply to any number of record-keeping situations. Designing a good database is a skill that you can develop with experience and knowledge of a few generally accepted design principles.

> You may decide to bring in a consultant to help with the design. But as you probably realize by now, the process will inevitably be a collaboration; the consultant can't do the whole job alone. A good consultant (Appendix A offers guidelines for selecting one) will know how to build a database, but you know how your business really works. the more you understand about database concepts, the better you'll be able to participate in the design.

Defining the Results First

Databases don't exist for their own sake—they must have a purpose. The purpose of most databases is to produce customized, meaningful information. The first step in database design is to lay out, as specifically as you possibly can, what you intend the database to produce. If the database will produce certain reports, for example, you should create mock copies of the reports you want to see. If the database will display information on the computer screen, draw diagrams of how those displays will look and the types of information that will be presented there.

Although your database probably will evolve over time, and although it may eventually produce reports that you cannot envision at the outset, you must still develop the clearest possible idea of your results before you delve into the more technical aspects of database design. Many a database has failed simply because its purposes were only vaguely articulated at first.

Data Modeling

Once you have clearly defined your database's intended purpose, you are ready to analyze and chart the information-handling structures and procedures that will produce the results you intend. This process is called *data modeling*.

There are two aspects to data modeling. First, you must describe the features of the various entities in your business that you will use to produce your intended result. For example, if you intend to produce a regular report of cash balances for your business, you will need to define the business entities that produce income and expenses: customer and purchase records to show how the money flows in, creditor and expense records to show how the money flows out.

In the real world, the number of business entities can be quite large and the relationships between them quite complex. If you find that your data modeling scheme is beginning to look like a large platter of mushroom linguini, you may need to simplify your goals. You can always model a specific, limited aspect of your business (for example, a simple purchase order system) rather than some larger scheme involving expense accounting. If you have a well-organized, simple foundation, a natural progress of evolution will be possible. Besides, simplifying to a foundation level is a good way to get past the bane of many a business: endless planning.

After you have defined the entities in your business, you must then define the relationships between them. For example, customers should be related to purchases; creditors to expenses. Figure 13.4 shows a chart of some simple business entities—customers and purchases from inventory—and how relations might be defined between them.

Defining Tables

If you have done a good job of defining your business entities, you will be able to use them as a basis for defining the tables in your database. From the previous example, you can see that a record of customer purchases would require at least three tables: one for customer records, one for purchase records, and one for inventory. Each of these tables requires certain columns.

FIGURE 13.4

Modeling customer and
purchase entities

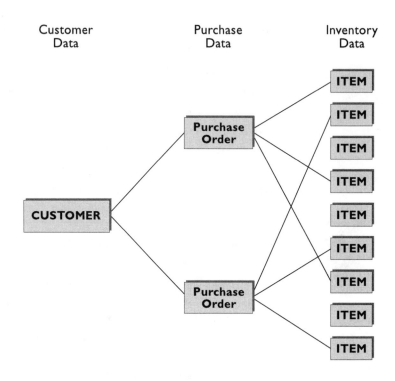

You would expect that the customer table would require customer names. It also might require shipping addresses and credit information. You would very likely want to include a customer identification number to use as a key field for relating the customer record to purchase records.

The purchase table would include key fields for customers and inventory items. The inventory table probably would include a key field plus a description of the item, various relevant features for each item, and the price.

An initial listing of your table columns for your customer purchase database might look something like this:

Customers	**Purchases**	**Inventory**
Customer ID	Customer ID	Inventory ID
First Name	Purchase Order No.	Description
Last Name	Inventory ID	Model

Customers	**Purchases**	**Inventory**
Address		Color
City		Price
State		
Zip Code		
Phone		
Credit Card		
Credit Rating		

Normalization

After you have listed the tables in your database, your next step is to *normalize* it. Normalization is simply a process of going over the columns you have laid out in your initial listing and eliminating any unnecessary redundancies and accounting for problems that may have surfaced during the process of defining the tables.

For example, in the customer purchase database as it is designed so far, there is a problem with the purchase order numbers. A system of numbered purchase orders could be important to your business, but the current purchase table introduces much repetition of customer ID and purchase order numbers, one set for each inventory item ordered.

One way to overcome this is to create a separate purchase order table, which will match a customer ID number with a purchase order number. Then you can revise the purchase table to include only a purchase order number with each inventory item.

Purchase Orders	**Purchases**
Customer ID	Purchase Order No.
Purchase Order No.	Inventory ID

Although adding a new table may seem at first to add a new level of complexity to the database, it actually makes the database more efficient by reducing redundancy. Remember that the process of accessing data from multiple tables is largely automated by a controlling database language so that multiple tables, which appear complicated to humans, can be handled very quickly and reliably by computers.

It is a fairly commonplace occurrence that, as you seek to reduce redundancy in your database tables, you create additional tables.

Normal Forms

Over time, as database designers have acquired experience designing efficient databases, certain rules have evolved regarding the normalization process. These rules are called *normal forms*, and they describe the structure of an efficient set of database tables. There are five normal forms, of which the first three are the most frequently used:

First normal form, no repeating columns   A table contains only single instances of each column element. For example, you should not add several columns for purchases to the customer table—this would limit the maximum number of purchases to the number of columns. If a customer exceeded the limit, your only recourse would be to add more columns, creating a bloated table structure. Creating a separate purchase table solves this problem.

Second normal form, columns depend on all key fields   If a table has two or more key fields (called a *composite key*), additional columns must be associated with the complete composite key, not just a portion of it. For example, in our original customer purchase system, the inventory ID was matched with a composite key: the customer ID and purchase order number. This was a violation of the second normal form because the inventory ID needed only to be matched with the purchase order number. Creating a separate purchase order table solved the problem.

Third normal form, non-key fields do not depend on each other All the columns in a table that are not used as the key field do not have dependencies upon each other. For example, suppose you have established certain ratings of credit-worthiness among your customers. You would violate the third normal form if you put both a credit-rating column and a credit-limit column in the same customer table. It would be more efficient to create yet another table, of credit ratings and limits, and keep only a credit rating column in the customer table.

The last two normal forms apply only to the largest and most complex databases:

Fourth normal form, key fields do not form interdependencies with each other In some tables containing more than one key field, one or more of the key fields may form a dependent relationship to another, leading to a situation in which key fields must be repeated within the table. For example, suppose your customer table included a column for credit-worthiness, which indicated a variable level of credit based on the total amount of each purchase. (In technical database terms, such a state of affairs is called a *multivalued dependency*.) In such a case, it would be more efficient to create a table for credit rating codes based on purchase amounts and relate those codes to the purchase order table, based on the total of the purchases in the purchase table.

Fifth normal form, multiple key fields do not form implicit selective dependencies This is an extension of the fourth normal form. It is possible that a multivalued dependency can imply additional dependent relationships that affect some key fields. For example, certain levels of credit may be allowed based on purchase amounts, while certain customers, based on their payment history, may have limited eligibility for credit. To track this type of interdependence efficiently, you create three tables: one for credit ratings based on total purchase amounts, as described previously, another for customer credit categories based on payment history, and a third to track the payment histories of customers.

Bear in mind that these five normal forms are guidelines for creating efficient databases. Exceptions to the rules abound, but you can justify them based on database performance and efficiency. In other words, go ahead and bend the rules of normalization, provided you can show that by doing so your database will save or make money for your business.

Charting the Relationships

The last step of the design process is vital and should not be over-looked, despite any temptation you may have to do so: Draw a picture of your tables and how they relate to each other. Figure 13.5 shows such a picture of the simple purchase system.

FIGURE 13.5

A chart of the tables in the customer purchase system

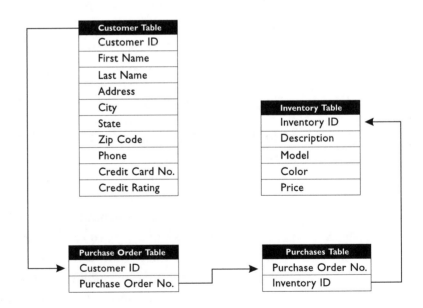

Drawing a chart of relationships is important not only because it may reveal weaknesses in your design (and better now than later), but also because it is the first step toward documenting your database. You will almost certainly want to refine and enhance the database as time goes by, to give it more features and power. To do this, you will need to know just how the various relations work between the database tables. A picture of your database is the best means to understand how it all fits together, when you come back to it weeks or months later to add those nifty enhancements.

Distributed Databases

A *distributed database* is one whose tables are divided between two or more computers. It also can refer to two or more databases with tables that are linked in controlled ways.

Distributing a database can yield some significant benefits. For example, consider the customer purchase database. The shipping department may access the customer information and purchase order tables more frequently than any other department, while the inventory department may access only the inventory table regularly, as it receives incoming shipments and updates the table. If the two departments are not located very close to each other, it may make sense to have the inventory table on a server that is local to the inventory department, and the purchase order tables on a server local to the shipping department. Meanwhile, the accounting department which needs to access the records less often, can access both tables remotely across the network.

Often, if you can place data tables on different local servers so that users who need them most often have local access to them, you will derive faster and more efficient performance. The performance gains come from reducing traffic across the network to a single server with all the tables. Fortunately, client/server databases are equipped with tools to go out over the network and assemble relationships between far-flung data tables when necessary.

Every business has unique ways of handling information. A database manager must carefully analyze who uses the information and how often and strike a balance in your networked database. On the one hand, you want all the performance gains you can get using local access to data tables. On the other hand, if your database becomes too widely distributed, you may lose performance because of all the network over-head required to assemble information from widely distributed sets of data tables.

Some distributed databases are created by default. The data is already stored in various locations throughout the network, and a client/server database system is brought in to tie it together. This type of installation often requires many compromises involving system performance, access to data, and the amount of meaningful information you may be able to extract. In short, you must weigh the time and effort of designing a completely new data-handling system from scratch against the compromises that come from tying separate, pre-existing data files together. Again, these are decisions you must make based on careful analysis of how your business works.

Distribution Methods

There are three common methods for managing data in a distrib-uted database. Each method has its own strengths and weaknesses, and usually a distributed database will use some combination of the three. They are:

Extraction   Also called *data downloading,* this is the process of copying some portion of the database to another location. You can copy an entire table, a set of tables, just a portion of a single table, or the entire database, to the second location. This approach can be efficient in situations where the user receiving the copy of the data does not have to modify it at all. For example, you may elect to copy a table of prices for inventory items to the order-entry department, which needs frequent access to the information but only refers to the table and never updates it.

Replication   This is also a process of copying some portion of the database to a different location, but here the user who receives the copy is also allowed to modify it. When data tables are replicated in this manner, the database system software must keep track of all modifications that are made to all the copies and update the original as soon as possible, if not immediately. If the database software does not keep modifications current throughout the system, the database is considered out of synchronization, and destructive errors can creep in.

- For example, suppose the order entry department can make spot changes to inventory prices on its copy of the inventory department's data table. If the inventory department is not made aware of these changes, it might prepare inaccurate reports of the sale value of the inventory for the accounting department, which in turn might produce inaccurate financial statements.

- Good distributed database software includes tools that you can use to automate the process of updating copies of data tables in a distributed database. However, you can expect that this process may involve some fairly complicated system design and programming, and there is virtually no way you can have a replicated database completely in synchronization all of the time. Replication is recommended on systems where the need for the best possible performance justifies the risks involved and the extra work required to configure, program, and debug such a system.

Fragmentation   This is a process of splitting a single table up and storing it in two or more locations. As with the other distribution systems, the goal is to enhance performance by providing local access to certain types of data. For example, on a wide area network, it may make sense to split a single customer database table between different servers in different regional areas so that local names and addresses appear on a server located where the customer calls.

- It is also possible to split a table by columns between two different computers, although this is done far less often.

- If you find that you need to split a table between servers, be sure that your controlling database software can reassemble a split table. A good database software system can access both locations and make the table appear as a single unified table without the user having to know the actual physical location of the data records.

Getting to the Data

Once you have designed your database storage layout and either placed all your data tables on a centralized server or distributed them to different servers throughout your network, your users must be able to get to that data as easily as possible.

Users normally access data using different kinds of application software. Their software retrieves the data, perhaps does additional processing on it, and then formats the results so that the information is useful.

However, it is common on a network to have many different types of applications, and they also may be running on different local operating systems. This makes access to a single database more difficult. For example, you may have users that come into your organization already familiar with a specific database front end: dBASE, Visual Basic,

Delphi, or other similar product. Can you get different products to access the same data tables? Also, you may find that, as your network evolves, you have reason to add a Macintosh machine to a PC-based network. In addition to the technical issues involved in making such a connection (see Chapter 9 for details), you must find a way to allow the Mac to access the PC-based tables.

Fortunately, there is a mechanism that allows all these different applications to access the same database, called an *application programming interface* (API). The API is a standard feature on every popular application designed to access network databases. Very simply put, this software mechanism operates as a type of translation device that receives instructions from the application and converts them into instructions that can be understood by the database's controlling software. The API does so by passing the application's instructions to a software driver that is programmed to do the translation.

If necessary, the application's API can pass the instructions to one of several different software drivers because it is possible to have more than one vendor's database attached to the network. If there is more than one type of database on the network, the application's API will need a separate driver for each. The API must be programmed to recognize which database should receive which instruction, and route each instruction to the correct driver.

The network database's controlling software recognizes the incoming instructions, accesses the data, and returns the requested results back to the application. The application's API then receives the resulting data and presents it in a meaningful way to the end user.

Front-end application vendors, understanding the importance of enabling their front-end products to access any underlying network database, continually update and expand their available API drivers. Of course, different vendors, in competition with each other, have developed different methods of carrying out this process of moving data between applications and databases. Some standards have emerged, however, making it easier for different application software vendors to supply reliable client/server access features with their products.

For example, one such *de facto* standard is Microsoft's *Open Data-Base Connnectivity* (ODBC) standard, which conforms to the model described above. If your chosen database product is ODBC-compatible, and your chosen applications are also ODBC-compatible, then you have a reasonable assurance that they will work together.

Another *de facto* standard is IBM's Distributed Relational Database Architecture (DRDA) standard. IBM developed this standard to define a means by which different application products could successfully access its mainframe database product, DB2. However, this standard has now been supported by several different network database products.

The DRDA standard governs the behavior of instructions that are sent to distributed databases from applications and how the receiving database should handle them. It defines four levels of access to distributed databases, with increasing levels of complexity:

Level 1: Remote requests   On this level, individual instructions access a network database on a single server. Each instruction either succeeds or fails, and the application is notified—no additional processing is required.

Level 2: Remote transactions   On this level, a series of instructions, called a *transaction*, accesses a database on a single server. The database software is programmed to handle the transactions as a group, and it can undo them if any one of the instructions in the group should fail.

Level 3: Distributed transactions   On this level, a transaction can access more than one database on more than one server, but each instruction within the transaction references only one database. Each database's controlling software must be able to undo the entire transaction should any individual instruction fail.

Level 4: Distributed requests   On this level, transactions access more than one database on more than one server, and each instruction can reference more than one database. This requires very complex controlling software, in which data from different servers is joined for processing and multiple updates throughout the system are tracked and recorded. Commands to commit or roll back the transactions must be included in every database's software.

Client/server databases are one area of networking in which standards can be extremely helpful to network administrators and users. Fortunately, there is a standard language for controlling a network database. Most network-aware applications that access databases include support for this language, called *Structured Query Language,* or SQL. The next section presents an overview of this standard database language.

SQL

The standard controlling language for accessing the in client/ server databases is called SQL. The letters SQL stand for *Structured Query Language* and are pronounced either "Sequel" or sometimes "Ess-Cue-El."

IBM researchers originally designed SQL in the 1970s (Edgar Codd, whom you met in the previous chapter, was highly influential in its early development). SQL quickly developed into a standard language for making queries in relational databases because it used a remarkably compact, English-like set of statements to perform complex sets of data access functions. SQL became a standard because its objectives are narrow, meaning that the language is used mostly for data queries and query-related processes. Simply put, you can use SQL to:

1. Create database tables

2. Define the relationships between them

3. Insert data into them

4. Extract the data in select, meaningful ways, based on the tables' defined relationships

Originally, SQL's developers intended to make complex database manipulation easy for end users. However, its developers were a bit too clever in condensing the language into a few powerful command operators and, in the end, undermined their own objective. SQL is so compact, it has become rigid. It is difficult for an average, non-technical user to master completely. In addition, it has only a few built-in functions for analyzing the data it extracts by queries.

Because of this, client/server database products use their own, more fully featured programming languages or interactive graphics-based interfaces as "front ends" for SQL. These languages execute SQL statements on the underlying database tables and then analyze and format the data returned by the SQL query statements. Unless you are a professional programmer, you need only be familiar with the conceptual fundamentals of SQL, rather than possess an in-depth understanding of its technical details.

SQL has great power to perform complex, sophisticated queries. It uses techniques such as nesting statements within each other, grouping key fields together, and applying built-in functions to narrow the range of records returned.

Locks

Multiuser access is the soul of client/server data processing, but allowing more than one user to access the data can allow errors to creep in. Database Management software like SQL provide tools for securing data when it is available to more than one user. A standard device for doing this is a system of *locks* to prevent more than one user at a time from making changes to rows in tables.

Here are some examples of problems that can develop if you don't use locks:

Unrepeatable reads   Suppose two users access the same data, one right after the other. The first user makes a change and issues a

COMMIT statement. The second user has no idea that the data has been changed. What is worse is that the second user is now working with incorrect data and doesn't know it. If this user reads the data a second time, it will be different. A database error (or at the very least, confusion in the mind of the user) may be the result.

Lost updates   A lost update occurs when two or more users access data in a row and both make changes. Simply put, the last user to record the change with a COMMIT statement "wins." The other changes are overwritten and permanently lost.

Access to uncommitted data   Suppose a user accesses some data and updates it but has not yet verified the update using a COMMIT statement. Suppose further that a second user accesses the changed, uncommitted data. If the first user backs out of the changes by issuing a ROLLBACK statement, the second user is suddenly working with incorrect data and as before, does not realize it. This situation can lead to bad business decisions based on bad data.

For example, to help prevent these problems, SQL places a lock on an entire row when a user accesses a field. SQL can issue two types of record locks:

Exclusive   An exclusive lock prevents other users from reading or updating data until the lock is released. When your database program detects an exclusive lock on a row, it displays a message indicating that the data is not accessible at this time and that the user should try again later.

Shared   A shared lock prevents other users from making changes to the data but allows those users to read it. When your database program detects a shared lock on a row, it displays some form of warning message. For example, the locked data might be displayed in a different color, or a special symbol might be added, warning the user that someone else has the data and may be updating it.

Deadlocks

SQL locks are effective, but they have problems of their own. One problem that may occur with SQL locks is called a *deadlock condition*.

Suppose a user accesses some data and places an exclusive lock on the row. Then, while the lock is still in place, the first user attempts to access another row.

However, another user has already accessed data in this second row and placed an exclusive lock on it. So far, so good; the system is working as it should. The first user must now wait until the second user releases the lock before accessing this second row.

However, the second user, while keeping the lock in place, attempts to access the original row, which still has the lock on it that the first user issued!

Now the second user must also wait for the first user to unlock the original row. Unfortunately neither user can unlock the rows, because their simultaneous locks and unfortunate timing have suspended them both in a perpetual state of waiting. They are waiting for each other to remove the locks on their rows, but neither can do this, because both need the other to unlock their rows first. Figure 13.6 shows how this deadlock condition comes about.

FIGURE 13.6

Creating a deadlock with locked files. Step 1: User A selects a row and locks it. Step 2: User B selects a row and locks it. Step 3: User A attempts to select User B's locked row and begins waiting. Step 4: User B attempts to select User A's locked row and begins waiting. They are both "locked out," each waiting for the other to release a row before they can continue.

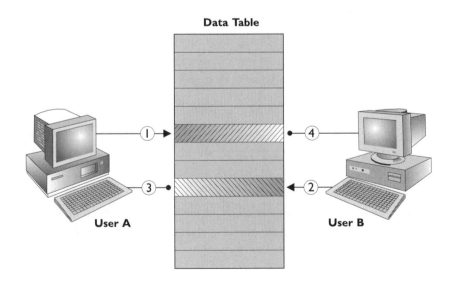

Data Table

User A

User B

Fortunately, client/server database products include mechanisms that detect such a condition and can override the users' locks and release them by sheer "brute force" and then roll back any changes that were not committed when the deadlock occurred. Both users can start over and hopefully not bump into each other again.

Where to Go from Here

If you manage a client/server database, you should expect that from time to time you will encounter SQL. For example, if you are evaluating competing database application products, the manufacturers will undoubtedly tout the advantages of their product as a SQL front-end and tell you how they implement SQL access for faster, more efficient, or more complete access to client/server data than provided by their competitors. They may demonstrate to you how well SQL is integrated into their product. This sampling of SQL in this chapter will give you a frame of reference for a better understanding of what they are talking about and for asking questions.

For Further Reading

- Bobrowski, Steve. *Mastering Oracle7 & Client/Server Computing.* 2d ed. Sybex, 1996.

- Gruber, Martin. *Understanding SQL.* Sybex, 1995.

- Martin, James, and Joe Leben. *Client/Server Databases.* Prentice Hall, 1995.

- Viescas, John L., Mike Gunderloy, and Mary Chipman. *Access and SQL Server Developer's Handbook.* Sybex, 1996.

CASE STUDY

GAB would like to get a handle on their client billing system. Traditionally, clients are billed on an hourly basis for services rendered and each employee keeps a log of hours of service performed. In the past, the office manager designed a spreadsheet template that employees used to enter their service hours, and then the office manager collected the spreadsheet files once a month and assembled the data into client invoices. The project was time-consuming, tedious, and prone to error. GAB begins work immediately on designing a central database to collect and store records of employee service hours.

For now, it does not appear necessary for GAB to acquire a large, formal database application, such as Oracle or SyBase. Instead, GAB will begin with a less expensive, simpler, network-aware application, (for example, Microsoft's Access or Borland's Paradox). GAB will start with three simple tables: one for general client information (with fields for names, addresses, and other relevant client-specific data), one for general employee information (names/addresses, salary information, and the like), and a third table for service data (including the type of ser-

vice performed, for whom it was performed, the date of the service, number of hours to be billed, and hourly rate charged).

GAB's database software includes tools for creating standard onscreen forms employees can use to enter service information and thus update their individual service logs quickly and easily. In doing so, they will be maintaining the centrally-stored service table, upon which GAB can base client invoices. The service table is related to the client and employee tables, allowing GAB to query for services performed for any given client within a given range of dates. The results of such queries will be imported into a spreadsheet or word processing template that will automatically format the raw data into finished client invoices.

Using this database, GAB's office manager can produce invoices in a fraction of the time it has previously taken to produce them. In addition, GAB will be able to store complete client case histories and employee work histories and generate additional reports based on this data.

GAB is starting out with a common-sense approach, using a simple, easy-to-understand database to produce useful results quickly. They can be reasonably sure that as they get used to working with databases, they will have a solid foundation for building more sophisticated record-keeping tools in the future.

PART

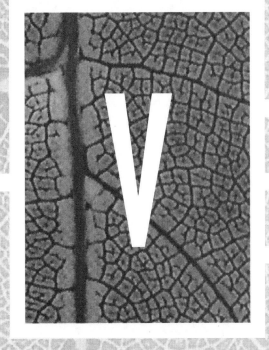

V

INTRANETWORKING

CHAPTER

14

Connecting Your Network
to the Internet

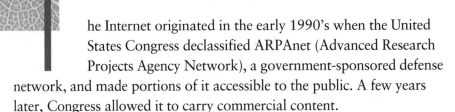

he Internet originated in the early 1990's when the United States Congress declassified ARPAnet (Advanced Research Projects Agency Network), a government-sponsored defense network, and made portions of it accessible to the public. A few years later, Congress allowed it to carry commercial content.

The subsequent rush to exploit this new means of commercial communication produced its astonishing growth and an extraordinary effect on worldwide commerce and culture. Businesses were quick to appreciate the value of such a large potential marketplace. At the time this is being written, there are approximately 30 to 40 million people using the Internet worldwide, with more coming online every day.

The profit potential represented by Internet growth has excited technology developers. The computer market has seen a flood of new software and hardware designed for Internet access. A surprising development has occurred along the way: Business technology managers discovered that Internet software and hardware tools could be used to manage information along local area networks. By adapting Internet tools to LANs, they could standardize their technologies and reduce network development and management costs. Thus was born the *intranet*, a private network that uses Internet technologies to process and exchange information.

The terms Internet and intranet look similar but have significantly different meanings. This chapter discusses the Internet: the world-wide application of ARPAnet-based technologies and protocols. The following two chapters will discuss intranets: the local, private use of these technologies and protocols.

The Elements of Internet Connectivity

There is no central controlling authority that regulates Internet content. Instead, the various networks that are connected to it at any given time determine what information is available and how that information flows from one point to another. This fully distributed structure makes the Internet flexible and capable of supporting an unlimited number of users. However, the Internet does require that all connected networks conform to certain fundamental standards.

These standards are maintained by a handful of voluntary organizations. For example, the Internet Architecture Board (IAB) reviews and approves transmission protocols and numbering standards. The Internet Engineering Task Force sets standards for the day-to-day operation of the network. The Internet Society publishes the various standards and is the point of contact between Internet supervising bodies, service providers, and users.

In this section, you will learn how you use these Internet standards to make world-wide connections from your local area network.

Service Providers

You will access the Internet by establishing a connection through an *Internet Service Provider* (ISP). The ISP acts as an Internet middleman, maintaining the actual connection to the Internet by means of an Internet router and licensing access, usually for a subscription fee of one sort or another (monthly and yearly fees are common). The user connects to the ISP's router by means of a telephone or dedicated leased line, which completes the user's connection onto the Internet.

Most ISPs are *direct providers*. Direct providers offer Internet access as their primary service to users. They charge a one-time startup fee plus the subscription fee and usually provide the software necessary to access their connection to the Internet. Direct providers differ widely in the kinds of additional features they may offer. Some provide only access to the Internet with no additional frills of any kind. Others will lease space for your personal Web site, offer sophisticated full-time direct connections, or help with Web site design and maintenance. There are dozens of direct providers competing for your dollars—some locally-based, others with nationwide access points. You can find listings and advertisements for these providers in computer magazines, newspapers, journals, and newsletters.

Online Services are another form of ISP. They provide special communications features in addition to Internet access (for example, stock quotes, weather reports, news, entertainment, and chat rooms). Although on-line services are available for businesses that use LANs, their client base consists mostly of individual home users or small home-based businesses, and their extra services are oriented toward this market. The two most popular on-line services are CompuServe and America Online.

Selecting Your ISP

Before you can select your ISP, you must decide how you intend to use the Internet. The type of connection you choose will be based on your anticipated usage. Following are typical ways businesses use the Internet:

Messaging and e-mail is the simplest Internet application. A connection that does nothing but messaging and e-mail is the easiest and least expensive type to install and maintain.

Domain access, also known as "surfing the Web," requires that you set up a mediated access account with your ISP, for which you will normally be charged a monthly or yearly subscription fee. This type of access is the most common for businesses that intend to use Internet resources only for gathering general information, conducting on-line research, or buying goods and services.

Client access is used to run Internet-based applications on workstations (for example, stock trading software that connects to a brokerage or communications software that manages real-time conferencing). These applications establish Internet connections on an as-needed basis while they are running.

Full-time direct access is used by businesses that offer their goods and services to the Internet community at large; for example, a clothing store with an on-line catalog and ordering capability or an airline with an on-line reservations system. This type of access is the most expensive and requires special installation by your ISP and higher usage fees.

After you have determined your usage style, shop around, first by collecting information from ISP advertisements, then by obtaining recommendations from business associates, friends, and vendors. ISP fees vary widely, and their stated fees may or may not include the exact services you need (for example, technical support, additional hardware, or access time over a given limit may not be included in an advertised price). It is very important to ask every silly question you can think of. (Silly questions can be useful; people can reveal a lot of information about themselves when they're confronted with a silly question.) Get all promises in writing before selecting your ISP.

Grill Your ISP

Here is a checklist of information any reliable ISP will be happy to provide:

- All installation and maintenance fees associated with ISP's services
- Required software and hardware and their costs
- Copies of manuals, documentation, and training materials, if any
- Minimum contract time period, if any
- Cost of installation/setup and lead time required
- Security features
- Availability of technical support
- Upgrade possibilities

Telephone Line and ISDN Connections

Messaging, domain, and client access connections require only *dial-up access* to your ISP; that is, you make the connection using standard telephone lines or ISDN lines, which are faster but cost more. (For general information on ISDN, refer to Chapter 7. Additional ISDN information with regard to the Internet is just ahead.)

After you have decided how you intend to use the Internet, you should decide how much of your own network resources you want to devote to Internet access. You may decide that you want to make the Internet available to only a few users or to all users on your network. If you want only a few users to have Internet access, you might consider setting up those users' workstations as if they were stand-alone computers; that is, install a modem in each workstation, configure those workstations to support TCP/IP-based data transfers, and have the users dial up the ISP directly. This approach saves time, is fairly easy to maintain, and does not require that you configure your entire network to support TCP/IP.

However, if you want Internet connectivity available throughout your network, you must configure your entire network to support TCP/IP data traffic. Instead of making the connection through a modem in a workstation, you make the connection using a *dial-up router,* a more sophisticated form of modem for networks. You install the dial-up router as a node on your network, and the router calls your ISP on command from workstations and maintains Internet connections to each workstation.

If you are making the connection with a router, bear in mind that concurrent connections from many network users will be extremely slow if you are using standard telephone lines. An ISDN line, though more expensive than a standard telephone line, costs far less than a dedicated leased line.

To use an ISDN line, you must make the connection in an area where ISDN is supported by the telephone company. You must install an ISDN-compatible dial-up router and pay a fee to the phone company for access to its ISDN equipment. In addition, you must use an ISP that provides ISDN access and pay their fees.

ISDN is a cost-effective alternative to leased lines if you have many users on your network that use the Internet but do not need 24-hour-a-day connections. ISDN rates are normally based on actual usage, versus a high flat fee for leased-line access. While you are planning your Internet connection, it is worthwhile to compare costs for each:

1. Ask the ISPs that you are considering for quotes on the cost of leased-line connections and their rate-per-minute for ISDN connections.

2. Estimate the amount of time you expect your users to be on the Internet.

3. Multiply this time by the ISDN rate-per-minute.

4. Make ISDN your choice if the result of step three is significantly lower than leased-line.

5. If the result of step three is close to the cost of a leased line, you are better to go ahead with the leased-line access—chances are good that the size of your network and the amount of Internet usage will both grow over time, making leased-line the better deal.

Leased-Line Connections

If you plan to offer a commercial Web site to the Internet community, full-time customer service, or any other business model that requires you to remain "open" on the Internet all the time, you will want to arrange for the purchase and installation of a dedicated *leased line* to maintain the full-time connection. If your ISP offers full-time Internet access capability, it will normally arrange for the leased-line installation with the local telephone company and pass the setup charges on to you. Thereafter, you can expect to pay a flat fee for maintenance of the connection. Leased lines are charged by the mile, so the closer you are physically located to your ISP's leased-line router, the better off you are.

The leased line is the two-way data carrier between you and your ISP. A special hardware device called a Channel Service Unit/Data Service

Unit (CSU/DSU) connects your network's Internet router to your end of the leased line and converts the network's serial data signal to the line's digital signal and vice-versa. Another CSU/DSU does the same job on the ISP's end.

Leased-line speeds are higher than dial-up connections. They range from 56kbps (56,000 bits per second) up to 45Mbps (45,000,000 bits per second). Most leased-line connections run at about 1.5Mbps.

Frame-Relay Connections

Some ISPs can provide an alternate means of full time connection, called a *frame relay connection*. This type of connection is a compromise between the expense of the leased line and the slower performance of dial-up access. Frame relay is a wide-area network technology that can dramatically speed up data flow. The maximum data-transfer speed under frame relay is just over 1.5Mbps, or 1,544,000 bits per second.

To establish a frame-relay connection, you must contract with an ISP that offers frame relay network access. The ISP sets up a permanent connection, called a Permanent Virtual Circuit (PVC), over existing digital telephone lines. Unlike with leased lines, where the data-handling capacity is permanent and always available, the data-handling capacity of the PVC is dynamic, which means that the PVC's data handling capacity is allocated on an as-needed basis. If there is little traffic on the frame-relay network when you are using it, frame-relay performance is very robust. But if a lot of traffic bottles up the network, performance can slow down considerably. Some ISPs can guarantee, usually for a fee, that their frame-relay network will not drop below a given minimum speed.

TCP/IP

TCP/IP stands for Transmission Control Protocol/Internet Protocol. The family of protocols that make up TCP/IP are the standard set of rules governing how information is transmitted safely along Internet connections.

The TCP/IP Family

TCP/IP includes the following protocols, which each handle specific types of data communications:

Transmission Control Protocol (TCP) breaks the communication stream into 64K packets, or datagrams, that can be transmitted and verified individually and resent if there is a problem.

Internet Protocol (IP) adds destination addresses and verifies the accuracy and correct sequential order of the datagrams.

Simple Mail Transfer Protocol (SMTP) processes electronic mail messages that contain only ASCII characters (letters, numbers, and standard keyboard punctuation marks) and a destination address.

File Transfer Protocol (FTP) transfers files, including binary files, and can be used to automate message sending.

Telnet is a set of rules that allows a person stationed at a computer on the network (called the *local terminal*) to access and run a different computer on the network (called the *remote terminal*). Telnet sends the local keyboard commands to the remote terminal and sends the remote screen's display of the command results back to the local terminal.

This section describes the fundamentals of TCP/IP. Awareness of TCP/IP will help you understand how and why the Internet works the way it does. The TCP/IP protocol suite was developed in the 1970's by the Department of Defense as a safe means of communicating over computer networks. The early, government-sponsored ARPAnet was developed to handle communications in emergency situations; but DOD realized that events such as wars or natural disasters could render the network unreliable. TCP/IP's purpose was not only to transmit the information but also to take control of its verification and insure its accuracy, independent of the platforms that were sending and receiving it.

What the DOD came up with was a system of chopping information into *packets* (also called *datagrams*), or small sections of data no more than 1,500 characters each, which could be sent and verified individually and rearranged at their destination. Fundamentally speaking, the TCP protocol chops the information into these datagrams, then verifies their accuracy and reassembles them on the receiving end. The IP protocol handles the addressing, sequence order, and sending.

These platform-independent safety features of TCP/IP make it ideal for the modern Internet. With forty million or so people using any number of different platforms, it's best to standardize error-checking in a protocol that can be supported by all.

TCP's mechanism for verifying the accuracy of a pack is a *checksum,* a number added to a header attached to each datagram. The checksum number represents the sum of the byte values of all the characters in the datagram. After adding the header, TCP passes the datagram to the IP protocol.

IP adds an *addressing header* to each datagram. The header includes the sending and destination address for each datagram and a number indicating its sequential order among the datagrams that constitute the original information. IP then passes the datagram to the sending computer, which uses its own protocol (for example, the Internet Point-to-Point or PPP protocol) to put the datagram and headers into a *frame.* The frame is a combination of yet another header, plus a footer, which is used to protect the datagram from errors as it passes through the Internet.

As the frame travels the Internet, it is handled by a series of Internet IP routers. Each router reads the destination address within the frame and selects the address of the next router required to pass the frame along to its destination. Because the flow of information on the network is constantly changing, a different set of routers might receive each frame. Also, different routers on the network might stop functioning for any number of reasons. If an IP router detects that an address is busy or not functioning, it chooses an alternate address to move the frame along.

What this all means is that frames can arrive at their destination out of order and must be verified and reassembled. When the frame arrives at the destination, the receiving computer first checks the frame header and footer to be sure that the datagram has arrived intact and then deletes the frame header and footer. IP checks the address and sequence number for each datagram, and TCP checks each datagram for accuracy by calculating a new datagram checksum and comparing it to the original checksum. If the checksums don't match, TCP assumes that the datagram has been corrupted somehow and sends a request that the corrupted datagram be resent. Once all the datagrams are received and verified, TCP realigns them in sequence, deletes the headers, and hands the information to the receiving computer for processing.

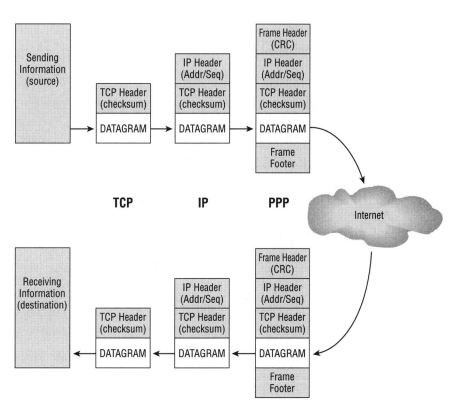

FIGURE 14.1

Basic TCP/IP protocol in action. TCP separates data into datagrams and adds a checksum header. IP adds addressing and sequencing headers. Internet protocols wrap the datagrams in header/footer frames for transport over the Internet. At the destination, the process is essentially reversed to recreate the original information.

IP Addresses

As you can imagine, a world-wide network of networks requires a sophisticated addressing system to route information to all its various destinations. The Internet Society has established a standard for addressing Internet destinations called *IP addressing*. An IP address contains four numbers, each in the range of 1 to 254, separated by periods. For example, the following is an IP address:

192.168.202.35

The numbers 0 and 255 can also appear in IP addressing schemes, but these numbers are reserved for special uses. The number 255 is used as a kind of wild card, for broadcasting datagrams to all computers on an IP network. The number 0 is used to specify addresses more narrowly. For example, suppose that the above example address indicated node 35 on network 192.168.202. Then 192.168.202.0 would specify only the network, and 0.0.0.35 would specify only the node.

The Cupboard Was Big; It's Almost Bare

The current IP addressing scheme allows for something in the neighborhood of four billion possible IP addresses, but it isn't enough. The Internet is growing so explosively that we are already running out. The Internet Society is hard at work on a new scheme, called IP Version 6 (IPv6), involving 128-bit IP addresses. (Using the current dot-delimited system, that would be an address of sixteen numbers instead of the current four.) It will take a few years to adopt IPv6 as the widespread standard because it will demand fundamental software changes and hardware upgrades on all IP-supporting equipment.

IPv6 will give us roughly 300,000,000,000,000,000,000,000,000,000,000,000,000 more IP addresses. How long before we use all *those* up, I wonder?

IP addresses can be manipulated to accommodate networks with only a few nodes or networks that have millions of nodes. To do this,

What These Numbers Mean to You

The numbers in an IP address represent 8-bit binary numbers or *octets*. The octets are read from right to left. In the above example, the first octet is represented by number 35. Following is the example IP address 192.168.202.35 in binary notation:

    11000000.10101000.11001010.00100011

Binary numbers allow you greater extendibility in assigning addresses to network destinations because you can manipulate individual 1's and 0's in binary numbers and develop addressing schemes that are more flexible than those using ordinary numbers. The process of manipulating network addresses with binary numbers is called *subnet masking*.

Subnet masking is used on complex networks with multiple servers to access different segments of the network. IP addressing requires each segment to have a unique IP network address. It is expensive to establish a unique IP network address for each segment of a complex network. With subnet masking, you combine a single network address with some of the binary digits in your node address to use as a network address for each server. You then use the leftover binary digits as node addresses for the nodes accessed by each segment's server. Using this technique, you can avoid the expense of having separate IP network addresses for each segment.

the Internet Society has defined three classes of networks, based on size. They are:

Class A: Large networks with millions of nodes   The first octet (the one on the right) represents the network address. The remaining three represent the node address.

Class B: Medium-sized networks with thousands of nodes   The first two octets (on the right) represent the node address. The other two (on the left) represent the network address.

Class C: Small networks with less than a thousand nodes   The first three octets represent the network address. The last octet represents the node address.

	Class	Type	Nodes	Net/Node Address
TABLE 14.1 Network Addressing Schemes; n=node address and N=Network address.	A	Large	Millions	nnn.nnn.nnn.NNN
	B	Medium	Thousands	nnn.nnn.NNN.NNN
	C	Small	Hundreds or less	nnn.NNN.NNN.NNN

You are assigned a unique IP network address by your Internet Service Provider. (Internet Service Providers are discussed in detail later in this chapter.) After that, it's up to you to configure your network for IP node addresses. Standard network operating systems, like Novell's InternetWare and Microsoft's Windows NT, have utilities that allow you to configure your network for IP node address.

Domain Name System

As you can imagine, it's considerably difficult to remember arcane, number-based IP addresses for each node on your network, let alone the entire Internet. For this reason, The Internet Network Information Center (InterNIC) was established in 1993 to manage the *Domain Name System* (DNS), a mechanism for substituting easily-remembered character-based *domain names* for numeric IP addresses. For example, it is a lot easier to remember a domain name like sybex.com than a literal IP address of 209.1.78.5.

When you establish an IP address on the Internet, you also establish a domain name and register it with InterNIC. Your domain name must be unique, not already used by another Internet address. Your name is added to a hierarchical database of all domain names. A domain name is a series of characters separated by periods, also known as *dots*; sybex.com (spoken as "sybex-dot-com") is the domain name for Sybex Books.

The rightmost portion of a domain name indicates the largest domain to which a specific address belongs, as well as the type of organization with which that address is associated. In the example just given, .com indicates that the address is a commercial site. There are several common domain types in the United States:

`.com`	Commercial
`.edu`	Educational organization; school
`.gov`	Government
`.mil`	Military
`.net`	Internet-related
`.org`	Non-profit organization

As of this writing, InterNIC is looking into the possibility of adding more domain types to this list.

Countries outside the United States generally have their own domain type, a two character code associated with that country. For example, `.fr` is the domain type for France, and `.nl` is the domain type for the Netherlands.

The characters preceding the domain type indicate the registered *subdomain name* associated with the IP address. In the above example, `sybex` is the subdomain name within the domain name `sybex.com`.

More complex numbers can have additional subdomain names added in order to address specific sections of the larger network. For example, `mail.telis.org` is the domain name for the mail server at Telis Nonprofit Educational Services.

Name Servers

Domain names are managed by a hierarchy of network *name servers*. Name servers store databases of domain names and their associated IP addresses. When a user on your network wants to connect to an Internet address, he or she enters a query to your network's local name server. The local name server first attempts to find the IP address in its own database. If it finds it, the server returns the IP address to the computer making the query, and the Internet connection is made. If the domain name is not found in the local database, the server refers the query to another server further up the hierarchy across the Internet. As long as the domain name is not found, the query continues until it reaches a *root name server*, a server containing domain names and IP addresses based on the domain name type, such as .com. Root name servers are located throughout the United States and are maintained by InterNIC. If the IP address is found, it is returned to the computer making the query. Otherwise, the server returns a message indicating that the domain name was not found.

As IP addresses are returned from root name servers, local network domain name servers maintain a cache of frequently accessed domain names in order to speed up processing and cut down on the number of requests they must pass along to root name servers.

Top-Level Domain Categories

Finally, domain names also include a *top-level category*. For example, www at the beginning of a domain name indicates that the site supports communications via the *World Wide Web* (more often simply called the *Web*), one of the largest site categories on the Internet. In order to be part of the World Wide Web, sites use a standard method of formatting documents, called *HyperText Markup Language* (HTML), which permits the documents to be displayed on any HTML-supporting computer. Web-based computers also use a protocol called *HyperText Transfer Protocol* (HTTP), which allows for the use of a technology called *embedded links* within HTML documents. Embedded links are coded instructions to move quickly and easily from one document on one Web site to another document on a different Web site. For more information on HTML and HTTP, refer to Chapter 15. There are millions of Web sites on the Internet today. For example, Sybex Books has a Web site located at www.sybex.com.

Another common top-level category is the *File Transfer Protocol* (FTP) site. These sites exist mostly to store and download datafiles. For example, a computer hardware company might maintain an FTP site to support its customers by supplying them with updated software driver and utility files, or a school might have an FTP site for maintaining datafiles as a virtual library. For example, the domain name for the software file server at the National Center for Supercomputing Applications (NCSA) at the University of Illinois is `ftp.ncsa.uiuc.edu`.

In this example, `edu` is the domain type, and `uiuc` is the subdomain name for the University of Illinois. This particular network is complex enough that an additional subdomain name, `ncsa`, is added to address the NCSA network, which is a subnetwork within the University's overall network.

Another common top-level category is the *newsgroup*. A newsgroup is a set of users with some common interest who access a central location to post related articles that can be read by other subscribers. Thousands of newsgroups exist throughout the world today. Taken together, these groups form a world-wide discussion database called *Usenet*.

Usenet access is handled by *news servers*, computers that specialize in the storage and transfer of Usenet databases and in communication with other news servers across the Internet. Most ISPs have some form of news server capability; if you intend to make use of Usenet newsgroup information, be sure to ask your ISP about their newsgroup capability before you subscribe to their service. You access newsgroups using a *news reader*, a feature that is built into modern Internet-access software.

Before you use your news reader, you must configure it to access the domain name of the news server provided by your ISP. After you have configured the news reader, you can start it and it will automatically log into the server and display the names of newsgroup databases stored there. (The display may take some time if you are connected over a modem; there are thousands of names of newsgroups to download to your reader.) Once the names are displayed, you can simply pick the ones that interest you and read the messages, replies, opinions, ideas, comments, rants, and other interesting articles contained therein. News readers also include commands that allow you to post articles of your own.

Domain names for newsgroups can begin with any one of a number of top-level categories. Here are some commonly-found examples:

alt	Topics that are generally not considered mainstream; can be controversial content
comp	Computer-related topics
misc	Topics that do not fit one of the standard categories
news	Newsgroup information
rec	Entertainment and recreational topics
sci	Scientific topics
soc	Sociological and cultural topics
talk	Matters of opinion: politics, religion, social issues, current events, etc.

You can find a list of Usenet newsgroups at http://www.cis .ohio-state.edu/hypertext/faq/usenet-faqs/bygroup/ news/lists/top.html.

Browser Software

You use a special software application called a *browser* to connect to the Internet. Browsers were originally designed to access documents from Web servers, but competition between software developers has led to the addition of more and more features. As a result, a modern browser has become an all-purpose Internet access application. The two most common browsers in use today are *Netscape Navigator*, published by Netscape Communications, and *Internet Explorer*, published by Microsoft. Both packages do a good job of accessing the Internet. Both include support for multiple Internet services such as HTTP, FTP, newsgroup readers, and electronic mail, plus support for older protocols like Telnet and Gopher.

Of these two browsers, Netscape was the first to fully implement and support the Java programming language, which is widely used to create various nifty browser-based applications, called *applets*. This early support for Java applets, combined with vigorous marketing, has helped Navigator maintain its firm position in the browser software market despite intense competition from Microsoft. For more information on Java, refer to Chapter 15.

To access an IP address on the Internet using a browser, enter the full domain name of the address where the browser prompts you. For example, if you were logged onto the Internet and wanted to contact Sybex, you would enter **http://www.sybex.com**, indicating that sybex.com can be found on the World Wide Web and is to be accessed using Hyper-Text Transfer Protocol. This addressing syntax is called the *Universal Resource Locator* (URL). The browser resolves the domain name to an IP address by connecting to a root name server as necessary and makes the connection.

Once the connection is established, the contacted site sends data to your computer, usually instructions to display information of some kind on your screen. This set of instructions, written in HTML, is the contacted site's *Web page,* or *home page.* The site's Web page can include text, pictures, sounds, animation, applications, or embedded links to other sites or additional Web pages at the same site.

Other protocols work in a similar way. For example, to access NCSA's FTP site, enter **ftp://ftp.ncsa.uiuc.edu**.

Internet E-Mail

Electronic Mail is the most widely used Internet service. It has the advantage of being fairly simple to set up and maintain and can provide fast, efficient communications to any part of the world where computers are connected to the Internet.

You can access Internet e-mail using mailing features built into your browser software; by using your network's native e-mail system, if it has one and if it can support TCP/IP-based communications; or by using stand-alone commercial software such as cc:MAIL or Eudora Pro.

After you compose an e-mail message and supply the domain name address of the recipient in the message header, your chosen software transmits the message to your network's mail server, which resolves the domain name to an IP address of a destination mail server and sends the message across the Internet. The destination server examines the message header and delivers the message to the recipient workstation or stores the message in a central location for pick-up at a later time by the recipient.

The standard protocol for transferring Internet e-mail is SMTP, or Simple Mail Transfer Protocol. SMTP establishes a mail transfer connection between the sending and receiving mail servers, breaks the message into sections, and verifies each section as it is sent.

At first, Internet-based e-mail could contain only ASCII text because the Internet messaging protocol could only recognize ASCII characters. Modern e-mail software incorporates compression schemes for translating binary files into ASCII-based formats and attaching these translated files to regular e-mail messages. One widely-used compression/translation scheme is MIME, which stands for Multipurpose Internet Mail Extension. E-mail software that supports MIME can send or receive binary files from any other software that also supports MIME. A modern Internet mail application will automatically translate attached binary files without special intervention from the user.

If your network already has local e-mail, you can expand your current e-mail system to include Internet mail by adding a *SMTP gateway*. The gateway is a device that translates outgoing e-mail into an SMTP-compliant format and reverses the process for incoming mail.

An alternative system is a provider-based system, wherein your ISP maintains mailboxes and your users connect to the provider to download their mail. If you implement this system, called *remote-access e-mail,* your software must support a remote access protocol such as POP3 (Post Office Protocol Version 3) or other electronic mail protocol as may be required by your ISP.

Where to Go from Here

The Internet has grown so quickly thanks to a rapidly-developing support technology that will continue to improve for some time to come. This development is spurred by competition among vendors seeking to exploit the computer market's rush to embrace the Internet's promise of fast communication and world-wide commerce. From a networking perspective, Internet technology has another promising aspect: the development of *intranets*, or the use of Internet-access tools to simplify local area networking. Depending on your circumstances, you may need only internet access, or you may want to investigate whether intranet technology is right for your business. Intranet technology is examined in the next two chapters.

If you are content to stick to Internet-based applications, the process of getting started is not all that complicated:

1. Determine how you want to use the Internet. You may want only to access information or only to use the Internet for your business's electronic mail, being essentially an Internet customer. Or, you may want also to launch your own Web site, being what amounts to an Internet supplier. You may want to access newsgroups. All this should be worked out before you take any further steps.

2. Determine what connection is most appropriate. Your two basic choices are direct-access and dial-up. The information in this chapter is intended to help you determine which technology best matches your intended usage.

3. Look for an Internet Service Provider that can meet your needs. You can find advertisements for ISPs in computer-related journals and periodicals. If you have a friend or colleague who is already online, ask for referrals or help finding an appropriate ISP using the Internet. If you need software or training, many ISPs can provide it for you as part of their service. A good ISP can help you

select any additional software tools you may need to get the most out of your connection.

4. Take time to experiment and learn. Don't rush to exploit the Internet. It's not going away any time soon, and your ability to use it profitably depends more on your ability with your chosen software than on how quickly you get on board. The Internet is already jam-packed—that's just a fact of on-line life. An ability to use this resource efficiently will serve you best in the long run, by enhancing your Web presence and helping you to stand out in an overrun field.

For Further Reading

- Crumlish, Christian. *The ABCs of the Internet.* 2d ed. Sybex, 1997.

- Ellsworth, Jill H. and Matthew V. Ellsworth. *The New Internet Business Book.* John Wiley & Sons, 1996.

- Hoffman, Paul E. *The Internet Instant Reference.* 3d ed. Sybex, 1996.

- Schwartz, Evan. *Webonomics: Nine Essential Principles for Growing Your Business on the Web.* Broadway Books, 1997.

- Stern, Morgan. *The NetWare to Internet Connection.* Sybex, 1996.

CASE STUDY

GAB studies what potential benefits the Internet may have for their business and comes to the conclusion that their initial use of the Internet will be confined to information-gathering and communications.

One reason they selected Windows NT as their operating system is that Windows NT provides well-integrated support for TCP/IP protocols, which should simplify how they configure their Internet capability. At this point in the process, GAB has concerns about their networking budget. A direct leased-line connection appears far too costly at this time; however, GAB will consider an ISP that can offer this capability at a later date if costs come down or if their own business expansion warrants it. For the time being, they will content themselves with dial-up access, even though they will be making a compromise in performance. They will look for an ISP with unlimited on-line time and fast modem access, and they will invest in a fast dial-up router.

E-mail is of great concern. Should GAB use commercial e-mail software and configure it for Internet e-mail, or should they use their ISP as an e-mail server? Both solutions have their advantages. Table 14.2 outlines the pros and cons.

In the end, GAB elects to purchase a commercial e-mail package, to take advantage of internal scheduling and conferencing features. They will have to configure it for dial-up access to the Internet. They will use their NT server as an Internet gateway. GAB is, in effect, beginning the process of developing their own Intranet by using TCP/IP protocols as the basis for their e-mail system.

T A B L E 14.2 Comparing e-mail options in GAB's case study	**Solution**	**Pro**	**Con**
	Commercial e-mail software	Flexible, expandable, fully-featured for internal conferencing, scheduling, and messaging	Difficult and expensive to implement and maintain
	ISP-based e-mail	Easy and inexpensive to implement and maintain	Can be costly over time as usage/subscription fees accumulate; limited features compared to commercial packages

CHAPTER

15

Implementing an Intranet

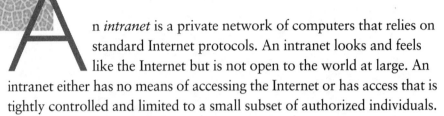

An *intranet* is a private network of computers that relies on standard Internet protocols. An intranet looks and feels like the Internet but is not open to the world at large. An intranet either has no means of accessing the Internet or has access that is tightly controlled and limited to a small subset of authorized individuals.

An intranet uses familiar Internet building blocks like HTML, HTTP, TCP/IP, SMTP, FTP, CGI, domain names, and Web browsers to collect and display information from Web servers throughout the enterprise.

An intranet is, at least for the foreseeable future, an add-on to a LAN, not a replacement. More mature LAN technologies (such as NetWare, Windows NT, Oracle, and Powerbuilder) offer a wider range of features, more flexibility, more sophisticated security, and generally don't require as much in-house development. Nevertheless, there is a clear trend towards using intranet technologics and tools to support a growing range of business functions. The reason for this trend is that intranets are especially well-suited to serve the collaborative aspects of business: communicating with colleagues via e-mail and conferencing, collecting, storing, and sharing up-to-date information with less day-to-day administrative overhead.

Web Pages

Intranets use a set of forms, called *pages*, which are text files that contain instructions to collect and display information in various formats. Pages can contain almost any kind of information in text or graphic-image format, and often the two are mixed together. An average-sized intranet will contain hundreds if not thousands of these pages. Intranet Web browsers work the same way they do on the Internet's World Wide Web: They access and read pages, and they display the page's contents on the screen as instructed.

When users turn on their computers and log onto the intranet for the first time, the intranet displays a default home page, which typically acknowledges the logon and introduces a basic set of choices for users to make as they navigate through the various pages.

Pages are related to one another by means of hypertext links (usually just called *links*). A link can be a snippet of text or a graphic image, and it can appear anywhere within the information on a page. The people who design Web pages try to integrate links within the information on a page so that the links stand out in some way and give the user a clear idea of what additional pages they represent. When the user moves the mouse pointer to the link and clicks the mouse, the browser retrieves the page represented by the link. Pages can be nested within each other to multiple, theoretically infinite, and often recursive levels, and the browser will happily display and re-display pages as the user points and clicks.

The term *Web* (as in Web server, Web browser, etc.) refers to the system of hypertext links that is the underlying structure of the Internet.

An intranet's pages are managed by a *Web server,* a computer that stores Web pages and displays them when instructed to do so by *Web browsers,* which are the Web server's clients.

Web pages can do more than just display information. Web pages can support embedded applications or access server-based applications that can collect information, process data, and display results in text or graphic formats.

The page-and-link structure for an intranet makes it easy to support otherwise incompatible platforms. It is not necessary that all intranet clients have the same operating system or hardware, only that they run an Internet-standard browser. Browsers are available for virtually any combination of hardware and operating system. So, for example, if one user is running a UNIX Web browser on a UNIX workstation and another is running a Windows Web browser on a Windows workstation, the Web server can recognize the standard protocols involved and supply the same page to both browsers. Both will see pretty much the same results. In practice, the different client types may show occasional idiosyncrasies in their screen displays or some rare incompatibility with embedded software; but on the whole intranets are reliably platform-independent. Meanwhile, new developments in intranet software are making communications between different platforms smoother and more reliable than ever.

How Do I Set an Intranet Up?

Understanding the Internet gives you a jump start on developing your company intranet, because the protocols and standards are the same. If you already understand things like browsers, TCP/IP, and domain names, you will be in familiar territory when discussing intranet options.

The process steps for implementing an intranet are similar to the basic process steps for any new computer project:

1. Determine how you intend to use your intranet.

2. Select the software that will help you accomplish your goals.

3. Select the hardware that will support your software.

Determining How to Use Your Intranet

LANs have advantages over intranets: they have sophisticated levels of security and they can share hardware resources (such as hard drives and printers) with more flexibility. However, they require significant overhead expense to maintain. Businesspeople approach the idea of building an intranet in hopes that it will save them money.

In general, LAN administrators try to run software at the client level, for the sake of speed, and store information at the server level, for integrity and security. Intranets blur the distinction between applications and information. A lot of application power can be embedded in browsers and Web pages, with the result that applications can be centralized along with information. By centralizing application power, your company has the potential to make meaningful savings in network administration and overhead costs. For example, upgrades can be made at a single location, and the effect is felt instantaneously throughout the enterprise. This one aspect of centralized applications can greatly reduce time and travel costs.

In general, an intranet supports collaborative processes more efficiently than traditional LANs, which rely on specialized and usually decentralized applications to do the job. If your business involves a large amount of collaborative processes and your existing LAN (if you have one) seems to be supporting these processes unsatisfactorily, you should look into building an intranet.

Some of the ways an intranet supports collaborative processes are as follows:

- Promoting on-line meetings between project collaborators, which can include such useful technologies as video conferencing and white board collaboration, making better use of individuals' time and reducing travel costs

- Developing standardized on-line company training, which can be offered in a one-on-one format, scheduled at will, self-paced, and can include trainee feedback, testing, and suggestions

- Allowing new employees to use a familiar, browser-based communications interface rather than an in-house e-mail system that may require training

- Providing real-time updates to shared information, even while such information is being used and displayed

An intranet can help you save a considerable amount of money if your company relies on paper-based documents. Although the ideal of a completely paperless office is still a long way off, an intranet may save on paper costs by:

- Posting electronic announcements and distributing them automatically throughout wide-area networks

- Creating an on-line library of product and research materials that can be accessed immediately on demand

- Replacing employee manuals, policy documents, administrative files, and other forms of paper-based company information with their on-line equivalents, saving paper and reproduction expenses

If you have need for an Internet connection, you might well want to build an intranet to maintain consistency and reduce the costs of moving on and off the World Wide Web.

Intranet development costs do vary, based on the number of users that you connect to your intranet and the degree to which you need to upgrade your existing hardware. If you have already implemented an Ethernet-style LAN, your hardware upgrades will be minimal. To whatever extent your employees are already familiar with the Internet and browsers, your training costs will be reduced.

Operating Systems for Intranets

The server software and Web browsers that form the heart of an intranet require some kind of operating system to run. Fortunately, just about any network operating system will support Web servers and browsers, and multiple operating systems can run intranet browsers that make sharing Web-based information a breeze. The reason for this is that your intranet's TCP/IP protocols are the same regardless of the operating system. If you are running a LAN, there is little reason to change your operating system just to implement an intranet. The current versions of the most commonly-used network operating systems at a minimum support the TCP/IP protocol suite and include Web server and client software. In some cases, you will need to upgrade. These operating systems include:

InternetWare, also called NetWare Version 4.11. This sophisticated operating system provides integrated intranet server and client software and a reliable platform for third-party intranet development tools.

Windows NT Server 4 supports intranet services via its *Internet Information Server version 3.0*, which supports TCP/IP protocols, plus a package of development tools: a search engine (*Index Server*), an authoring tool (*FrontPage*), and a client browser (*Internet Explorer*). There are also built-in connections to optional intranet features, such as relational databases, mail server, catalog server, certificate server (for managing public encryption keys), and proxy server.

Windows NT Workstation 4 includes a limited version of the Internet Information Server called *Peer Web Services*, suitable for small intranets. Other development tools can be added using third-party products such as those described later in this chapter.

UNIX is the operating system of the Internet and thus support for intranet protocols is virtually guaranteed. There are flavors of UNIX that run on all standard hardware. A recent flavor of UNIX, called Linux, is available for free and has acquired a good reputation for reliability. UNIX-based Web servers include *WebForce* by Silicon Graphics and *Netra* by Sun Microsystems.

Windows 95 has built-in support for TCP/IP and Internet Explorer. It can be used as an intranet platform, but it is less robust. If your intranet has only a small handful of users, you can use Windows 95 as your server platform and run Internet Explorer as your client. However, performance will be noticeably less than what you would expect from, for example, Windows NT.

Intranet Software

Other intranet development applications that you will probably find useful include: a Web page authoring tool; a document manager and search engine for locating data within those many Web pages you soon will have; and a translator to move data between existing network databases and Web-based format. If you plan to develop your own intranet applications, you will need an Internet applications development tool, such as Java.

Web Page Authoring Tools

Web pages are built using a standard formatting language called Hyper-Text Markup Language (HTML). HTML uses commands, called *tags*, embedded within the content of a Web page to instruct browsers how to display that content. Content can include text, graphics, sound, video, animations, and various interactive forms, such as fields into which a user can enter information. This combination of tags and content is called the *source text* of a Web page. Figure 15.1 shows how raw HTML source text looks. Figure 15.2 shows how the same source text is displayed within a browser.

Although the HTML source text uses only ASCII characters, the language's tag structure and syntax make it a bit tedious and time-consuming to write directly from a keyboard using a text editor. Fortunately, there are several good HTML editors on the market that allow you to generate HTML source text by displaying content and formatting it using a graphics-based, drag-and-drop interface. These tools allow you to design a

FIGURE 15.1

A fragment of the HTML source text used to generate the home page for www.sybex.com

```
</HEAD>
<BODY BGCOLOR="#FFFFFF" TEXT="#004080" LINK="D70404" VLINK="#9F5F9F"
ALINK="#FFFF00">

<! --Computer Books/Software Downloads / Book Catalogs /
Programming / Technical / Mastering / Network press /
Strategies & Secrets / ABC / No experience required /
Developer Handbooks / MCSE / Games / Publishing / Self Help /
Tutorial Learning / Java / Windows NT / Windows 95 / NetWare /
Internet / Intranet / Multimedia / Hardware / Microsoft / Lotus /
SAP / Duke Nukem-->

<BASEFONT SIZE="3">
<CENTER>
<FONT SIZE=+1><I><B>Use this virtual desktop as your guide.
</B></I></FONT><BR>
<BR>

<A HREF="/cgi-bin/maps/index.map">
<IMG ISMAP SRC="/graphics/home1.jpb" BORDER="0"
ALT="The Sybex Home Page"></A>

<BR>
<H6><I>This area is maintained by
<A HREF="mailto:webmaster@sybex.com">The SyMaster</A></I></H6>
<H6><I>Copyright &copy; 1997 Sybex Inc.</I></H6>
<BR>
<BR>
<B><FONT FACE="Century Gothic" COLOR=#0080000 SIZE=-2>
Designed &amp; Develoepd with <A HREF="http://www.theavocado.com">
The <FONT SIZE=-1>Avocado</FONT></FONT></B></A>
</CENTER>
</BASEFONT>
</BODY>
</HTML>
```

page dynamically, all the while seeing how it will look in a browser. It is much more efficient to use one of these tools than to laboriously type up HTML text in a text editor and load it over and over into a separate browser to see how it will be displayed. HTML editors are indispensable for creating Web pages without wasting time.

As is the case with many programming tools that automatically generate source code, it is still enormously helpful if you have a working understanding of HTML. Often you will find it convenient to edit the generated source text in a text editor when you are ready to fine-tune your results.

FIGURE 15.2

How the HTML source text in Figure 15.1 is displayed in Internet Explorer Version 3.0

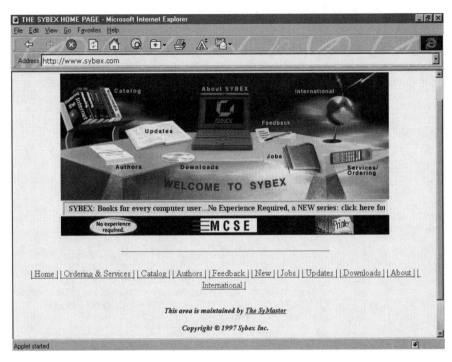

A good Web-authoring tool allows you to see and edit the source text in both its browser-displayed and raw-text forms. The authoring tool should include an easy way to generate links to other pages. Beyond this basic functionality, Web-authoring tools differ in the types of convenience features they support: Some will convert graphics files from non-supported formats like TIFF and BMP to browser-supported formats (GIF, JPEG). Some will perform useful error-trapping, like verifying that the links you are adding to a page can be found on your intranet Web site.

Here are a few commercial Web-authoring tools you may want to consider:

FrontPage (Microsoft Corp.) is a fully-featured Web site development tool and includes extensive graphics-editing capabilities. It uses a "wizard" interface to guide you through routine tasks, such as building and testing links, as well as more complex development tasks, such as discussion groups and interactive forms.

NetObjects Fusion (NetObjects, Inc.) looks and feels like a traditional desktop publishing program and includes tools for developing site-wide page definitions, to help your site's pages keep a consistent look.

SuiteSpot Server (Netscape Communications) is a package of intranet tools you use to organize intranet files, author Web pages, develop applications, and connect to network databases.

Visual InterDev (Microsoft Corp.) looks and feels like an Office 97 product. It is especially adept at creating pages that make extensive use of Microsoft's ActiveX controls, which are embedded applications that help perform tasks such as accessing databases on any server and displaying the results of queries in HTML format.

Web Factory Pro Image (Thunder & Lightning Co.) includes a split-screen window for simultaneous display of source text and Web page, a site management tool for checking page links, plus graphics editing and conversion. It is well suited for beginners because it includes several templates that offer basic Web site functionality right out of the box.

Word Processors as Web Authors

Commercial word processing applications are now assimilating Web page authoring applications the same way that they assimilated desktop publishing applications a few years ago. It's possible that stand-alone Web page authoring applications may soon no longer exist, having become features in word processors. Check out the Web page development features in the most recent versions of Corel's WordPerfect, Lotus's Word Pro, or Microsoft's Word 97. You may find that upgrading your old standby word processor is all you need to incorporate an adequate Web page developer into your intranet toolkit.

Search Engines

A search engine is software that gathers information from Web pages in an intranet. A search engine opens Web pages, extracts their links, and builds an indexed database of links and a summary of the content of the linked pages. Thereafter, you can access the search engine to extract specific links to Web pages that match various search criteria you specify.

From time to time, it is necessary to update the indexed database returned by the search engine. Depending on the size of your intranet and the degree to which you add and update Web pages, this can be a automated, daily task or one that can be done far less frequently, perhaps once every few weeks or so.

Different types of search engines can be programmed to retrieve greater or lesser quantities of information as they roam the intranet and build the indexed database. Some will exhaustively examine every link on every page that they find, then test the validity of the link, working down through the entire structure. Some will examine links more selectively; for example, the software can be programmed to bypass those links that lead only to pictures or sound files.

Search engines can gather different amounts of content from Web pages. They can read every single word in every page, a preset number of words from each page, just titles and headings, or simply the link name itself. The more information your search engine incorporates into the indexed database, the more complicated your searches through that index can be.

To start a search, call up a Web page in your browser that activates the search engine software. This Web page will include a form into which you enter a *search key* that will narrow the search in some way. For example, you might search for a key phrase that can appear in various pages' content, or a key topic likely to be found in a page's heading or title, or simply a range of dates when pages were created. Whatever the search key criteria used, the search engine must have built an index based on it or be able to build a compatible index on the fly.

The search engine displays the links that it finds in a results Web page. When the user clicks on of the displayed links, the browser displays the corresponding Web page.

Popular search engines such as Yahoo!, Alta Vista, and Infoseek are intended for use over the World Wide Web and as such have proven to be indispensable tools accessed by millions of users each day. The indexed databases maintained by these search engines are updated frequently, but there is no guarantee that a link to an Internet site will be active, or even still exist, when it is returned. Intranet search engines, on the other hand, are smaller and more reliable because of the private, closed nature of an intranet.

Here are two popular intranet search engines:

Excite (Excite, Inc.) is easy to install, supports natural-language searches ("How many salespeople are in Idaho next week?"), and sorts search results according to a weighted scale, estimating the accuracy of the match between the search key and the linked page. The database created by Excite's indexer is huge and requires about half again the amount of space currently occupied by your intranet pages.

Index Server (Microsoft Corp.) is included in the Windows NT Server 4 package and supports a full range of keyword queries, although natural-language queries are not available. It maintains its search index full time but requires that the NT server be running at all times. Index Server will also run under NT Workstation 4's Peer Web Server.

Common Gateway Interface

Business databases on local area networks exist in binary formats that are optimized to make queries as fast as possible, given the massive amounts of information they are designed to hold. (Refer to Chapter 13 for details on networked business databases.) As network technology developed, software vendors produced more and more front-end applications designed to make access to all that information easier than ever.

Owing in part to the binary nature of large business databases, Web software has lacked any native ability to access that information. However, vendors are now providing solutions to the problem in the form of database translators, software that translates Web-server queries into commands that the database server can understand and translates the results of those queries into HTML-compatible formats so that Web browsers can understand query results. The most popular of these translators is the *Common Gateway Interface,* also called CGI.

CGI is not a programming language. It is a programming standard for language commands that allow programmers to bridge the gap between traditional LAN database servers and Web-based browsers. A Web software programmer usually writes a script, or series of CGI commands, using a compiled language such as Java or C++ or an interpreted language such as UNIX's Perl. The script is then placed on your Web server in a directory reserved for CGI applications, usually named \CGI-BIN. The programmer or Web author may then include a link to the script on a Web page.

A *compiled* language requires that the programmer use a *compiler* to create a machine language executable from source code before the program can be run. An *interpreted* language will run in source code format with the assistance of a separate piece of software called the *language interpreter.* Interpreted languages like Perl are favored for creating CGI scripts because they can be tested and debugged on the fly, without the intermediate step of compiling a machine-language version each time the slightest change is made.

When a user clicks on a link, the Web server launches the script. For example, the script may display a form in the browser that asks the user to set up a query or collect new information to add to the database. After the user fills in the form, the application may test the data for accuracy and perform a variety of handy error-trapping routines before processing it any further.

At this point, the CGI script acts as a client to the network's database server. It makes a connection to the business database server and commands the server, using a database language like SQL, to honor the user's query or instruction.

The database server returns some result after executing the instructions. The CGI program on the Web server receives the result and reformats the data using whatever HTML tags are required and displays the result in the Web browser. The user may now treat the returned HTML page just like any other page in the Intranet.

Accessing Legacy Data

Many older networking technologies, especially mainframe systems, were developed without support for TCP/IP; it can be a challenge to find ways to use an intranet to access the information on these systems. In some cases, CGI scripts may work. The drawback to CGI scripts is that they tend to be database-specific, meaning that they are written to interact with one particular database server and will not necessarily work with other servers or mainframes. If you must collect data from a variety of older systems, you may need to write separate versions of CGI scripts for each one.

CGI scripts can be written to access data on mainframe systems. If you so desire, the CGI program can be written to include onscreen objects, such as pick buttons, to replicate the functions of the mainframe's terminal keys. The CGI program translates the data stream so that it appears to the mainframe as if coming from a terminal. The CGI program reformats information returned from the mainframe with HTML tags for display by the browser.

Another way to connect to mainframe systems is to use *terminal emulation software*. Terminal emulation software acts as a gateway to translate the data stream flowing over a connection between a TCP/IP browser and the mainframe. The emulation software translates TCP/IP instructions from the user into mainframe protocols (for example, IBM's Systems Network Architecture protocols sent to a 3270 mainframe), and the data returned by the mainframe is processed into normal TCP/IP datagrams for the intranet users. The result is that, while the connection remains active, the TCP/IP computer looks and acts like one of the mainframe's terminals.

If a connection to the legacy mainframe exists, and the above solutions aren't practical for some reason (you can't afford the programmer, time is of the essence, etc.) a manual, "brute force" solution can be employed:

1. Use available network commands to dump the data from the mainframe to text files on the intranet server.

2. Import the files into Web authoring tools and reformat them into HTML pages.

This takes the mainframe system "out of the loop." It works provided that you're no longer employing the mainframe to make changes and updates to the data or at least not doing it too often. If you use the mainframe to make changes to the data, you'll have to repeat the process for whatever data was changed.

Java

Java, a programming language developed by Sun Microsystems, has quickly evolved into the development language of choice for intranet and Internet developers. The main reason for its popularity is its platform-independence. A Java application is compiled like other compiled languages, but the compiled application still requires the services of a small, platform-specific Java interpreter before it will run. Java interpreters are available for just about any platform: PC, Mac, UNIX, OS/2, SPARC workstations.

At first it may seem clumsy that compiled software needs an additional interpreter to run, but it is a boon for developers. Once a Java interpreter is installed on various different platforms, a Java application need be compiled only once, and it will run fine on each platform (see Figure 15.3). Also, Java interpreters are small and can be embedded seamlessly within a Web browser, as is the case, for example, with Netscape Navigator. Once your Java-supporting browser is up and running, a Java program will run within it.

In addition to the time saved by not re-compiling an application separately for each platform, the independence of Java makes it a natural for distributing software across an intranet or Internet or for downloading on demand from a Web server that may be accessed by browsers running on different platforms.

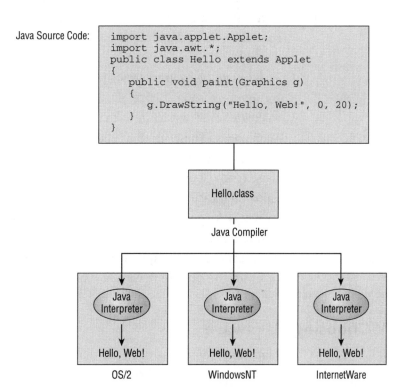

FIGURE 15.3

A single Java applet (HELLO.CLASS) can be compiled once, and it will run on different platforms because each platform has its own Java interpreter.

Java Source Code:

```
import java.applet.Applet;
import java.awt.*;
public class Hello extends Applet
{
    public void paint(Graphics g)
    {
        g.DrawString("Hello, Web!", 0, 20);
    }
}
```

Hello.class

Java Compiler

Java Interpreter — Hello, Web! — OS/2

Java Interpreter — Hello, Web! — WindowsNT

Java Interpreter — Hello, Web! — InternetWare

Java is an object-oriented language much like C++, with which it shares a number of syntactical similarities. It uses blocks of code that combine conceptual *properties* (buttons, scroll bars, intelligent icons) with *methods* (things that happen when the user does something) into various programming *objects* that are combined on the computer screen in a graphical user interface, to achieve some result when the user performs some action (clicking on an object with the mouse pointer, for example).

Unlike other object-oriented languages, Java is quite rigid in how the programmer can allocate memory. Java interpreters create a *Java Virtual Machine* (JVM) in which the application runs. The JVM gives the Java interpreter extensive control over the application's behavior, and it can monitor the Java application to be sure that it does not violate its boundaries, unintentionally create havoc, or accidentally crash the computer. Programmers used to traditional object-oriented languages have to make some adjustments to get used to the Java interpreter's rigid memory rules.

Java can be used to create just about any application; and as long as the interpreter is available, the application will run. Java is commonly used to create small applications that run within browsers and can be linked to Web pages. These small applications are called *applets*. Applets can scroll text across your screen, animate icons, or produce sounds. While these types of applications add interest to Web pages, they have limited value on most business intranets. On an intranet, Java is more often used to access corporate databases or update, in real time, corporate information retrieved from the Internet. For example, many financial information intranets use a Java applet to reproduce a scrolling stock market ticker or up-to-the-minute news headlines on the browser's screen.

Choosing Hardware

Hardware requirements for intranets are virtually the same as those for local area networks: You will need a Web server, client workstations, Ethernet cards, and cabling. One notable exception: If you have a Macintosh LocalTalk network, you will need to upgrade to an Ethernet-based system.

A capable Web server would have a fast processor, such as a Pentium II CPU running at least 133MHz, 64MB RAM, and 2GB hard disk storage space. If you plan to allow direct access to the server, rather than across the network, add a medium-quality PCI video card with at least 1MB of VRAM, moderate VGA resolution (800×600 is adequate) with a compatible VGA-style monitor.

Intranet client hardware should be geared toward fastest possible graphics display. A fast CPU will help; again 133MHz is a good starting point. A large RAM will also help performance; 32MB is safe minimum if your current client machines can accept it; otherwise, get the most that your current machines will accept. Economical video cards with 2–4MB VRAM are available and are a good value for their performance. Unless your business calls for it, you probably can get by without the ultra-high performance video cards usually reserved for engineering and graphic arts workstations. Large hard disks are a must; get the biggest you can afford. 2GB is a good starting point.

Monitors are a matter of individual taste. Most standard VGA monitors sold by reliable vendors will not cause eye strain; but if you are shopping for new monitors, make comparisons and let the users choose the ones they like best. High graphics resolution (1800×1200 and higher) and large monitors are nice because browsers tend to use up onscreen real estate and you will want as much screen area as you can get to display the content of your Web pages. However, this type of video adds considerably to your costs if you have to buy it for new machines or add it to existing machines.

Web pages can include some very sophisticated sound and animation. Most businesses don't need this kind of multimedia functionality; but if yours does, be prepared to add sound cards and speakers to the price of your purchases or upgrades. Sound cards and speakers, like monitors, are largely a matter of individual taste. In general, try to avoid these bells and whistles when you're starting out; developing animations and sound for your internal business pages can result in some very distracting features, not to mention that they eat up money and development time. You can always add them later when you've acquired more experience developing your intranet and can see where such niceties would actually be profitable.

Hardware requirements are the same for servers and clients, so you can refer back to Chapter 6 for more information on servers and Chapter 4 for more information on workstation clients. The information about network hardware requirements in those chapters applies equally well to intranets.

Intranet Applications

Intranet Applications is a fast-growing industry. As this book is being written, several vendors are competing to introduce a new style of client workstation called the NetPC: essentially, a "GUI-based dumb" terminal that will not process data on its own but rather access and process remotely-stored data entirely via Internet/intranet protocols. In theory, the NetPC will eliminate the administrative headaches associated with currently-in-use "smart" workstations. Smart workstations process independently of the network and require frequent individual attention from support staff. To make the NetPC workstation a practical reality, vendors will have to make it profitable to run sophisticated business applications like spreadsheets, word processors, and databases within browsers across TCP/IP connections.

Currently, the most widely-used intranet applications support collaborative processes. These include intranet e-mail and various groupware services, such as discussion software, videoconferencing, and training software.

Intranet E-Mail

Intranet e-mail is based on the Simple Mail Transfer Protocol (SMTP), a specialized protocol in the TCP/IP protocol suite that is reserved for delivering messages to workstations, or Post Office Protocol (POP), which stores messages on servers for collection by recipients. Traditional LANs use mature e-mail systems such as cc:Mail, Lotus Notes, or

Microsoft Mail. These mail applications are rich in formatting, addressing, storing, and security features and can be used to generate intranet mail messages. However, if you need only straightforward, point-to-point messaging between intranet workstations, you may want to look into other less-expensive mail message generators, such as Eudora Pro and Pegasus Mail, which may be adequate for your needs.

Intranet e-mail messages are created on client workstations, using a TCP/IP compliant message-generating application called a *mail user agent* (MUA). The mail applications mentioned in the previous paragraph are all capable of generating mail messages for intranet transfer. MUAs have, at a minimum, simple text-editing features for composing e-mail messages, plus features like address books and abbreviated domain names that make addressing your messages easier.

After the user composes the message and specifies an address, the MUA sends it to the Web server. The Web server includes special software called a *mail transfer agent* (MTA), which checks the message's address and forwards it to one of two places: If the message is to be sent out over the Internet, the message is directed to the Internet gateway. If the message is addressed to a workstation on the intranet, the message is directed to another Web server program called the *mail delivery agent* (MDA).

The MDA transfers the message to the recipient workstation, where the recipient's MUA collects it and alerts the recipient workstation that a message has been received. The recipient can read the message at once or store it in a file for reading later.

Some intranets use Post Office Protocol to store messages in separate directories on the Web server. Each client uses a MUA to access the server's mail directory from time to time to collect messages.

E-mail messaging has become a major means of business communication and is now required to handle transfer of pictures, sounds, spreadsheets, and word processing documents, which are all stored in binary files. Unfortunately, the SMTP protocol is designed to handle transfer of plain ASCII text files only. To send binary files over an intranet, you must translate them into their ASCII equivalents. There are a variety of encoding methods available, and modern MUAs have the most common encoding methods built right in.

Two common binary coding schemes are:

UUENCODE/UUDECODE is a coding system originally developed for UNIX and ported to other platforms. Nowadays, it is used with message systems that don't have their own built-in encoding schemes.

Multipurpose Internet Mail Extension (MIME) uses a coding scheme called *base64,* which is more robust and designed to be platform-independent. It is the standard built-in encoding scheme for modern MUAs.

If you are using an up-to-date MUA, you need only instruct the MUA to attach a binary file to the message and the MUA will handle the encoding process automatically. The recipient's MUA must have the same coding features as the sender in order to decode and read the binary file; with modern MUAs, this is not likely to be a problem.

Intranet Groupware

Intranet groupware is a term that encompasses a growing body of sophisticated collaborative applications; for example, two possible applications are described in this section: discussion software and videoconferencing. Intranet groupware helps people share common documents securely and efficiently and communicate ideas more freely using standardized Web-based interfaces.

Discussion Software   Discussion Software is similar to the newsgroup software found on the Internet. Discussion messages are retained indefinitely on a server; and as users reply to messages, the software links these replies together into a database that can be searched, sorted, and archived. A set of linked messages in this database is called a *message* *thread.* Most discussion software packages attempt to link to existing e-mail systems, in order to eliminate the need to learn new interfaces.

Because group discussion packages are built around databases, they can also be used to manage non-message-based information, such as an internal corporate bulletin board or a suggestion box.

Messages in discussion software can include links to Web pages. When a user clicks on the link, the browser is launched and the Web page appears automatically. Messages threads can extend beyond the intranet to the Internet, through server gateways. Message threads can be public (meaning accessible to everybody on the intranet) or private (usually meaning restricted by passwords). In some cases, highly confidential message threads may be locked behind firewalls. Refer to Chapter 16 for more information on intranet firewalls.

Discussion software is overseen by a network administrator, sometimes called a *threadmaster.* Threadmasters control access to, as well as the content of, message threads on the server. These two products also act as historians and librarians, archiving old message threads or deleting those that serve no further purpose.

Examples of discussion software include:

Lotus Notes (Lotus Development Corp.) and **TeamWare** (Team-Ware), which include discussion group features in their extensive set of collaborative group functions. These two products are useful if you are considering the purchase of a full-featured, turnkey group collaboration system.

Collabra Share (Collabra Software) and **TeamTalk** (Trax Softworks) work by adding discussion functions to existing e-mail programs.

Conference+ (The Mesa Group) adds discussion functions to Microsoft Mail only.

Videoconferencing   Videoconferencing combines real-time video transmissions and sound to create virtual meetings, demonstrations, and training over intranets. Videoconferencing requires additional hardware—video cameras, sound cards, and microphones—plus software to display video-based images through workstations' graphics cards.

The earliest (and still one of the most popular) of videoconferencing applications is CU-See-Me. CU-See-Me runs on workstations with attached video cameras and microphones. The input from workstations is managed on the server by software called the *multimedia reflector*. The reflector manages multiple conference participants, and each one can see all the others in a particular conference. The videoconference data is not transferred using TCP/IP protocols. Because it is "live," there is not much purpose in asking that corrupted packets of data be re-sent. Instead, the data is transmitted using User Datagram Protocol (UDP), which simply passes the data along without checking for errors.

The video camera and microphone translate analog video images and sounds into digital code, then CU-See-Me compresses the digital information and transports it across the intranet. The same software on the receiving end directs output of the digital signals on the recipient's monitor and speakers.

The reflector is configurable by the network administrator who can control access like a threadmaster can control it in to discussion software: For example, the administrator can password-protect private conferences and scheduling conferences in advance. The administrator can also control the degree to which the intranet's communication capability can be devoted exclusively to videoconference signals. This allows the administrator to balance the need for high-quality conference signals with the need to not completely tie up an intranet's bandwidth with videoconferencing signals.

One-to-one videoconferencing is easier because a reflector is not required. If you are having a videoconference with only one other user, you can use the CU-See-Me software to make a direct link to the other person's workstation.

You can use reflectors in creative ways. A reflector has the capability of sending real-time signals to multiple workstations, and it is possible to use them to "broadcast" more than just video and sound. You can use CU-See-Me software to broadcast the content of shared files of any type to collaborators. The collaborators can edit these files normally, and others in the conference can see the changes in real-time. This process is sometimes referred to as *whiteboard conferencing.*

While reducing the need for in-person collaborations, this technology can increase the amount of collaboration that can take place, by reducing the scheduling and travel efforts necessary to get people together. This technology, which uses live collaborators or video and sound recordings, can be used to train employees at their workstations, keep them informed, and provide instant feedback to managers. While still in the development stage, this intranet application shows tremendous potential.

When businesspeople imagine the possibilities of videoconferencing, they naturally visualize conferences between far-flung collaborators many miles apart. Wide-area intranets do exist, but for many businesses, linking collaborators that are miles apart will involve using the Internet rather than an expensive, wide-area intranet. Internet-based videoconferencing is possible today, but unfortunately the performance leaves much to be desired because of the Internet's limited bandwidth, which is already crowded in the extreme. But the trends are clear, and the development of high-performance Internet videoconferencing is not that far in the future.

Where to Go from Here

Do you need an intranet? If you have a LAN and are completely satisfied with its ability to help your business run profitably, then you may be able to get by without one for the time being. On the other hand, if you are just setting up your network, if you would like to see your employees collaborate and communicate more efficiently, or if you are planning to move your business presence onto the World Wide Web, an intranet is in your near future. The information in this chapter is intended to give you some idea how an intranet may be able to support your business and make it more productive.

If you currently use a LAN, you will be happy to know that developing an intranet does not require that you scrap your investment. Intranets expand the abilities of existing LANs and in many way complement them. If this seems interesting to you, the first step is to see how you can configure your existing LAN to support TCP/IP protocols, if it does not do so already. Windows NT has the advantage here; but NetWare has developed many tools that allow you to create a powerful corporate intranet. UNIX-based LANs are natural intranet platforms and will accommodate TCP/IP-based software with little if any trouble.

If you are developing a LAN from scratch, be aware that many traditional network applications, particularly e-mail and conferencing, are being replaced by less expensive and easier-to-maintain intranet applications. You will still need a robust network operating system, and many business applications (for example, spreadsheets, word processors, large server databases) are not yet browser-based. When evaluating any network hardware and software, consider features that support intranet-based collaboration as a plus.

Intranets, because of their open and accessible nature, present very special security and management problems. You will look at these issues in the next chapter.

For Further Reading

For the moment, intranets are *the* hot topic. There are hundreds of books on the subject, and you can be sure every bookseller that carries computer books has a large selection. The following list is nowhere near exhaustive or even representative, but these books are worth a look if you're planning to delve deeper into the topic. It will be worth your while to invest some time browsing and skimming through the titles you find in various bookstores.

- Davis, Stephen R. *Learn Java Now*. Microsoft Press, 1997.

- Dyson, Peter, Pat Coleman, and Len Gilbert. *The ABCs of Intranets*. Sybex, 1997.

- Gaskin, James E. *The Complete Guide to NetWare 4.11/ IntranetWare*. 2d ed. Sybex, 1996.

- Kabir, Mohammed J. *CGI Primer Plus for Windows*. Waite Group Press, 1996.

- Minasi, Mark, Christa Anderson, and Elizabeth Creegan. *Mastering Windows NT Server 4*. 4th ed. Sybex, 1997.

- Morris, Bruce. *HTML in Action*. Microsoft Press, 1996.

- Ross, John. *The ABCs of Microsoft Internet Explorer 4*. 2d ed. Sybex, 1997.

- Stern, Morgan and Tom Rasmussen. *Building Intranets on NT, NetWare and Solaris: An Administrator's Guide*. Sybex, 1996.

- Weisskopf, Gene. *The ABCs of FrontPage97*. Sybex, 1997.

CASE STUDY

Everyone at GAB has reason to be interested in developing an intranet on their NT LAN platform. They see three advantages in particular:

- Intranet e-mail offers the potential of easy-to-manage conferencing and scheduling.

- Discussion software will allow them to keep track of collaborations and meetings.

- Digital forms will help them cut back on the vast amount of paper they use.

Mature, complex collaboration software like Lotus Notes is probably overkill for an office as small as GAB's, even though its range of features is tempting. A more economical approach would be to implement a simpler system like Microsoft Mail and to add a robust program like Collabra Share to manage their discussion databases and scheduling. GAB's office manager is especially excited about reducing the company's paper load. Already she is planning to convert GAB's marketing materials to Web pages. For example, GAB's mailers and advertising brochures, which always seem to require

updating before they can be used, can be kept up to date online and printed in smaller quantities as needed, saving time and avoiding waste. As GAB develops its much-anticipated Web site, marketing Web pages can be made accessible from the World Wide Web, with the addition of forms to retrieve information from potential customers and handle queries from existing customers. Such Web-based interactivity reduces both paper and mailing costs. Many of GAB's internal business records can be transferred to non-paper-based formats. Employee policy manuals and memoranda, employment history files, and client files can be kept online, saving paper and space. Search engines will make it easier to look up records.

Most importantly, GAB, as an accounting office, uses hundreds of paper forms. Most of these forms (especially tax forms) are already available in digital format. All these forms can be stored on the Web server and accessed, either to print out as blank forms whenever needed, or filled out over the intranet and stored in GAB's database. With digital forms, GAB saves money and time, has a much easier time keeping accounting forms up to date, and even reclaims some space in the office because stacks of forms no longer have to be stored on site.

CHAPTER

16

Maintenance & Security

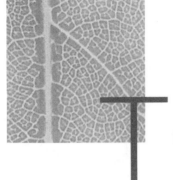

The keys to a successful intranet are:

- Clear, simple design
- Relevant, up-to-date content
- Appropriate levels of security

An individual, called a *Webmaster,* can administer a small (20–40 users) to medium-sized (40–70 users) intranet and handle the design, content, and security tasks. Much larger intranets will require a team-based approach, wherein the Webmaster maintains standards and supports users and receives assistance from part-time or full-time content authors, page designers, and programmers. This chapter discusses common issues Webmasters are likely to confront regarding intranet design, content, and security.

Design

Your intranet has two design levels: page layout and link organization. If you have never done it before, you may think it would be difficult to design a good intranet, but in practice the task need not be all that daunting. Just follow two classic business rules: Plan ahead and keep things simple.

Using Standard Client Software

Although an intranet will support all kinds of different hardware platforms, you will find it easier to maintain your intranet if everyone uses the same version of the same Web browser. Although different Web browsers have remarkably similar features and capabilities, minor differences do occur and they can affect the performance of your intranet. There are many advantages to standardizing on a single brand of Web browser:

- It takes less time to design and test Web pages because you know that one page will work consistently throughout your intranet.

- Implementing browser upgrades is easier, faster, and less costly: If everyone has the same browser, you can post an upgrade on the server and users can download the latest version from their client workstations.

- Training is easier and less costly. You need to maintain only one browser-training program for your whole company.

- Software support is easier. If users discover a problem with a Web page, they can report it over the intranet to the Webmaster, who can fix the offending page. The solution or work-around is instantly distributed company-wide.

Web Page Layout

Clarity and content, not dazzling visuals, are what count most on your company's in-house Web pages. Unless your page content is extremely complex, you probably don't need a professional Web site designer to format your in-house Web pages. However, it may be well worth your while to hire a professional designer to create marketing and advertising Web pages, whose purpose is to impress potential customers as well as impart corporate information.

If you are truly design-impaired, a number of good books will show you enough of the basics to get you started; for example, *Mastering Web Design,* by John McCoy, published by Sybex, is a good place to start. Remember that the design rules that make your real-world business office attractive and productive make intranets attractive and productive as well: Both offices and intranets should be clean, uncluttered, and unified in look and feel. Figure 16.1 shows an acceptable design for an intranet home page. Notice that there are no fancy graphics, just a simple logo and some separator lines to draw the eye into the page; other than that, this home page is all business.

Compare this home page with a typical commercial home page on the Internet, such as the Sybex home page illustrated in Figure 16.2. The Internet home page is much flashier so that it will excite potential customers and promote book sales. A promotional-style page, although much more fun to design, is simply too distracting for internal business use.

FIGURE 16.1

A typical home page is simple, with lots of white space and a menu of links to content-driven pages.

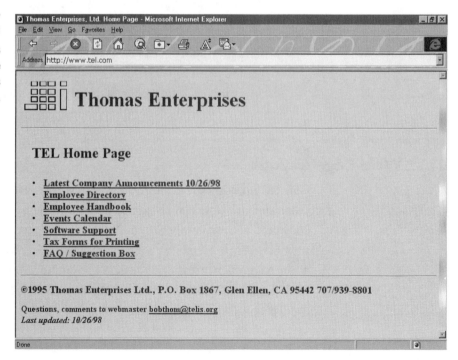

FIGURE 16.2

A commercial home page

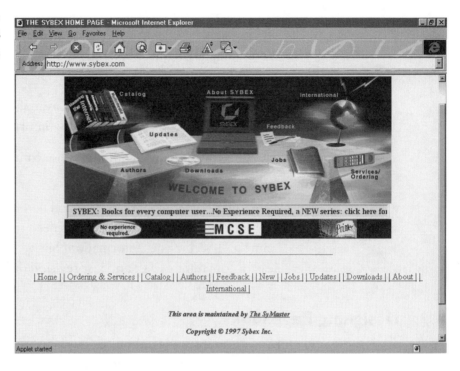

How Not to Design a Web Page

Just for fun, try visiting one of the many Web sites devoted to collecting examples of truly terrible Web page designs. You can learn a lot from studying the mistakes of others. For starters, try

        http://www.gormon.org.uk/bad.html

Most sites that collect bad pages have links to other sites with similar intent, enabling you to surf merrily through the worst of the Web until you finally can't take it anymore. Ironically, some of the "elect" represented on these sites take pride in having been named among the very worst—proving yet again there is no accounting for taste.

A good home page will include at least the following:

- Your company name, phone number, mailing address, and e-mail address.

- An overview of what information is available on the site, plus links to the various categories of company information.

- How to contract the Webmaster: phone number, extension, and e-mail address.

- Copyright owner, copyright date and date the page was last revised. (Not all of your Web pages need to repeat your company name and Webmaster information, but all of them should have at least a copyright owner and last-revision date.)

Designing Page Links

Before you start inserting links into your intranet pages, walk away from the computer and lay out your intranet's *site map* on paper. The site map is simply a diagram of the links between Web pages. Figure 16.3 shows how a site map might look.

This preliminary site map need not be pretty. It only needs to convey to you a sense of how your Web pages fit together intuitively and logically. While setting up your site map on paper, you can focus on making sure your pages' links serve your intranet's overall organization. Experiment with alternative structures. Do all this before sitting down to the keyboard and embedding links in pages.

Different types of information require different organizational methods. If you are putting together a training site, create a linear design, moving progressively from one topic to the next, plus a table of contents containing links to all topics so that a trainee can leave and return to a specific page if training is interrupted. If you are putting together a catalog of pages (for example, an employee directory, a parts and supplies list, or group technical support bulletins), set up a hierarchical design for

FIGURE 16.3

A Site Map

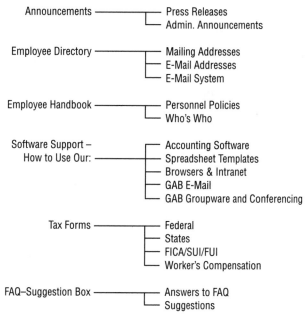

your page links, with a catalog page of general categories leading to pages with lists of links to more specific items of information.

All pages on your intranet should contain a link back to the home page. This link is really an "escape hatch" that prevents the user from getting stuck on some remote Web page with no way to get back other than repeatedly clicking their browser's Back button.

Intranets are in a constant state of evolution. As your intranet grows, you may confront organizational issues that force you to reevaluate your design. It is important that your intranet reflect the way your company uses information and will likely use it in the future so that it can evolve in a natural, logical progression. Be flexible, but don't go overboard on linking. Follow a logical pattern. Don't link because you can, link because you must. Finally, never link to sites that say "under construction"—it annoys users. Don't make mention of a new page until it's ready to be visited.

Content

What should users find on your intranet? It is usually not difficult to come up with information that ought to go on your intranet; more likely, the problem is making time to get it all in there as quickly as you can.

You can begin to develop content by constructing pages that replace or at least replicate your company's print-based information. Here are some typical examples:

- Personnel Handbook

- Corporate Policies

- Administrative Forms

- Employee Directory

- Announcements and Bulletin Board Items

- Training Manuals

- Newsletter

- Calendar of Events

- Minutes of Meetings

- Frequently-Asked Questions

- Intranet Site Map

- Contact Database, with forms for entering and updating

- Meeting Schedule Database

- Chat Room (welcome to the virtual water cooler)

- Suggestion Box Database

- Software Upgrade Page

- Technical Support Page

- File Download Page

If your intranet is typical, the number of additional ideas for content will snowball quickly. As your users become accustomed to the convenience of intranet-based sources of information, you can expect plenty of feedback regarding what content they need and how well you're living up to their expectations.

Maintenance and Troubleshooting

Maintaining your intranet involves several key tasks:

- Backing up intranet pages and other critical files

- Installing and configuring browsers, servers, and software

- Optimizing performance

All of this requires a great deal of time and energy and some money. Certainly, designing and implementing your intranet is a full-time job. Testing and deploying Web pages can take hours.

Every intranet is unique in some way (just as every company has its own unique features), so no one can tell you precisely how much time you will need to keep your mature intranet up and running. You can expect to spend more time if your users are inexperienced or if your system is large or complex. In the long run, it is cheaper to keep your intranet simple at first and let it grow slowly. Many companies will find that even though an intranet is simpler than a full-scale local area network, its upkeep is a full time job.

Network backups were discussed in detail in Chapter 12, and everything that applies to backing up networks in general applies to backing up your Web pages. Maintaining a regular backup schedule, as described in Chapter 12, is far easier and cheaper than losing critical data.

Installing and Configuring Intranet Browser Software

Browser software is easy to install, but a little tricky to configure. The two major browsers, Netscape Navigator and Internet Explorer, are easy to obtain and upgrade. Navigator is economically priced and available from just about any software distributor; or, if you have an Internet connection already, you can download Navigator from Netscape's site:

```
http://cgi.netscape.com/cgi-bin/123.cgi
```

Explorer can be downloaded for free from Microsoft's Internet site:

```
http://microsoft.com/ie
```

Both have easy-to-follow, menu-driven installation programs with extensive help menus.

To upgrade either one of these browsers, revisit their sites from time to time to see if a new version has become available. You will find a lot of information on upgrades plus other information on interesting add-on products you can download.

If possible, try to schedule your downloads early in the morning or late at night. There are fewer people accessing these popular sites during off-peak hours, and your download will likely go more quickly and smoothly.

Installing and Configuring Intranet Server Software

Netscape's Web server software is called *FastTrack Server*. FastTrack Server requires either Windows NT or Windows 95 as its operating system, and your server hardware must have at least 32MB of RAM available.

FastTrack Server includes many important intranet management features:

Server Settings allows you to view and optimize server performance.

Access Control allows you to verify users and restrict access to specified files.

Encryption allows you to encode transactions for security purposes.

Programs allows you to run Java and CGI applications and specify their location on the server's hard disk.

Server Status allows you to monitor activity on your intranet and generate reports on usage and errors.

Content Management allows you to specify the locations of your intranet's content pages and manage URL addresses.

Microsoft's Web server software is called *Internet Information Server* (IIS). It is bundled with Windows NT Server, and your server hardware should make at least 32MB of RAM available for NT plus IIS.

IIS expands Windows NT's standard file system and security features to include support for IP addressing of intranet connections. You can manage settings for the following IIS-specific features:

Service Properties allows you to specify service timeouts, maximum number of users, and user passwords for logging on.

Directory Properties allows you to specify a default startup document to appear in browsers that do not request a specific document when logging on and whether to allow users to browse directories by means of a hypertext listing.

Logging Properties allows you to monitor user activity in a log file.

Advanced Properties allows you to restrict access based on users' IP addresses.

Messages Properties allows you to specify the content and visibility of system messages to users that appear when they log on, log off, or a maximum number of connections has been reached.

Optimizing Performance

Computers are faster than ever; blindingly fast compared to the computers of just a few years ago. Yet, no matter how fast these machines run, sooner or later they seem to be too slow. Performance is perception.

The best way to monitor your intranet's performance is to use it yourself, often. When you are a regular user, you have a user's perspective and will see ways to improve things that may not be so obvious from a developer's or administrator's perspective.

On the hardware level, your intranet server will run fastest with the most RAM and the fastest possible hard disks you can afford. Performance will also vary from workstation to workstation, depending on each client's RAM size, video card type, VRAM size, bus type, and hard disk speed. Improving performance at the hardware level is usually constrained by budgetary concerns. However, there are some things you can do to help your intranet run at top speed, no matter what hardware you are using:

Use graphics sparingly. Graphics should convey information, not just "enhance" your pages or make them more interesting.

Keep graphics files small. Line art and charts in small GIF-format files will load faster than scanned full-color photographs stored in big JPEG-format files.

Keep pages at a reasonable length. Most users will prefer clicking on a series of links to pages that load quickly, rather than waiting for extra-large pages to load and then scrolling and scrolling through a seemingly endless page searching for information. Pages, on average, should be a maximum of two or three screenfuls in length.

Don't run TSRs on the server. Memory-hogging, terminate-and-stay-resident software (for example, that fancy screen saver) steal performance resources. (Turn the server's monitor off instead.)

Turn off unused services. Some server software turns selected services on by default, but you may not need them on your system. For example, if your Web server doesn't have a printer attached, turn off the server's print queue. If you don't need extra protocol services like FTP and Gopher, turn those off as well.

Time out inactive users. Sooner or later, some users will walk away from their desks while the intranet connection is active. If a user has had no activity for a reasonable amount of time, have the system log them off automatically.

Diagnostic and performance monitoring utilities are available for the network operating systems described in this book. They all are designed to analyze network usage and report how network resources are being allocated. For example, Windows NT Server includes four:

Task Manager will report how each application and thread on your system is using memory and the percentage of processor time devoted to each.

Performance Monitor reports how well each system component is performing and can signal you when performance drops below a specified level.

Network Monitor captures and displays packets from the network's data stream. You can analyze the displayed data to detect the source of problems relating to protocol incompatibilities or possible corruption during transmission.

Server Manager keeps track of how users are deploying network components, such as shared printers or storage devices.

Add-on server software is available that will examine the header of every packet that is sent along your intranet and store the results in a database for later analysis. Software of this type will allow you to select the types of packets that will be tracked and which types will be ignored; it all depends on what information you, as the administrator, deem important enough to monitor this thoroughly. For example, you might track e-mail and HTTP packets only and ignore FTP and audio/video packets because there are too few to be of much concern.

Using packet-monitoring software, you can determine which sites are being visited most often and when and how heavy the data traffic is at any given hour or between any given set of sites. You can use this information to determine if additional servers might be useful to handle traffic between specific sites or to specialize in certain services, like e-mail.

Whatever tools you elect to use, generate reports regularly and store the results in your network system log. You may spot interesting usage trends over time, and this information can suggest ways to adjust your network's configuration settings to improve performance.

Test, test, and test again—this golden rule of computing applies to your intranet as much it does to any other aspect of network development. Try bringing in a few select users with different levels of expertise and have them run your setup, offering their comments and criticisms, especially with regard to ease of use and intuitive understanding. Do this before giving access to all your network's workstations.

Security

If your business is like most, the data on your intranet is most at risk of accidental loss or damage through simple carelessness or misunderstanding.

Employees may sometimes snoop or attempt to expunge embarrassing information, but few want to do malicious harm. Reliable backups are of supreme importance. However, most managers will want to go beyond simply keeping good backups, to limiting access to certain types of information. In some cases (for example, your employees' personnel files or company trade secrets), information is of such a personal or sensitive nature it must be kept confidential.

Any risk of malicious damage to your data is likely to come from outside your company via the Internet. The Internet is something like a new Wild West. A small number of ill-intentioned individuals have the potential to do great damage, and the threat they represent, whatever its statistical likelihood of affecting your company, must be taken into account. You could, of course, simply not connect your intranet to the Internet and thus completely eliminate that aspect of the risk. Beyond that, there are four essential ways you can restrict access to information on your intranet from internal and external sources:

- Access control

- Enhanced passwords

- Encryption

- Firewalls

This following sections offer you a brief introduction to each of these security measures.

Access Controls in Server Software

Any good Web server software will allow you to include and exclude users based on some set of unique criteria. For example, Internet Information Server in Windows NT Server 4 allows you to identify ranges of IP addresses to include or exclude using the advanced tab on its Service Properties Sheet. You can choose to allow access to all except those addresses you specifically exclude, or you can deny access to all except those addresses you specifically allow.

This is IIS's first line of defense. It checks the IP header of every packet it receives against this list to see if it is from a permitted site, before sending it on to its intended destination or rejecting it as not from an approved IP address. You can also further restrict access from any particular IP address to only a specific set of users, who identify themselves using passwords as being able to legitimately log on from any given IP address.

Netscape FastTrack works in a more traditional way: by building a database of user names and passwords and allowing you to control what kinds of access each user has to any given set of files. You can block access to a site, or a specified set of sites, from all users except those you specifically name. Alternatively, you can allow anyone to have access except those you specifically exclude. FastTrack eases this process by allowing you to classify users into named groups (with group titles like Administration, Accounting, Shipping/Receiving, and the like).

Security Features in Web Browsers

At the browser level, there are some means of keeping data on workstations secure. The primary threat to workstation data comes from applets, small programs downloaded from the Internet and designed to run within browsers. Most applets downloaded from the Internet are benign, but it is possible for an intruder to download an applet whose purpose is to destroy data or reveal confidential information. To combat this, browsers include some means of checking applets for possible danger to your system.

The current version of Sun Microsystems' Java programming language allows programmers to add digital signatures to their applets, as a means of verifying the legitimacy of their source and thus their benign intent. A digital signature is an identification code embedded within an applet. These ID codes are registered with an independent software certification company, such as VeriSign, a Silicon Valley company that performs security checks on commercial software developers and issues licenses to use registered digital signatures.

In its default setting, Internet Explorer checks for digital signatures in all downloaded applets. You can configure your browser to restrict downloading of applets to those that carry specific digital signatures that you have approved. If an applet's digital signature is not on your list, your browser can provide warnings, allow you to add the new digital signature to your approved list, or refuse the download altogether.

Netscape uses a similar technology, called object signing, to restrict downloads. In addition, object signing allows you to restrict which areas of your hard disk may accept downloaded applets, keeping applets from having access to sensitive areas of your hard disk.

If your intranet design includes Internet access and you want the convenience of applet technology, you should look into software that manages applet security across intranets. For example, a program called UniShield, by Network Information Technology, allows you to analyze and classify downloaded applets according to user-configurable levels of security. Access to applets on your intranet can be restricted based on the security classification assigned by the intranet manager.

Enhancing Password Protection on Your Intranet

Most access control schemes require some kind of password system to determine who has legitimate access. General rules for managing network security and password systems were discussed in Chapter 12; these ideas apply equally well to intranets. However, as you have seen, the open nature of intranet protocols and standards makes it easy for you to configure intranets for access by remote users; in doing so, you make your intranet more vulnerable to unwanted intruders. Intruders can, with a moderately high degree of skill, eavesdrop on intranet traffic using just about any connection that is made available by the server. They do this using the same monitoring software used legitimately by managers to analyze packet traffic, then they replay copies of selected packets back to the server, mimicking the legitimate session at their own address. If you believe your intranet may be vulnerable to such a threat, you can add additional security measures, such as *remote call backs* and *challenge handshaking*, to your battery of password-based security measures.

A call back system can be useful if your intranet needs to be accessed by employees who telecommute from a fixed location (such as a home office) using a modem. The employee dials up your intranet, logs in, and enters the correct password. After the server verifies the password, it ends the connection and calls the employee back, using a previously stored phone number linked to that particular password. This insures that no one calling in from a remote location is attempting to masquerade as the employee, since the server will always dial back to the predesignated return number.

Challenge handshaking is a system whereby the server continually tests the client computer as long as the connection is active. This system helps prevent unauthorized users from using monitoring software to pick up packet traffic along the network, and replaying it to the server to "trick" the server into believing that the additional session is legitimate. In a challenging handshaking system, when a user first logs on from any location, the server generates a random encryption key. After the user enters the password, the server encrypts the password according to the key and stores the results on the client. Thereafter, from time to time, the server again compares the encrypted password in its own records with the one stored on the client. If they still match, the session continues. If the encrypted client password can't be found or no longer matches the server password, it means that an unauthorized user is monitoring the session. The server immediately disconnects.

A hardware-based challenge handshaking system can be especially useful when a remote user must call up on a portable machine from different areas. In such a case, the server cannot call back because there is no way to know the call back number in advance. Such a user could carry a card similar to a bank ATM card, with an encrypted password on a magnetic strip in the back. To enter the correct password, the user slides the ID card through an attached card reader. After the user has logged into the system, the server may ask the user to periodically reinsert the card to verify the password and the legitimacy of the connection.

If the correct password is not returned to the server after a specified amount of time, the server takes this as evidence the session is being monitored and cancels the session.

Encryption

Encryption is another means of frustrating the attention of unwanted eavesdroppers on your intranet. Encryption is a system of translating messages into random-looking unintelligible characters, using a *key*. Keys are special character strings or complex mathematical formulas that replace characters in messages. The encryption keys are so complex that unless you have the key, you cannot decrypt the message. Both the sender and the receiver must know the key before they can communicate with encrypted messages.

When sender and receiver are using the exact same key, the encryption is called *symmetrical*. A one-key system like DES is sufficient for private data-sharing over your intranet, but it is difficult to implement if you are accessing the Internet at large; if you send an encrypted message to someone who doesn't already have the key, at some point you must also send the decrypting key. If you send the key over the Internet, you risk making it vulnerable to eavesdroppers, and you pretty much defeat the purpose of encrypting the message.

To overcome this problem, you can use a two-key, or *asymmetrical*, system. A two-key system encrypts messages using a pair of keys; messages that are encrypted by one can only be decrypted by the other. One key is called the *public* key and is freely distributed. The other key is called the *private* key and is kept completely secure.

Two-key encryption systems can be used in a variety of ways. One of the most popular ways is called *RSA encryption* (named after its inventors: Ronald Rivest, Adi Shamir, and Leonard Adleman). RSA encryption works like this:

1. A sender begins by passing a message through a special algorithm called a *hash function*. The hash function returns a number called a *message digest*, similar to a checksum; it can be used to verify that the original message has not been tampered with.

2. The sender then uses a private key to encrypt the message digest. This produces an encrypted *digital signature*: that is, the encrypted message digest, which could only have been encrypted by the sender's private key.

3. The sender then generates a completely new random key. The sender uses this new key to encrypt the original message along with the digital signature. Only this new random key can decrypt the message, and at this point, only the sender has it.

4. Next, the sender uses a copy of the intended recipient's public key to encrypt the random key; this encrypted random key is called the *digital envelope*. Only the recipient's private key can decrypt the digital envelope; what this means is that now only the intended recipient can get to the random key and decrypt the sender's message. Even the sender has no way to decrypt the message.

5. The sender sends the digital envelope, the encrypted message, and the digital signature.

6. The recipient uses the private key to decrypt the message's digital envelope, which yields the random key.

7. The recipient uses the random key to decrypt the message.

8. The recipient uses the sender's public key to decrypt the digital signature.

9. The recipient then runs the message through the same hash function as the sender, which yields a new message digest.

10. The recipient compares the new message digest with the message digest in the digital signature. If they are exactly the same, then the message is genuine.

PGP, or *Pretty Good Privacy,* is a popular variation on the RSA encryption model written by Paul Zimmerman. It can be downloaded for free over the Internet. To download the free PGP software, contact `http://web.mit.edu/network/pgp.html`. For more information on the latest versions of PGP, contact `http://www.pgp.com`.

Message Security as a Management Issue

Message encryption is more than just a technical challenge—it is a way to implement important checks and balances that can protect the integrity and privacy of e-mail messages across your network.

For example, consider that a Webmaster or network administrator typically has access to folders and files that are unavailable to the company at large or has enough technical proficiency to access and read otherwise unavailable information. For the sake of employees' peace of mind, it is important that persons with this level of access implement security features even they cannot bypass.

Fortunately, most people are fair-minded and honest (and for that matter, most e-mail content is fairly dull, businesslike, and thus innocuous). However, sooner or later, we all hear stories that tell us how some compromise in e-mail security brought about damaging results.

Some organizations use filtering software (similar to the kind that home users employ to block access to objectionable Web sites) that blocks e-mail going outside the company if it contains certain key phrases or words. This helps the company check for and prevent the release of secure content such as trade secrets, confidential price proposals, competitive strategy plans, and the like.

The important thing to remember is that your company must institute clear and consistent policies regarding what is appropriate content for electronic correspondence and what actions can result from violations of that policy. If you are working for a company and cannot be fully aware of whether or how your e-mail is secured, assume that your e-mail is fully public (the digital equivalent of tacking a sheet of paper on a bulletin board in the hallway) and compose your messages accordingly.

Firewalls

A *firewall* is a combination of hardware and software that prevents access to your intranet from the Internet, while at the same time allowing you to gain access to Internet resources from your intranet. Firewalls are built with a combination of routers and servers, plus specialized software to run them. The most common type of router is called a *filtering router*. There are two types of firewall server, a *proxy server* and *bastion host*.

Filtering Routers

A filtering router is installed between the Internet server and the rest of your intranet. It examines every datagram and compares its source and destination IP address to addresses listed in a *filtering table*. The filtering table is set up by the intranet manager. If an IP address is not an approved address in the table, the datagram is dropped from the network.

Filtering routers can approve IP addresses for any combination of one-way or two-way access between your intranet and the Internet. A few examples:

- They can allow a datagram with a particular source or destination address to travel freely to and from the Internet.

- They can allow a datagram with a particular source address to go out onto the Internet but not allow an incoming packet to go to that address.

- They can allow a datagram with a particular destination address to come into the intranet but not allow a packet coming from that address to go out onto the Intranet.

Filtering routers can also be used to prevent internal users from accessing restricted data within your company's intranet. For example, they can prevent all departments except the personnel department from accessing or downloading employee records.

Proxy Servers

Proxy servers are like sentinels that manage all traffic between your intranet and the Internet. Typically, proxy servers are used on large intranets with many clients and multiple servers that have connections to the Internet, where the job of managing traffic security on each individual server would require too much time and money.

A proxy server examines traffic in complete detail, even down to individual keystrokes if necessary, between the servers on your intranet and the Internet. It analyzes each datagram to approve the legitimacy of source and destination, evaluates all content for possible dangers such as viruses or hostile applets, and keeps detailed logs of the activity that it monitors.

The proxy server is transparent both to your intranet's users and to outside users who want to get in. To the users, everything looks like a normal Internet connection. If an outside user attempts to access restricted files, the proxy server intercepts the message and denies the request.

A proxy server is also useful for increasing performance and providing firewall security. It can store a large cache of Web pages from the Internet; when a request is made for any given page, the proxy server can check the cache first before seeking the page out on the Internet. If the page is stored in the cache, the proxy server returns the stored page, which is much faster than doing an Internet search. Of course, Internet pages do get updated from time to time, so a proxy server can be programmed to recheck pages after a specified period of time or at any time the manager programs it to do so.

A very determined intruder might attempt to get past your proxy server. To prevent the most aggressive and sophisticated attacks, a proxy server can run as software on a *bastion host*. A bastion host is a hardware server that has no access to your intranet. It serves only as a shield between the proxy server and the Internet at large—it has no login services, no user accounts, no intranet file access. Normally, a bastion host keeps a log of all activity to and from the Internet and continually updates a backup copy of that log on a separate machine that is dedicated solely to storing the backup copy. Because there are no user accounts on a bastion host, no one can log onto it and take control of it—it is controllable only by direct, in-person access. If an outside intruder were somehow to connect to it, there would be no network services to access and thus no means to go further, not to mention that the intruder would likely leave a record of the attempt and a backup of that record on a separate machine that would be difficult to find. Figure 16.4 shows how a firewall works.

FIGURE 16.4

An intranet firewall. A bastion host shields the proxy server from intruders. The proxy server analyzes and approves content. The filtering router analyzes and approves IP addresses in both directions. The Internet server directs traffic to other intranet servers that handle Internet-based information.

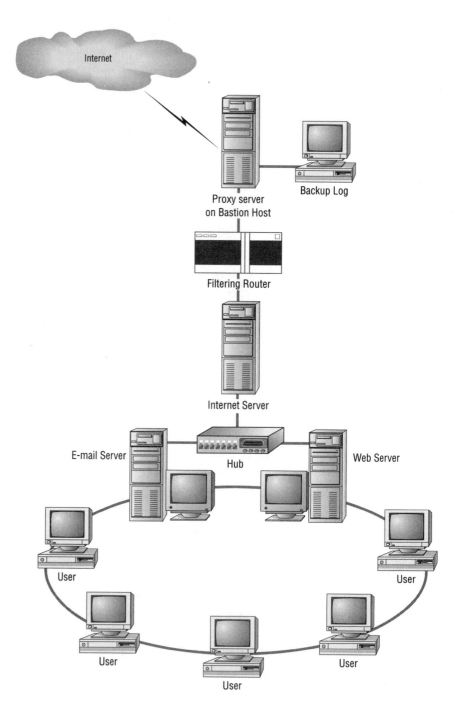

For Further Reading

- Black, Roger, and Sean Elder. *Web Sites That Work*. Hayden Books, 1997.

- Coleman, Pat, and Peter Dyson. *Mastering Intranets The Windows 95/NT Edition*. Sybex, 1997.

- Gross, Michael. *A Pocket Tour of Law on the Internet*. Sybex, 1995.

- Jaworski, James. *Do-It-Yourself Web Publishing with HoTMetaL*. Sybex, 1996.

- Lipschutz, Robert P., and John Garris. *Mastering Netscape Fast-Track Server*. Sybex, 1996.

- McCoy, John. *Mastering Web Design*. Sybex, 1996.

- Stallings, William. *Protect your Privacy: The PGP User's Guide*. Prentice Hall, 1995.

CASE STUDY

GAB needs security, but extensive hardware-based security is beyond their small company's budget. Accordingly, GAB implements the following safeguards:

A rigorous schedule of automated backups   A full backup will be made at the end of each work week and archived off-site. This backup will be supplemented by two daily incremental backups: one made at lunchtime and the other made at the close of business.

Adequate training for all users   Adequate training allows users to be as productive as possible and minimizes the risk of inadvertent data loss.

An especially rigorous system of password-protected access control   Access by both internal and remote users must be carefully controlled. GAB will restrict access to confidential information, require call backs for remote access, and secure their Web browser software.

GAB's confidential files (specifically, GAB's client financial records and personnel files) will be stored on password-restricted directories. Passwords will be assigned to users by the network manager and changed every thirty days.

GAB does not use a roving sales force. Taking advantage of this, GAB will restrict all remote access to calls from employee's homes or client offices, by requiring automated call-backs. Employee and client telephone numbers can be stored on secure directories on the server. The manager will configure the remote-access software to call back in every instance. No other remote access will be allowed.

GAB has chosen Internet Explorer as their browser because they have already decided to use Windows NT. GAB will configure their browsers to the highest level of downloading security: Applets will not be downloaded unless they carry digital signatures approved by the intranet manager. To enable centralized, secure control of browser security settings, GAB's intranet manager visits Microsoft's Internet site, then registers for and downloads the *Internet Explorer Administration Kit* (IEAK), a software tool that allows the manager to customize the browser and distribute it to workstations from the central server. Using this kit, the manager can restrict users' access to the browser's security settings and prevent individuals from updating the list of approved digital signatures. In this way, GAB will prevent inadvertent downloads of possibly harmful applets from the Internet.

GAB's intranet manager finds information about IEAK at `http://www.microsoft.com/ie/ieak`. Groupware messages will be difficult to secure because message threads, to be useful, must be made freely available to all. For the time being, employees are advised that the company groupware and collaborative messaging system is the equivalent of a completely public bulletin board, visible to anyone inside and outside the company, and they are advised to use it accordingly. Private e-mail can be sent to employees' password-restricted directories. Each employee is solely responsible for maintaining his or her own password to a private e-mail address. As a matter of company policy, even the system manager is not allowed to know an employee's private e-mail password. If an employee forgets his or her private e-mail password, the mail stored there is utterly irretrievable. All the manager can do about it is open a new private e-mail address for that employee—there

is no other recourse. If an employee leaves the company or there is no possibility that an employee will remember a forgotten password, the manager can delete the private e-mail directory but can not open and read its files.

Employees who discover weaknesses in GAB's security procedures will be encouraged to report them and rewarded for doing so. As GAB gains more experience using their intranet, the company will consider the possibility of adding encryption to their e-mail and message system and later installing a filtering router and a proxy server.

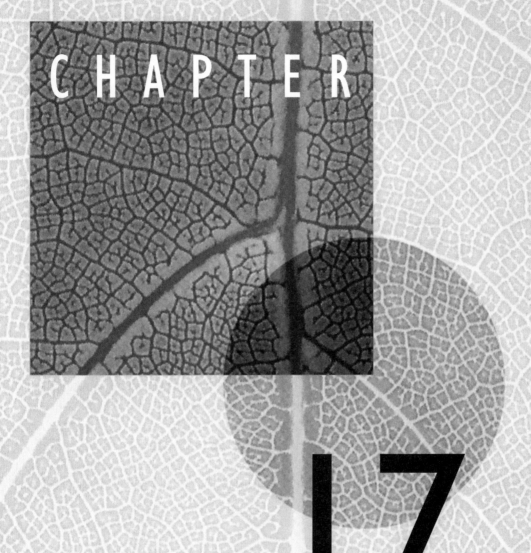

CHAPTER

17

Where to Go from Here

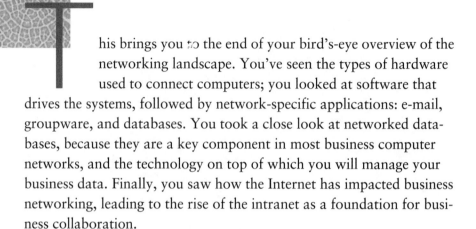

This brings you to the end of your bird's-eye overview of the networking landscape. You've seen the types of hardware used to connect computers; you looked at software that drives the systems, followed by network-specific applications: e-mail, groupware, and databases. You took a close look at networked databases, because they are a key component in most business computer networks, and the technology on top of which you will manage your business data. Finally, you saw how the Internet has impacted business networking, leading to the rise of the intranet as a foundation for business collaboration.

Where do you go from here? It's time to begin planning and designing your network system or modifying your existing system to make your business work better. The information in this book is a frame of reference, a foundation for further inquiry, to help you understand the enormous amount of sometimes-conflicting information that is out there, to cope with the rapidly evolving technology, to help you seek out the most able helpers, ask the right questions, and understand the answers you receive.

Making the Right Choice

The networking industry will continue to evolve rapidly. You have every right to expect that networks will become easier to use, even as their inner workings become more complicated. This has been the general trend of the computer industry from the beginning; there is every reason to expect that trend to continue for both hardware and software.

This book has focused on the underlying principles of networking. The most important of these is that hardware and software work together to make the technical details of network data transfer as transparent as possible—just as an automobile engine generally runs with only basic maintenance on the part of the driver, who probably isn't thoroughly versed in its inner workings. Your job is to purchase the appropriate system, drive and maintain it properly, and keep up with the changes in the industry.

This book is intended to focus your attention on a comparison of features and capabilities between different types of systems. As you have learned about different types of hardware and software, you may have developed more of an interest in one type of system over another; a particular system may appear more likely to be effective for your style of doing business. For example, you may lean toward a Macintosh-based system for its relatively easier installation and maintenance. Or you may be leaning toward a NetWare or Windows NT system for their rich feature sets and greater emphasis on data control and security. You may be leaning toward a peer-to-peer system because communications and file sharing are most important for your business, or you may be leaning toward a client/server system because your business requires shared access to a large-scale, centralized database.

In all cases, the process of choosing the appropriate type of networking system depends on your clear understanding of how you do business and how you need to manage your information, rather than on any flashy features or on the latest, greatest, gee-whiz technology. Begin with the closest possible examination of how you do business and why.

Analyzing Your Business

A theme stressed throughout this book is that the network you choose should lend support to—and reflect—the way you do business. Despite our desire that our networks run our businesses for us while we happily push our mice around our desktops, networks will not do that. We must run our businesses, using our networks to help us.

Keep the information you have learned from this book in the back of your mind as you review and analyze how your business manages information, seek to improve your management processes, and visualize how your network will support those improvements. By all means, get your users involved in the analysis as early as possible. Encourage them to make suggestions about how your business can work better, not just about their software and hardware preferences.

Getting More Information

Once you have clarified your business goals and the rules you use to attain them, you will want to obtain more detailed information about which system seems to be best for you. There are traditional avenues through which you can obtain detailed information about network hardware and software.

User Groups

All over the world, there are groups of people who meet to exchange information and advice on popular (or even not-so-popular) hardware and software. You can obtain information about these groups by visiting local computer stores and picking up a copy of computer magazines and newsweeklies printed in your area. Most user groups run classified advertisements in these local periodicals. Also, your local library may have information and access to periodicals.

Even if you don't have access to these types of periodicals, you can find a wealth of information by joining an on-line service such as Prodigy, CompuServe, or America OnLine; or, if you already have an Internet connection, try using your browser's search engine to connect to an intranet-related newsgroup. Here are two you might try:

```
comp.infosystems.intranet

misc.news.internet.discuss
```

On-line user forums function as world-wide user groups and can yield much valuable information.

For example, you could post a question like this on a forum for any popular networking product: "I have a small design and construction business with 20 employees, and I am looking to network my desktop computers. My employees need shared access to computer-based drawing plans as well as customer billing services and project scheduling. On the basis of my own research so far, I am inclined to believe that [Windows NT, NetWare, LANtastic, or whatever product] is right for me. Has anyone had experience using this product under similar circumstances?" Questions like this have been posted before, will be posted again, and have often received surprisingly helpful responses.

Advertising

Provided that you take the information found there with a large grain of salt, you can learn about product features in manufacturers' and vendors' promotional material. Of course, they will all say that they have the perfect solution for you; be skeptical and make them prove their claims before you spend any money. Many software vendors and developers offer demonstration disks, and there is nothing wrong with collecting these demos from as many vendors as will offer them to you. The more software you've evaluated, the better informed your decisions will be.

Vendors and Consultants

It's always best to obtain as much reliable information as you can on your own before talking to vendors about your needs. This is good for both you and the vendor; they are in the business of selling systems, after all, and it is appropriate that they save time and money by steering absolute beginners toward classes, promotional seminars, or books like this one.

However, it is also a fortunate aspect of this industry that many vendors are willing to offer solid, objective advice, to users of all levels.

This is good business practice as it builds customer loyalty. Look for a vendor that can explain different alternatives to you and does not talk down to you, rather than a vendor who promotes a single solution as a cure-all for every customer's problem.

Consultants are paid to offer a beginner objective and up-to-date advice. In addition, you can hire them to help you with your needs analysis, planning, scheduling, and system design. A good consultant can save you money if you hire and use them well. Refer to Appendix A for more details about hiring a network consultant.

Move Slowly

Make your moves slowly. This is classic financial investment advice, and a computer network certainly qualifies as a financial investment. There is an art to looking carefully at your alternatives and making your commitment to a chosen system at just the right moment.

There is no compelling reason to rush into buying a system. Those beginners who are too impatient to get started with some system—any system—are more likely to get stuck with a system that doesn't fit their business model. Those who rush in too quickly are prey to cure-all salesmen who tout the advantages of one particular system, make their money on the sale, and won't follow up with service and support when the problems arise.

On the other hand, there are good reasons to go slowly: Technology is constantly improving, meaning that networks get easier to use as time goes by and prices on existing systems tend to fall as newer, flashier systems move to market.

If there is no need to rush into networking, there is no need to be too timid either. Remember that you don't need to be a complete technical expert to get started, just someone who has taken the time to learn the basics. There are great rewards to be gained from implementing a network system that's exactly right for your business. The introductory material in this book has given you solid information to use as you pick your way through the dense mix of technical facts and marketing hype that has always characterized this industry.

The Future

If your business depends on any form of shared information, communications, or collaboration, there probably is a computer network in your future. The initial purchase costs for networking hardware and software may go down, but the cost of maintaining your information technology, as a percentage of your business overhead, will always be significant. In other words, networking will never be all that cheap or easy, but it will be indispensable in terms of your business's competitiveness and productivity. With indispensability come unique problems and payoffs.

Fifteen years ago, the average PC had an 8088 processor running at 8MHz, a 20MB hard disk, and maybe as much as 1MB of RAM. Now the average PC has a Pentium processor running at 160MHz, a 2GB hard disk, and 32MB RAM. At this rate of development, you can expect CPUs of the future to run at thousands of megahertz (KMH), with thousands of kilobytes of storage (KGB—an interesting acronym for mass information storage), and with thousands of megabytes of RAM (KMB). Much of this newfound processing power will be devoted to data communications and transfer between machines at increasingly remote locations.

NetPC

An attempt is already well underway to take all configuration and administration tasks off of your desktop and onto a centralized management authority. To this end, there is already a marketing push underway on behalf of the NC, or "net PC." Simply put, the NC substitutes the network and server for the local hard disk on your desktop machine.

Under this model, your NC will, upon boot-up, check in with the central software server for its operating system and applications, either via a LAN, an intranet, or even the Internet. The server in turn will poll your PC to determine if you have attempted to configure it in a non-standard way (if you have any means to configure it at all), or if you have attempted to install any non-standard or incompatible applications (if you have any local storage at all). The payoff for this type of completely centralized model is a dramatic lowering of network maintenance costs.

If all this sounds too centralized for your comfort level, be aware that many users at all levels in your organization will greatly appreciate its upside: All the daily, burdensome data-management tasks to which we have become accustomed—and accomplish with varying degrees of skill and success—will have been lifted from our shoulders. In theory—as yet unproved—the costs of network management and administration will be lowered dramatically.

Beyond the implications of authoritarian rule over information, the result of NC-related technology will be that computers simply occupy a position of reduced cultural importance. In other words, they will become part of the background static of business, more like the other business appliances we take for granted: telephones, copiers, fax machines, calculators, intercoms, and the like.

Wide Area Networking

Wireless LANs offer an enticing vision of an always-networked future. Rather than being dependent on cables and phones for connectivity, you will be able to connect to centralized data warehouses from anywhere, via satellite-based data broadcasting systems. This technology will support and intensify a trend that is already underway, of a mobile workforce outside a central office, working out of homes or in distributed worksites.

New data-transport technologies promise greater speed and throughput to support more widespread communications. For example, the recent release of 56Kbps modems allows remote connections at speeds about half of full-speed ISDN but without ISDN's associated high costs. Also, the core infrastructure for 56Kbps service is already in place, making it deployable right now. There are drawbacks: There are no 56K hardware and software standards in place, and your Web server or ISP must support the proprietary standards for whichever 56Kbps scheme you are using. In addition, you must have a high-quality phone line into your office, and you must be within a mile or two of your phone company's switch (which rules out 56K modems for many rural areas).

Other emerging technologies, such as satellite data service, digital subscriber lines, and cable modems offer the promise of greater speed and lower costs than currently-available digital technologies but lack recognized standards. Also, they require significant investments in existing telecommunications infrastructure to become practical.

Satellite data service requires a receiving dish connected to your PC; you can receive data at speeds up to 400Kbps. However, direct-to-satellite transmitters are still in the development stage. To send data you must use a normal, 56K modem connection to a transmitting service provider.

Digital subscriber lines provide dedicated digital connections, similar to leased lines, running over high-quality copper wiring that must be installed by the phone company. This type of connection can run at speeds up to 8Mbps, but your access to this technology depends on your phone company's willingness to upgrade its equipment.

Cable modems are similar to digital subscriber lines in that they provide high speed, dedicated digital connections. In the case of cable modems, these connections use an installed cable transmission system similar to cable TV. Whereas cable TV uses one-way cabling to pipe signals into your home, cable modems would require two-way signals for business content. The technology holds great promise—speeds of up to 27Mbps—but, as with digital subscriber lines, your ability to access this technology depends on cable companies' willingness to make a large investment in upgrading their infrastructure.

A Final Word

Since the beginning of the technological age—which occurred somewhere just past the peak of the industrial age—we have been subjected to glib predictions about how rosy our future will be in the warmhearted embrace of advancing technology. So far, however, the technological age has been a mixed blessing. In many ways the technological tools we have been given have made our lives easier, but in exchange for all its wonderful tools technology has extracted its toll on our lives. For example, most people would agree that life is more stressful and our future more uncertain than previous generations', even though for many of us, our lives are more comfortable as well.

In the future, we will face the same question with which we started this inquiry: Why *are* we in business, anyway? To make money, sure, but this answer is likely to leave a certain unfinished aftertaste. Most human beings have deeper, more universal desires in common: to find fulfilling connections with each other, to transcend everyday experience by acquiring insights into what our experiences mean, to have our lives in the end count for something more than our own survival. Our business activities can be as much in the service of these deeper needs as profit-making.

The line between our professional and personal lives is not as well defined as it was for an earlier generation, largely because of the way in which we have embraced technology: cellular phones, pagers, laptop computers, and the ability to network these tools together. The tools we use to communicate and collaborate can bring us closer together, or they can become walls of separation over which we toss the digital equivalents of messages-in-bottles.

We will always find a way to control the tools of our trades, and to some extent we will be willing to allow those tools to control us. To what degree we retain or relinquish that control is a shifting choice we make on a day-to-day basis. By trial and error we will find a way to fulfill life's most fundamental purposes; but we can minimize our lives' trials as well as its errors if we keep those purposes uppermost in our mind when we make choices about how we work and relate to one another.

APPENDICES

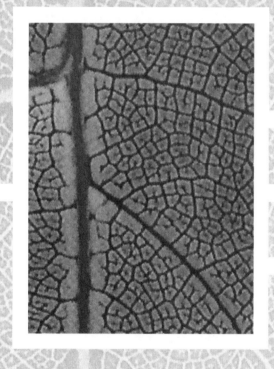

APPENDIX

A

Hiring a Network Consultant

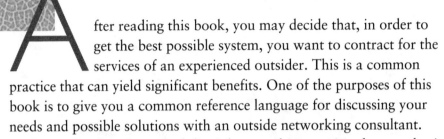

After reading this book, you may decide that, in order to get the best possible system, you want to contract for the services of an experienced outsider. This is a common practice that can yield significant benefits. One of the purposes of this book is to give you a common reference language for discussing your needs and possible solutions with an outside networking consultant.

If you take the time to find the right consulting services for your business, you can save a great deal of money in the long run. To make and keep the consultancy cost-effective, you should spend a lot of time at the outset interviewing as many different individuals and firms as possible and negotiating hard regarding schedules and fees. Do this before you bring your chosen consultant on board and pay money. Above all else, you will be looking for a individual, work team, or firm that is compatible with the type of business you run and with your unique style of doing business. This appendix offers some advice on selecting the right networking consultant.

What Kinds of Consultants Are Out There?

There are many different types of consultants available. The market is crowded because of the great demand for their services from companies who have discovered that computer networking is more complicated than simply buying computers and stringing them together.

For large companies, there are large consulting firms, like Andersen Consulting or Hewlett-Packard, who employ thousands of consultants and are available nationwide. On the other hand, a small business could easily get by with the services of a smaller, one- or two-person shop, found by scanning the advertisements in local computer newsweeklies and the Yellow Pages. Many of these smaller companies provide surprising value, as long as you are persistent and patient in your search, evaluating them and comparing what they offer according to the criteria described in this appendix.

Different kinds of consultants provide specific types of services. Although the terms used to describe consulting services are imprecise, they generally fall within one of the following categories:

Consultants are advisors. They provide needs analysis (as discussed in Chapter 11) and make recommendations for solutions. They can also perform data modeling and network systems design.

Systems Integrators are hardware and software installers. They can set up new systems or work with existing systems to upgrade, optimize performance, or add new features. They can provide management training, but they are generally not called upon to do day-to-day management and maintenance themselves.

Outsourcers are third-party managers. They control a network and manage it on a day-to-day basis. They are called *outsourcers* because they do not work from within your company. They may manage several different systems within a given locale or license a particular system that they own and maintain.

There can be some overlap between the descriptions given above. It is important only that you be familiar with how these terms are generally used as you interview and evaluate different consulting service providers.

Making the Choice

You can locate possible consultants by looking for them using two traditional channels of information: recommendations from colleagues and advertisements in locally available media (for example, business journals, professional directories, chambers of commerce, and the Yellow Pages). As you might expect, the Internet is a good source for locating prospective consulting help. For starters, try the following URL:

```
http://www.yahoo.com/Business_and_Economy/Companies/Computers/
Networking/Consulting/
```

You solicit a consultant by calling and arranging for an initial interview. You should be prepared to interview several before selecting one and paying any fees for services.

Following is some advice for selecting and hiring a consultant. Although some of it is pure common sense, you may find a suggestion or two here that you haven't thought of before:

Spend the most time in the planning stages. If you plan well, the implementation will go a lot more smoothly. If you plan hurriedly or sloppily, you will pay dearly in the implementation phase.

Check references. There are many ways to learn about the qualifications of a prospective consultant:

- Some networking vendors have implemented programs for training and certifying individuals who can install, configure, and support their products. Novell supports a training program for Certified Network Engineers (CNEs). Microsoft supports a program of examinations that certify professional expertise in their products. Individuals with these credentials offer you at least some preliminary assurance that they have the knowledge to do the job.

- Look for an individual or firm that has done your type of project before. By all means, ask for references to previous clients and call on them. When calling on a reference, ask specific questions: "What specific services did the consultant perform for you? Was the project completed on time and within budget?

Did the consultant keep you informed at every stage of the project? Did the consultant communicate clearly in terms you could understand? Was the consultant readily available throughout the project? Was the project unduly disruptive?"

- If you are hiring a consulting company rather than an individual consultant, ask the company representative for information on the training, background, and experience of the individuals who will be doing the actual work for your company.

Have clear, concrete, and detailed goals. If your stated goal is "installing a network to handle the records for the Marketing, Retail Sales, Customer Fulfillment, and After-Sale Support Departments," it is not specific enough. A good consultant would consider such a goal a *mission statement*, a reference point for working with you to discover the concrete, real-world results you are looking for. How do the various departments work together right now? How will the system facilitate that, or should it change the way you do business? What does the final output look like? Who sees it first? Who sees it next? What evidence is there that the new system will save or make money? Answers to questions like these are the basis for the all-important (and all-too-often neglected) data modeling process.

Get a concrete, detailed proposal. This is the flip side of the previous advice. Perhaps you have no idea what you want; you may need the consultant to analyze your business and tell you. A good consultant will provide you with a proposal that offers alternatives, breaks the project down into a series of steps, includes a timeline for implementation of each step, describes each step's methodology, and estimates each step's cost.

Negotiate realistic cost estimates. Be firm about what you can afford, and be prepared to negotiate costs and consulting fees individually for whatever specific services may be required to complete your project.

The relationship is more important than the cost. Notwithstanding the above, remember that installing or upgrading a network is a long-term project. You need a productive and reliable business relationship with your hired help. Of course, you need to stay within a budget, but if you focus only on dollar costs at every step of the project, you run the risk of entering into a business relationship that is not really right for you. The result could be a bad system, more costly in the long run.

Get everything in writing. A written contract should include incentives for meeting intermediate goals or penalties for not meeting them. Incentives work better.

Keep schedules flexible and costs firm. There are plenty of unforeseen pitfalls down the road. You will get a better system if you can allow time to react to unexpected events. You don't necessarily have to build such time into the contract; but if you keep it quietly in reserve, you will sleep better at night. On the other hand, be firm regarding the dollar costs that you have negotiated. Once the cost estimate is given in writing, insist that you stick to it.

Don't throw good money after bad. There is always the possibility that things might not work out as planned. Build an *escape clause*, a basis for ending the relationship, into the initial contract. Good consultants work under contracts with such escape clauses for themselves—and so should you. Second-guessing your consultant during the project is a sure sign that you have hired one that is wrong for you or that you could have done the job without one in the first place. Don't stay in such a relationship; if the consultant doesn't recognize the unworkable situation and bow out, invoke the escape clause and bow out yourself. You will be doing both the consultant and yourself a favor.

Hiring a consultant does not have to be a daunting task. As the client, you are in control of the process. You have the most control during the selection and interview phase, so take your time and negotiate firmly. A satisfactory long-term relationship with a reliable consultant will require little supervision and, in the long run, may well turn out to be the best networking bargain you can make.

APPENDIX

B

A Glossary of Networking
Acronyms and Jargon

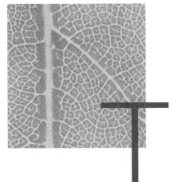

The following is an alphabetical listing of the acronyms and technical terms used in this book, with a brief explanation of each.

10BASE 10Mbps Baseband. A common cable designation that indicates coaxial cable capable of handling 10 megabits data transmission per second. *See also* 10BASET.

10BASET 10Mbps Baseband Twisted-Pair. A common cable designation that indicates twisted-pair cable that can transmit 10 megabits data transmission per second. *See also* 10BASE.

100BaseX An extension of the traditional Ethernet standard, supporting 100Mbps baseband transmission. Also called Fast Ethernet.

100VG-AnyLAN A 100Mbps networking technology, built on a star topology, which combines support for Ethernet frames and Token Ring packets.

3COM Computers, Communications, Compatibility. Logo of the 3COM Corporation in Santa Clara, California, makers of networking hardware.

Access control list A file used by a network operating system to specify rights of access to other files, directories, disks, printer ports, and other workstations.

Access rights   The limitations placed by a network administrator on the ability of users to locate, read, and modify data files on the network.

Active hub   A device that accepts, amplifies, and forwards data transmissions along a network. *See also* Passive hub.

ADSP   AppleTalk Data Stream Protocol. An AppleTalk protocol that monitors and verifies the flow of data between computers.

AFP   AppleTalk File Protocol. An AppleTalk protocol that handles requests for data files and manages file security.

Analog   A communications method that represents signals by continually changing properties such as voltage or amplitude. *See also* Digital.

Anonymous ftp   A method for downloading publicly-available files from Internet sites, called anonymous because it does not require a logon account at the file site.

AOL   America OnLine. A commercial OSP that offers access to information databases, Internet access, and direct communications between users. *See also* CIS, OSP.

API   Application Programming Interface. A software mechanism used to develop machine instruction code.

Applet   A small application, often run within browser software, that normally performs a single or limited set of functions.

AppleTalk   A suite of communication protocols for Macintosh systems.

Application layer   The seventh layer of the OSI/RM networking model, a description of specifications for the environment in which network applications communicate with network services.

Application server   A machine that manages access to centralized application software; for example, a shared database.

Archie   An Internet search engine for locating publicly available files on anonymous FTP sites.

ARCnet   Attached Resource Computer Network. An inexpensive desktop computer networking system that uses hubs to connect workstations and printers.

ASP   AppleTalk Session Protocol. An AppleTalk protocol that verifies data sent across a network in sections.

Asymmetrical encryption   A two-key system to encrypt messages using match pair of keys; messages that are encrypted by one key (the public key) can only be decrypted by the other (the private key).

Asynchronous transmission   A method of transmitting data using special data bits, called start bits and stop bits, to control the flow of data without regard to the time intervals involved.

ATP   AppleTalk Transaction Protocol. An AppleTalk protocol that verifies the accuracy of network messages.

Attribute   A code attached to a datafile that describes limits on its availability to users or its capability of being modified.

Backbone   A cable configuration in which workstations, servers, and even entire networks are connected to a main cable, for the purpose of minimizing the flow of network data traffic between them.

Bandwidth   The capacity of a network to handle simultaneous data transmissions. The larger the number of simultaneous transmissions, the greater the network's bandwidth.

Baseband A cable that carries a single signal. *See also* Broadband.

Bastion host A hardware server positioned between a proxy server and an Internet connection, to serve as a security shield against unauthorized access to a network.

Baud rate The measurement of speed of data transmissions using a modem, measured as the maximum number of bit changes (1 to 0, 0 to 1) the modem can handle per second.

BBS Bulletin Board System. A usually informal system in which a single computer with one or more modems manages communications and file sharing between callers who establish links using modems.

Bit Binary Digit. The smallest unit of information that a computer can process.

Block A pair of 8-bit data bytes. *See also* Byte.

BNC Bayonet Connector. A metal cylinder used connect cables with computer network interface cards, or other nodes on the network.

Bridge A hardware device used to link two or more LANs and manage the flow of communication signals between them. *See also* Gateway, Router.

Broadband A type of cable that can carry more than one signal at a time. *See also* Baseband.

Browser All-purpose Internet/intranet access software.

Bus The electronic pathway that carry signals from one component to another inside a computer. *See also* EISA, ISA, PCI.

Bus master   A peripheral device, such as a network interface card, with the capability of transferring data without requiring services from a computer's CPU.

Business rule   A business process that specifies some action that must occur as the result of another. For example, if a shipping order falls above a certain minimum quantity, shipping costs are then free.

Byte   A group of eight data bits, representing a binary number.

C/S   Client/Server. A network system in which one or more computers (called servers) are dedicated to sending, receiving, storing data files, and managing the system, while other computers (called clients) are dedicated to receiving and processing data from servers.

Cable   An insulated wire used as the pathway for network data traffic.

Cable modem   A modem designed to carry data signals along a dedicated, wide-area, cable communications infrastructure.

Cache   Computer memory that stores most frequently used instructions so that they can be accessed as quickly as possible.

Category 5   A specification for cable certified to carry data up to 100Mbps, using four twisted pairs of copper wire. Sometimes referred to as Cat 5.

CD-ROM   Compact Disk Read-Only Module. A hardware device used to read computer data from laser disks. Sometimes this acronym is used as a generic term for laser-readable disks.

CGI   Common Gateway Interface. A programming standard for language commands that allows programmers to bridge the gap between traditional LAN database servers and Web-based browsers.

Challenge handshaking A security system whereby a server continually tests a client computer as long as a connection is active, to verify that the client is an authorized user.

CHAP Challenge Handshake Authentication Protocol. An Internet-standard protocol for verifying encrypted passwords.

Checksum A number, generated on-the-fly as data is processed, which represents the sum of the byte values of all the characters in the data. The checksum is used to verify that data has not been corrupted during processing.

CIS CompuServe Information Service. A commercial enterprise that offers access to huge databases of information and communications between users, including access to the Internet. *See also* AOL, OSP.

CISC Complete Instruction Set Computer. A term used to describe a chip with a fully featured internal architecture. *See also* RISC.

CLI Call Line Identification. A protocol that identifies a calling telephone number and checks against a stored list of authorized callers before making the link to a computer.

Client A computer that has been configured to receive data on a network.

Client/Server *See* C/S.

CNA Certified NetWare Administrator. An individual who has passed a course of study in everyday management of a Novell NetWare network.

CNE Certified NetWare Engineer. An individual who has passed a course of study in the design, installation, and technical maintenance of a Novell NetWare network.

Coaxial   A type of communication cable that uses a single insulated wire surrounded by insulation and a braided copper shield.

COM   Communications port. An acronym used to name computers' peripheral ports, which send and receive data in serial (single-bit) format.

Communication port   A hardware receptacle for cables connected to peripheral devices, such as printers or external modems.

Compiler   An application that translates program source code into machine instruction code.

Configuration   The process by which a computer component (hardware or software) is modified so as to make it work with another component.

Constraint   A specification that disallows obviously improper data entry into database fields.

Content   A general term used to describe information stored in Web pages.

CPU   Central Processing Unit. The combination of random access memory, storage device, and processing chip used to manage digital electronic data.

CSU/DSU   Channel Service Unit/Data Service Unit. A special hardware device that connects a network's Internet router to the end of a leased line, converts the network's serial data signal to the line's digital signal, and vice-versa.

CU-See-Me   A videoconferencing application that runs on workstations with attached video cameras and microphones.

Database   A set of raw data elements organized into tables of rows and columns, which define common features of the data, and can be accessed and modified by one or more users to produce useful information. *See also* DBMS, NDBMS, OODB, RDBMS.

Database administrator   An individual responsible for programming and maintaining a large multi-relational database in a networked environment and facilitating access to the database by individuals on the network.

Datagram   A small section of data, no more than 1,500 characters in length, which is transferred from one computer to another and verified individually at its destination.

Data link layer   The second layer of the OCI/RM networking model, which describes processes for detecting and correcting low-level data errors during transfer of data between the physical layer and the layers above the physical layer.

Data modeling   A process of analyzing and charting information-handling structures and procedures.

DBMS   Database Management System. An application that organizes data into a structured framework, consisting of tables containing columns and rows, and uses that framework to provide access to the data and a vehicle for processing it. *See also* NDBMS, OODB, RDBMS.

DCC   Direct Cable Connection. A data link that uses either a parallel or serial cable to connect two similarly configured computers using their built-in communication ports.

DDP   Datagram Delivery Protocol. The data handling protocol at the heart of the AppleTalk protocol suite.

De facto standard   A term used to describe a specification so broadly accepted in the marketplace that competing vendors must support it in order to market their products.

Deadlock   A situation in which two or more computers attempt to access data currently held by each other and become completely inaccessible as each waits for the other to release the data.

Default page   The first page displayed upon access to a Web site. Also called the home page.

Dial-up connection   A process for establishing a remote data connection using existing telecommunications technology (for example, modems and telephone lines).

Dial-up router   A hardware device, installed as a node on a network, that specializes in making dial-up remote connections; for example, establishing a connection to the Internet.

Differential backup   A system of data backup that makes copies only of those files that have been modified since the last full backup was made. *See also* Full backup, Incremental backup.

Digital   A communications method that represents binary values by measuring electronic states. *See also* Analog.

Digital envelope   A randomly generated encryption key, itself encrypted with a public key, then added to a secure data transmission.

Digital signature   An identification code embedded within a secure data transmission. Also, a registered ID code embedded with an applet sent across the Internet, which is used to verify the applet's original author.

Digital subscriber line A dedicated wide-area digital connection, similar to a leased line, running over high-quality copper wiring installed by the phone company.

Directory A means of representing related files as being grouped together on the hard disk under a unique directory name.

Direct access A wide-area network technology that uses a dedicated, leased telephone line to complete the necessary connections.

Discussion software An application that manages a database of linked user messages on a server. *See also* Message thread.

Disk mirroring A process by which duplicate hard disks are run off the same controller and data is copied to both disks simultaneously.

Distributed database A set of data tables that is typically located on different servers throughout the network and which can be accessed and controlled as a single unified system.

Distributed processing A system in which different users on a network handle the separate tasks that, taken together, make up a single unified process involving shared network data.

DLC Data Link Control. A limited-use protocol designed for connections between LANs and IBM mainframe computers.

DMA Direct Memory Access. Special circuits on some hardware components that allow users to bypass the microprocessor for certain data-transfer operations.

DNS Domain Name System. A mechanism for substituting easily remembered, character-based names for numeric IP addresses.

Domain (Windows NT) A group of computers that operate as a single workgroup within a larger network and can be accessed as a group using an identifying unique name.

Domain name An easily remembered, character-based substitute for a numeric IP address.

DOS Disk Operating System. A standard operating system for non-networked computers.

DRAM Dynamic Random Access Memory. A memory chip that uses tiny capacitors to store electrical charges that represent data in binary format.

DRDA Distributed Relational Database Architecture. A standard developed by IBM Corporation that allows different applications to access IBM's mainframe database, DB2, along with other DRDA-compatible database products.

Drive mapping The process of assigning drive letters to network nodes for faster and easier access to them.

DSS Directory Services Server. A machine that keeps track of the locations of stored data files on large-scale systems.

Duplex A control setting for the display of transmitted characters on the sender's monitor.

Dynamic bandwidth An optimization technology for ISDN remote-access connections, in which the remote node server monitors the rate of transfer for various types of data. When data is dense and the designated speed of transfer falls below a predetermined level, another communication channel is opened to accommodate more data and speed up the transfer rate.

EDC   Error Detection and Correction. A memory feature that verifies RAM output, and resends output when memory errors occur.

EDO RAM   Extended Data-Out Random Access Memory. Memory chips that are designed to take advantage of faster motherboards, like those found on high-speed Pentium systems.

EISA   Extended Industry Standard Architecture. A 32-bit design that is an enhanced version of ISA. *See also* Bus, ISA, PCI.

ELAP   *See* EtherTalk.

E-mail   Electronic mail. A network communication system for transferring messages between users.

Embedded link   Coded instructions to a browser written into a Web page, normally launched by clicking on a displayed symbol or text string.

Encryption   A system of translating messages into random-looking unintelligible characters, based on a secret digital key. *See also* Key.

Enterprise   A complex network of computers—often including other networks—which is organized around a shared business mission.

EP   Echo Protocol. An AppleTalk protocol that repeats messages back to the sending node to verify its integrity.

Ethernet   A widely used protocol and cabling scheme, developed by Xerox in 1976, used as the basis for various types of computer networks.

EtherTalk   A specification for running AppleTalk protocols over an Ethernet system at the physical and data link layers.

Fast Ethernet   *See* 100BaseX.

Fax server   A machine that specializes in managing facsimile (fax) transmissions across a computer network.

FDDI   Fiber Distributed Data Interface. A laser-light network topology using optic fiber cabling and specialized communication hardware.

Fiber line driver   A hardware device that permits connections between fiber-optic and wire-based cables.

Fiber-optic cable   A cable type that uses a fiberglass core to transmit pulses of laser light that represent binary data bits.

File server   A computer on a network that stores and sends data files to other nodes. *See also* Server.

Filtering   A process that increases data transfer efficiency by reducing unnecessary data traffic between two networks.

Filtering router   A security device installed between an Internet server and an intranet. It verifies the source and destination IP addresses of datagrams and drops those not listed in its filtering table.

Filtering table   A list of authorized IP addresses stored in a filtering router, used to secure remote access to an intranet.

Firewall   Either software or hardware or a combination thereof, which prevents unauthorized access to an intranet from the Internet, while at the same time allowing authorized user to make connections to the Internet from within the intranet.

Flat-file database   A database composed of a single table.

Frame   Data combined with headers and footers used to protect it from corruption as it passes over a wide-area network connection.

Frame relay   A high-speed, wide-area network technology based on sending data in small, verifiable packets.

FTP   File Transfer Protocol. A communications protocol used to process complex messages and data files sent over a network and to automate message processing.

Full backup   A data protection method that makes copies of files on the hard disk, regardless of whether they have been modified since they were previously backed up.

Gateway   A hardware device with its own processor and memory that connects networks with more complex systems using different communications protocols. *See also* Bridge, Router.

GB   Gigabytes. One billion bytes of data, used as a unit for measuring larger hard disks and RAM. *See also* MB.

GIF   Graphics Interchange Format. A de facto standard for storing pictures in digital systems for display on computer screens. A graphics file type commonly used on the Internet because of its relatively small size. *See also* JPEG.

Gopher   An application that simplifies Internet access by presenting common Internet features as a series of onscreen menus.

GOSIP   Government Open Systems Interconnection Profile. Technical specifications and requirements established by a government and made available to manufacturers who wish to sell products to it.

Groupware   Network software that manages the collaborative communications (scheduling, messages, shared data) of business workgroups.

GUI   Graphical User Interface. Software that allows the user to control computer services by means of graphical objects displayed on the screen and selected using a digitizing device such as a mouse or tablet.

Handshaking   A process by which two computing devices determine a commonly supported protocol and transmission rate in order to exchange data.

Hash function   A security algorithm used to protect the integrity of an encrypted message.

Header   Identification information attached to the front of a packet or datagram prior to transmission across a network.

Hierarchical database   A set of tables linked together in a linear, one-directional relationship.

Home page   The first page displayed upon access to a Web site. Also called the default page.

Host   The machine that accepts a connection from another machine.

HTML   HyperText Markup Language. A set of text commands embedded within the content of a Web page to instruct browsers how to display that content and form links to other Internet/intranet services.

HTTP   HyperText Transfer Protocol. The standard protocol for establishing links to Web pages on the Internet or intranet.

Hub   A device that accepts signals from an attached network node and passes them along to another attached node. *See also* Active hub, Passive hub.

Hypertext links   A snippet of text, graphic image, or symbol that is displayed by a browser. When accessed by a pointer click, the hypertext link launches an Internet or intranet service; for example, displaying another Web page, running an applet, or sending an e-mail message. Often simply referred to as a *link*.

IAB   Internet Architecture Board. A standards organization that reviews and approves transmission protocols and numbering standards for the Internet.

IAC   Interapplication Communication. A process that allows applications to access data from other applications.

IDP   Internet Datagram Protocol. The basic protocol in XNS, similar to TCP/IP. *See also* TCP/IP, XNS.

IEEE   Institute of Electric and Electronics Engineering. A body of experts that establishes electrical specification standards for just about every electrical device.

IETF   Internet Engineering Task Force. An oversight committee that sets standards for the day-to-day operation of the Internet.

Incremental backup   A data backup technique that copies only those files that have been created or changed since the last incremental backup. *See also* Differential backup, Full backup.

Internet   A world-wide, free-form network using telephone lines, made up of millions of users all over the world who make connections via modem and communicate with each other on just about any subject imaginable.

Internet Society   A standards committee that serves as the point of contact between Internet supervising bodies, service providers, and users.

InterNIC   Internet Network Information Center. An organization that registers and maintains domain names for Internet IP addresses.

Interpreted language   An uncompiled programming language that requires a separate application, called an interpreter, to execute its programmed instructions line-by-line.

Interrupt   A means by which a computer can temporarily suspend current processing in order to accept a request for services that must take priority.

Intranet   A system that uses Internet technologies, such as browsers and Web servers, to manage communications and collaborations over a private network of desktop computers.

IP   Internet Protocol. A communications protocol for verifying the accuracy and address of network data. *See also* TCP/IP.

IP address   Four numbers, each in the range from 1 to 254, separated by periods, and used to identify Internet sites.

IPv6   A revision of the original Internet Protocol to include support for 128-bit IP addresses.

IPX   Internetwork Packet Exchange. A standard protocol, similar to TCP/IP, that handles data verification and addressing responsibilities between NetWare and other networks.

IS   Information Systems. A business workgroup responsible for managing communication of business information. Also called MIS.

ISA   Industry Standard Architecture. A 16-bit standard for transmitting data inside a workstation. *See also* Bus, EISA.

ISDN   Integrated Services Digital Network. A set of telephone-wire technologies that allow specialized data pathways to coexist with voice pathways.

ISO   International Standards Organization. A body of experts, based in Geneva, Switzerland, that define global standards for networking and data exchange.

ISP   A vendor that provides users with connections to the Internet, usually for a subscription fee.

Java   A platform-independent programming language developed by Sun Microsystems that has quickly evolved into the development language of choice for intranet and Internet developers.

JPEG   Joint Photographic Expert Group. A graphics file format that compresses photographic images into digital files for transmission across networks, including the Internet. Sometimes abbreviated to JPG. *See also* GIF.

JPG   *See* JPEG.

JVM   Java Virtual Machine. An area of RAM dynamically allocated for running Java-based programs.

KB   Kilobyte. One thousand data bytes. A standard unit for measuring the size of floppy disks and smaller data files.

Key A complex sequence of characters or a mathematical formula used to encrypt electronic messages, rendering them unreadable until decrypted using a required decryption key.

LAN Local Area Network. Two or more computers that can exchange data via cables or broadcast devices. "Local" is a relative term; it means that the computers on the network are located within reasonable physical proximity of each other. *See also* WAN.

Leased line A dedicated telecommunications line used as a two-way data carrier between a network and an Internet service provider.

Linear bus A common network topology in which nodes are connected by a single length of cable.

Linux A variation of the UNIX operating system, available as freeware.

Lock A digital mark associated with data (such as a database record, datafile, or directory) that acts as a signal to alert other users that the data is in use and prevents other users from making changes to it until the original user is finished.

Log in To establish a connection as a user on a network.

Log out To end a connection as a user on a network.

Logical topology A description of the behavior of computers on a network, from the perspective of its human operators.

Login script A series of commands, stored in a data file, used by a network operating system to set up environment parameters for workstations logging in. Also called a logon script.

Logon script *See* Login script.

LPT   Line Printer. An acronym used to name computers' peripheral ports that send and receive data in parallel (8-bit) format.

Mac   A Macintosh computer, one of several models manufactured by Apple Computer, Inc.

Macro   A series of application commands listed in a data file and executed in sequence, thereby automating more complex application procedures.

Mail server   A machine dedicated to managing e-mail traffic on a network.

Mainframe   A large, multiprocessor computing system designed to allow access by a large number of users and process especially large amounts of data.

Map   To assign a drive letter (E:, F:, G:) to a node or file directory on a network.

MAPI   Messaging Application Programmer's Interface. A standard for formatting and displaying electronic messages, developed by the Microsoft Corporation.

MAU   Media Attachment Unit. A device used to connect computers to a shared cable.

MB   Megabyte. One million bytes of data, used as the unit for measuring the size of hard disks and random access memory. *See also* GB, KB.

Mbps   One million bits per second, the unit of measurement for dial-up data connections.

MCA   Micro Channel Architecture. A 32-bit design for transmitting data within a workstation, developed by IBM. *See also* Bus.

MCP Microsoft Certified Professional. A program of standardized exams sponsored by the Microsoft Corporation to certify required knowledge and skills using Microsoft Products.

MCSE Microsoft Certified Systems Engineer. An individual that has passed a set of certification exams proving ability to implement and maintain computing environments using Microsoft networking products.

MDA Mail Delivery Agent. Network server software that transfers messages to recipient workstations.

Message digest A number, similar to a checksum, returned by a hash function and used to verify that an encrypted message has not been tampered with or corrupted in transmission.

Message thread A set of related newsgroup or groupware messages linked together for easy reading in sequence.

Method Computer instruction codes linked to fixed data in order to form a programming object.

MHS Message Handling System. A standard electronic mail and messaging system developed by Novell Corporation.

MHz Megahertz. One million cycles of a vibrating crystal in the microprocessor, used as the unit for measuring its speed.

Millisecond One-millionth of a second. The unit of measurement for the data-access speed of a hard disk.

MIME Multipurpose Internet Mail Extension. A coding scheme that allows binary information to be sent on networks, such as the Internet, which normally accept only ASCII-based data.

Mirrored file server   A performance and data-protection system in which data is stored on a primary file server and immediately transferred at high speed to a secondary file server.

MIS   Management Information Systems. A business workgroup responsible for managing communication of business information. This is an older term normally associated with mainframe systems. Also called IS.

MLID   Multiple Link Interface Driver. Software for allowing compatible hardware to accept data using more than one protocol. *See also* ODI.

Modem   A hardware device that translates digital signals to analog signals, and vice-versa, to enable communications over analog telephone lines.

Motherboard   A desktop computer's main circuit board.

MS   Millisecond. One-millionth of a second. Measures the time it takes the hard disk to find data.

MS-DOS   *See* DOS.

MSAU   Multistation Access Unit. A special hub on token-ring networks used to connect workstations.

MTA   Mail Transfer Agent. Server software that checks e-mail message addresses and forwards it to a local network address or onto the Internet.

MUA   Mail User Agent. Client software for composing and sending e-mail messages.

Multimedia reflector   A device that transmits data from a single source to multiple recipients.

Multiprocessing   The ability of hardware or software to perform more than one process simultaneously.

Multiprocessor   A server with more than one processing chip, used to provide greater power and efficiency to the network.

Multivalued dependency   A relationship between database tables in which data in one table is variable and derived from data in a separate table.

NAC   Network Adapter Card. A hardware device inserted into a slot inside the computer, which manages the flow of data between the computer and the rest of the network. Also called NIC (Network Interface Card).

Name server   A machine that stores and manages a databases of domain names and associated IP addresses.

Nanosecond   One-billionth of a second, the unit of measurement of the speed at which computer chips process data.

NBP   Name Binding Protocol. An AppleTalk protocol that translates user-defined network node names into network node addresses.

NCB   Network Control Block. Instruction code sent by network software to a computer's network-aware operating system.

NCP   NetWare Core Protocol. A NetWare protocol that manages the flow of data between NetWare clients and file servers for maximum efficiency.

NCSA National Center for Supercomputing Applications. Located at the University of Illinois.

NDBMS Networked Database Management System. An application that synchronizes multiple users' access to centralized databases. *See also* DBMS, OODB, RDBMS.

NDS NetWare Directory Services. A system for organizing network locations into a hierarchy, used in NetWare version 4.

NetBEUI NetBIOS Extended User Interface. A small protocol suitable for networks where all nodes establish direct links with the server. *See also* NetBIOS.

NetBIOS Network Basic Input/Output System. A standard developed by the IBM Corporation for accessing network services by means of a computer's operating system.

NetPC A terminal that accesses remote applications and processes remote data via Internet/intranet protocols.

Network administrator A person responsible for the day-to-day operation and maintenance of a computer network.

Network database A multiple-table database in which any table may be related to any other table.

Network layer The third layer of the OSI/RM networking model, which describes processes for routing data between network addresses and for verifying that messages are sent completely and accurately.

News reader Software for accessing Internet newsgroups and for reading and posting messages.

News server   A computer that specializes in the storage and transfer of Usenet databases.

Newsgroup   A set of computer users with some common interest who access a central location to post articles to read by others.

NIAS   NetWare Internet Access Server. A proprietary TCP/IP gateway in Novell's NetWare 4.11.

NIC   *See* NAC.

NLM   NetWare Loadable Modules. A NetWare application designed to run in the background while the operating system is active.

Node   A connection to the network made by any type of device (including workstations, shared printers, modems, and the like).

Normal form   A rule that describes the structure of an efficient set of database tables. There are five normal forms.

Normalization   The process of eliminating redundancies and maximizing efficiency in the relationships between database tables.

NOS   Network Operating System. Software that directs data traffic throughout the network, manages security, and handles requests for network services.

NS   Nanosecond. One-billionth of a second, used as the unit for measuring the speed of random access memory chips.

NuBus   A proprietary bus used by Macintosh computers.

Object   A specialized form of data in which information is stored together with code that executes when the information is accessed. *See also* OODB, OLE.

Object-oriented database   A database that stores information joined to instruction code that acts on that information when it is accessed.

Object signing   A security technique for restricting areas of a hard disk that may accept downloaded applets.

Octet   An 8-bit binary number, commonly used in IP addressing.

ODBC   Open DataBase Connectivity. A standard developed by the Microsoft Corporation for moving data reliably between application programs and databases.

ODI   Open Datalink Interface. A software standard for allowing compatible hardware to accept data using more than one protocol. *See also* MLID.

OLE   Object Linking and Embedding. A protocol developed by the Microsoft Corporation that allows applications to exchange data in the form of objects that are either stored in separate files and linked to the application, or embedded as copies within applications. *See also* Object.

OODB   Object-Oriented Database. A database that links instruction code directly with stored data. *See also* DBMS, NDBMS, RDBMS.

OSI/RM   Open Systems Interconnection Reference Model. A seven-layer standard developed by the International Standards Organization, an international body of experts who define a variety of different technical standards for governments. The purpose of OSI/RM is to demonstrate how the parts of a network communication system should work together.

OSP   Online Service Provider. A large scale enterprise that offers access to huge databases of information and communications between users. *See also* AOL, CIS.

Packet   A block of data sent over a network, which includes both raw information and protocol-specific code used to identify and process the block.

PAP   Password Authentication Protocol. An Internet-standard protocol for verifying passwords from remote callers.

PAP   Printer Access Protocol. An AppleTalk protocol that monitors the flow of data that is sent in a continuous stream instead of in sections.

Parity   A form of error checking based on data bits, which helps synchronize communication between computers.

Passive hub   A device that is used to make connections between nodes on a network but does not act upon the signal in any way. *See also* Active Hub.

Password   A series of 8–10 characters (letters, numbers, and symbols) used to restrict access to data to those individuals who know the character string.

PCI   Peripheral Component Interconnect. A bus design developed by the Intel Corporation to take advantage of the advanced processing power in systems that use 80486 or later microprocessors. *See also* Bus, EISA, ISA.

PDL   Page Description Language. A set of functions used by printers to control the formatting of text on paper.

Peer-to-peer   A form of computer networking in which workstations are permitted to act as both clients and servers. *See also* C/S, Client, Server.

PEP   Packet Exchange Protocol. An XNS protocol that processes messages for transport along a network. *See also* XNS.

PGP   Pretty Good Privacy. A variation on the RSA encryption model written by Paul Zimmerman.

Physical layer   The first layer of the OSI/RM networking model, which describes the electrical, mechanical, and functional specifications for handling network data.

Physical topology   The layout of computer network hardware.

PIN   Personal Identification Number. A memorized number used as a password in PIN-based security systems.

POP   Post Office Protocol. A data transfer protocol that manages stored e-mail messages on network servers.

Port   A hardware device used to make connections between a computer and a peripheral device, such as a printer or modem.

Port address   A hexadecimal number used by a workstation to select a local electronic circuit through which it directs the NIC's incoming and outgoing data.

Post office   A central database that contains electronic addresses of message senders and recipients.

Power supply   An electrical device that acts as a transformer between a computing device and a standard electrical source.

PPP   Point-to-Point Protocol. A data transfer protocol within the TCP/IP family that transmits IP packets over telephone lines.

Presentation layer   The sixth layer of the OSI/RM networking model, which sets rules for formatting data transmissions.

Print queue   A utility that stores print job requests and directs them to the print server in order.

Print server   A computing device that handles requests for printing servers across a network. *See also* Server.

Private key   A complex sequence of characters or a mathematical formula, known only to a message recipient, which is used to decrypt electronic messages that have been encrypted with a corresponding public key.

Programming object   *See* Object.

Properties   Data that describes the appearance of a programming object (for example, a button, scroll bar, or icon) within a computer's graphical user interface.

Protocol   A rule, or set of rules, that allows computers to transmit and receive data, maintain consistent timing, and check for errors.

Proxy servers   A security device that manages and verifies network data traffic between a computer network and the Internet.

Public key   A complex sequence of characters or a mathematical formula, publicly distributed, which is used to encrypt electronic messages. The resulting encrypted messages can only be decrypted using a separate private key, known only to authorized recipients.

PVC   Permanent Virtual Circuit. A dedicated wide-area network connection whose data handling capacity is allocated on an as-needed basis.

Query   The process of extracting meaningful information from a database.

Rack-mount system   A storage technique that stacks and connects network hardware devices in a limited physical space.

RAID   Redundant Arrays of Independent/Inexpensive Disks. A system that uses more than one disk to make additional copies of the same data at the time it is being stored.

RAM   Random Access Memory. That part of a computer where actual data processing takes place.

RAS   Remote Access Server. A network hardware device that manages a connection from a remote PC so that the remote PC functions as any other node on the network.

RCP   Remote Courier Protocol. An XNS protocol that allows software to run services available on other network nodes. *See also* XNS.

RDBMS   Relational Database Management System. An application that organizes data into a structured framework of tables containing columns and rows, and sets up linked relationships between those tables. *See also* DBMS, OODB, NDBMS.

Redirector   Software that controls the flow of data between the various nodes on the network.

Referential integrity   The overall validity of relationships between elements in a relational database.

Refresh rate   The speed with which a computer's processor can access and restore a DRAM chip's data image.

Registry   A special database containing information about Windows NT or Windows 95 overall configuration.

Relational database   A data storage technique that breaks data down into fundamental units, which are arranged according to common attributes, in rows and columns called tables, and forms relationships between tables based on links between data attributes.

Remote   The computer that initiates a dial-up connection to another computer.

Remote access   The process of making connections to a network or workstation from distant locations using common-carrier or dedicated telephone lines.

Remote call back   A security technique in which a server verifies a password, ends a dial-up connection, and calls the remote caller back using a previously stored phone number.

Remote management   The technique of managing a network server and operating system from a client workstation.

Repeater   A hardware device, similar to a hub, which amplifies network data traffic and reduces electrical interference.

Replication   A security technique for copying data to more than one location as processing takes place.

Resistor plug   A small cap that absorbs a data signal at the end of a network cable.

RG-11   A cable specification for thick, sturdy, coaxial network cable.

RG-58   A cable specification for thin coaxial network cable.

Rights *See* Access rights.

Ring network A network topology in which workstations are joined to each other in a closed circle of cable connections.

RIP Routing Information Protocol. An XNS protocol that establishes the best data path for messages from one network node to another. *See also* XNS.

RISC Reduced Instruction Set Computer. A term used to describe a chip with internal architecture that has been simplified and optimized for the most common types of internal operations. *See also* CISC.

RJ connector A plus used to join twisted-pair cabling to hardware devices.

Rollback A technique used to reverse a series of computer instructions in the event of an error.

Root name server A server containing domain names and IP addresses based on the domain name type, such as .com. Root name servers are located throughout the United States and are maintained by InterNIC.

Router A hardware device that can send and receive data between multiple linked networks. *See also* Bridge, Gateway.

RPS Redundant Power Supply. A secondary computer power supply that takes over in the event that the main power supply fails.

RSA A popular, two-key encryption system named after its inventors: Ronald Rivest, Adi Shamir, and Leonard Adleman.

RTF Rich-text format, which allows users to send graphics, sound, and animation with their messages.

RTMP   Routing Table Maintenance Protocol. An AppleTalk protocol that monitors the location of nodes on the network and maintains a database of reliable connections between them.

SA   System Administrator. A person or department that manages the day-to-day operations of a computer network. *See also* CNA.

SAP   Server Advertising Protocol. A NetWare protocol that monitors the process of logging on and off the network and manages the transfer of data throughout the network.

Satellite data service   A communication method for receiving data on a PC at the fastest possible speed.

SCSI   Small Computer Systems Interface (pronounced *scuzzy*). A standard for the electronic circuitry controlling a computer's peripheral hardware such as hard disks and tape backup devices.

Search engine   Software that gathers information from Web pages in an intranet or the Internet.

Server   A dedicated computer that stores data and processes requests to access or transmit the stored data. *See also* File Server, Print Server.

Session layer   The fifth layer of the OSI/RM networking model, which controls the transfer of data, handling transmission and transport errors, and managing records of transmissions sent.

SFT   System Fault Tolerance. A three-level data protection scheme that provides variable safeguards for networked data on the NetWare network.

SIMM   A RAM Chip configuration that stores 8–32MB RAM on a single small card.

Site licensing   A software selling agreement in which a single copy of the software is granted rights to be copied onto a predetermined number of machines in an enterprise.

SMB   Server Message Block. A protocol that translates computer instructions into NetBIOS instructions. *See also* NetBIOS.

SMF   Standard Message Format. A standard for formatting electronic messages, developed by the Novell Corporation.

SMP   Symmetrical Multiprocessing. A feature that integrates more than one processor into a single file server.

SMTP   Simple Mail Transfer Protocol. An e-mail protocol that establishes a mail transfer connection between the sending and receiving mail servers, breaks the message into sections, and verifies each section as it is being sent.

SMU   Symmetric Multiprocessor Units. A file server that uses more than one central processing chip for greater speed and efficiency.

Sneaker net   A means of transferring data in non-networked businesses by physically carrying data from one machine to the next on floppies.

Software suite   A package that includes several of a vendor's business applications (most often a word processor, a spreadsheet, some kind of graphics or presentation package, and a database management system) bundled together and sold as a unit.

SPP   Sequenced Packet Protocol. An XNS protocol that verifies transmitted network data. *See also* XNS.

SPX Sequenced Packet Exchange. A NetWare protocol that uses NetWare functions to verify the accuracy of data.

SQL Structured Query Language. A standard language for managing client/server databases. *See also* DBMS, NDBMS, RDBMS.

SRAM Static Random Access Memory. Fast memory chips that do not require capacitors and do not need to refresh their electrical charge.

Star network A network topology in which workstations are independently connected to a central hub or server.

Star ring Two or more star topologies are linked together and accessed in sequence, using a central hub. At first glance, this configuration looks like a star topology joined into a larger star topology.

STDA StreetTalk Directory Assistance. A feature of VINES that lists node names on the network.

Stop bit A delay after a character is sent, to indicate to the receiving modem that the single-character transmission is complete.

STP Shielded twisted-pair cable. The cable's shielding protects it from electrical interference.

Subdomain name Characters preceding the domain type, separated from the domain type by a period, in an IP domain name. For example, sybex is the subdomain name within the domain name sybex.com.

Subnet masking A process of manipulating network addresses with binary numbers. For more details, refer to Chapter 14.

Suite *See* Software suite.

Symmetrical encryption   A security technique in which messages are encrypted and decrypted using the same key.

System log   A paper-based listing of a network's essential components and configuration, including such items as hardware specifications, boot files, directory structure, user profiles, system login scripts, configuration diary, software diary, hardware and software standards, backup schedules, printing configuration, and security procedures.

T-connector   A small device used to join workstations in a ring or daisy-chain topology.

T1   A specification for telephone cable that handles data (non-voice) transmissions only, providing twenty-four separate channels of communication, each channel transmitting data at a rate of 64Kb per second.

T3   A specification for telephone cable that handles data (non-voice) transmissions only, providing 672 separate channels for communication, each capable of transmitting data at 64Kb per second.

Tap   A device that connects a workstation cable to a main or backbone cable. Also called Vampire Tap.

TCP   Transmission Control Protocol. A host protocol for processing data sent along a network and over telephone lines. *See also* TCP/IP.

TCP/IP   Transmission Control Protocol/Internet Protocol. A communications protocol used as the basis for the Internet and supported by most network operating systems.

Telecommuting   A process by which users perform day-to-day computing tasks from home via remote access rather than personally appearing at the workstation site. *See also* Remote Access.

Telnet   A protocol that allows a person stationed at a workstation to access and run a different computer at a remote location as if that person were sitting at the remote computer's keyboard.

Thick Ethernet   A coaxial network cable (approximately one centimeter thick) used to connect large networks with nodes that are up to 1,000 meters apart.

Thin Ethernet   A coaxial network cable (approximately 5 millimeters thick) used to connect local area networks with nodes that are less than 500 feet apart.

Threadmaster   An individual who controls access, regulates content, and links messages for a newsgroup.

Time-domain reflectometer   A cable-testing device that transports a signal down a cable and measures the time it takes the signal to reflect back from blocked points.

Token Ring network   A network topology in which data traffic is regulated by passing a special electronic signal, called a token, between nodes. The token controls which nodes can send and receive data.

Top-level category   A series of characters at the beginning of a domain name or newsgroup name that indicates a specific type of site. For example, www. is a top-level category indicating that the site is part of the World Wide Web.

Topology   The layout of a network. A physical topology describes the real-world connections between network nodes. A logical topology describes the data paths used by the network operating system.

Transaction processing   Database management using tables to store processing instructions. If necessary, these tables can be used to reverse the instructions and restore the data to some selected previous condition.

Transport layer   The fourth layer of the OSI/RM networking model, which includes functions for establishing appropriate connections, initiating data transmission, and releasing the connection after the transmission is complete.

Trust relationship   A communication link between two Windows NT domains. When a trust relationship is established, the first domain (called the trusting domain) allows access by users in the second domain (called the trusted domain).

TSR   Terminate–and–stay-resident software. Software that remains in RAM and continues processing as a background operation; for example, a screen saver.

TTS   Transaction Tracking System. A NetWare system that keeps records of network processes and can roll back, or undo, the processes in the event a system crash damages the integrity of data on the network.

UDP   User Datagram Protocol. A communication protocol that does not perform validity checks on the data. UDP is used in videoconferencing, when validity checks on real-time video signals would degrade picture quality.

UNIX   A widely used computer operating system, which is also the base operating system for the Internet.

UPS   Uninterruptable Power Supply. A hardware device that provides continuous electrical power to the server, usually for a short time, in the event of a external electrical power failure. (Also United Parcel Service, a commercial mailing and shipping service sometimes called upon when a network fails.)

URL   Universal Resource Locator. An IP addressing scheme that resolves domain names to IP addresses.

Usenet   A world-wide database of discussion newsgroups.

User licensing   A marketing technique in which vendors charge a fee for permission to run software.

User profile   A datafile containing workstation configuration data; for example, program items and groups, window sizes and locations, screen colors, and printer connections.

UTP   Unshielded twisted-pair cable. An inexpensive cable that is not insulated against electrical interference.

UUENCODE/UUDECODE   An older coding system originally developed for UNIX and ported to other platforms. Nowadays, it is used with message systems that don't have their own built-in encoding schemes.

VGA   Video Graphics Array. A screen resolution standard for color monitors.

Videoconferencing   A networking technique that combines real-time video transmissions and sound to create virtual face-to-face meetings, demonstrations, and training over intranets. Videoconferencing requires additional hardware: video cameras, sound cards, and micro-phones, plus software to display video-based images through worksta-tions' graphics cards.

VIM   Vendor-Independent Messaging. A standard for formatting elec-tronic messages, developed by the Lotus Corporation.

VINES   Virtual Network System. A file-server based network oper-ating system designed as an extension of the UNIX, developed by Banyan Incorporated.

Virtual circuit A function that creates a direct connection between two computers on a network, bypassing the operating system's addressing mechanisms.

Virtual memory A maneuver used when a machine has insufficient standard RAM available for processing. Instructions and data are swapped to and from RAM and a reserved area on the hard disk as necessary to complete the required processing.

VLM Virtual Loadable Module. Software that controls a limited set of processes on a NetWare network.

VRAM Video Random Access Memory. Specialized chips used on video controller cards to process the digital graphics data into an analog signal for display on the system monitor.

WAN Wide Area Network. Two or more computers that can exchange data via cables or broadcast devices. Wide is a relative term, it means that the computers on the network are located outside of a reasonable physical proximity of each other. *See also* LAN.

Web *See* World Wide Web.

Web browser *See* Browser.

Web page A text file containing instructions for the formatting and display of text, graphics, and hypertext links within a browser.

Web server A computer that manages Internet and intranet connections across a network, stores Web pages, and displays them when instructed to do so by client Web browsers.

Web site administrator *See* Webmaster.

Webmaster   An individual responsible for implementing and maintaining the content and style of the company's Internet site, keeping the information accurate, up-to-date, and interesting.

Whiteboard conferencing   A technique for simultaneously displaying shared data to multiple nodes on a network, and updating that data in real time.

Windows NT   Windows New Technology. A client/server operating system developed by Microsoft Corporation.

Wireless transport services   A technology that manages network connections using radio or infrared signaling devices, eliminating the need for cables.

World Wide Web   A system of text pages in HTML format, which are stored on millions of computers throughout the world, then accessed and displayed by individuals using the Internet. *See also* HTML, Internet.

Workgroup   A set of individuals who collaborate, usually across a computer network, in the fulfillment of a business mission.

Workgroup manager   An individual responsible for problem solving, implementing standards and solutions, reviewing performance, and facilitating the efficiency of a workgroup.

Workstation   A user-accessible computer on a network.

WRAM   Window Random Access Memory. Memory chips are found on expensive high-performance workstations that intercept and process Graphic User Interface data, freeing more of the system's on-board resources for general information processing.

WTS   Wireless Transport Services. Hardware for managing network connections using radio or infrared signaling devices.

WWW   *See* World Wide Web.

X.400   An international standard for formatting electronic messages, developed by the International Consultative Committee of Telephony and Telegraphy, which defines the standard components of e-mail addresses.

XNS   Xerox Network System. A simplified communications protocol suite developed by the Xerox Corporation.

ZAP   Zone Information Protocol. An AppleTalk protocol that analyzes the network configuration and collects device addresses into groups to establish efficient access.

Index

NOTE: Page numbers in *italics* refer to figures or tables; page numbers in bold refer to primary discussions of the topic.

O

S

T

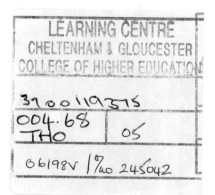

LEARNING CENTRE
CHELTENHAM & GLOUCESTER
COLLEGE OF HIGHER EDUCATION

3700119375

004.68
THO | 05

06198V | %wo 245042

SYBEX BOOKS ON THE WEB!

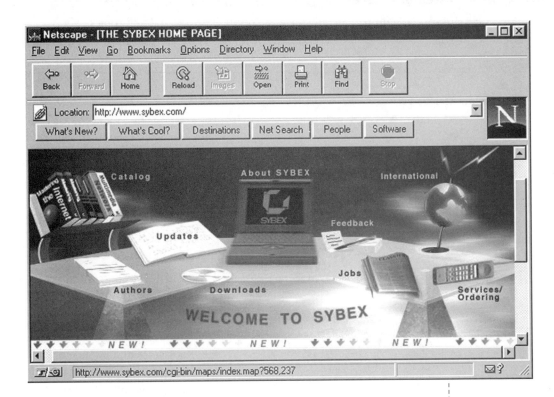

Presenting a truly dynamic environment that is both fun and informative.

- download useful code
- e-mail your favorite Sybex author
- preview a book you might want to own
- find out about job opportunities at Sybex
- order books
- learn about Sybex
- discover what's new in the computer industry

http://www.sybex.com

SYBEX®

SYBEX Inc. • 1151 Marina Village Parkway • Alameda, CA 94501 • 510-523-8233

More Internet Sites of Interest

The following sites provide up-to-date coverage of specific network-related topics. Many of these sites include links to related sites, plus e-mail addresses where you can ask questions and get expert advice:

Topic	Address	Description
ATM	http://www.ics.uci.edu/~atm/links.html	Good starting point for information on asynchronous transfer mode.
Cabling	http://www.cis.ohio-state.edu/faq.html	Good source of information on cabling standards, technical specifications, installation, and testing.
CGI	http://www.jmarshall.com/easy/cgi	A short introduction to adding CGI capability to Web applications; for programmers only.
	http://hoohoo.ncsa.uiuc.edu/cgi	The full technical specification of CGI
Commercial Websites	http://www.3com.com http://www.banyan.com http://www.microsoft.com http://www.netscape.com http://www.novell.com	These sites are maintained by vendors of networking hardware and software and include much useful information. (In general, you can find a major vendor on the Web by entering http://, plus the vendor's corporate name, followed by .com.)
Ethernet	http://wwwhost.ots.utexas.edu/ethernet	Wide range of technical information on Ethernet.
Fast Ethernet	http://alumni.caltech.edu/~dank/fe	Rich source of technical information on Fast Ethernet technology.
Firewalls	http://pandoras-box.bgsm.wfu.edu/digital_technology/firewall.html	Concise collection of fundamental information on building intranet firewalls, plus links to firewall vendors.
HTML	http://www2.wvitcoe.wvnet.edu/~sbolt/html3	Up-to-date information on the latest version of HTML.
	http://www.w3.org/pub/www/markup	Information on learning and using HTML.

[GRID STAMP ON PREVIOUS PAGE]

3703703228

Learning Wireless Java ™

WITHDRAWN

Related titles from O'Reilly

Database Programming with JDBC™ and Java™

Developing Java Beans™

Enterprise JavaBeans™

Java™ 2D Graphics

Java™ & XML

Java™ and XSLT

Java™ Cookbook

Java™ Cryptography

Java™ Distributed Computing

Java™ Enterprise in a Nutshell

Java™ Examples in a Nutshell

Java™ Foundation Classes in a Nutshell

Java™ I/O

Java™ in a Nutshell

Java™ Internationalization

Java™ Message Service

Java™ Network Programming

Java™ Performance Tuning

Java™ Programming with Oracle SQLJ

Java™ Security

JavaServer™ Pages

JavaServer™ Pages Pocket Reference

Java™ Servlet Programming

Java™ Swing

Java™ Threads

Learning Java™

Java™ RMI

Also available

The Java™ Enterprise CD Bookshelf

WITHDRAWN